MW01178226

Marching On . . .

SONJA DAVIES

Marching On . . .

RANDOM
HOUSE
NEW ZEALAND LTD

To the memory of my children
Penny and Mark

Acknowledgements

Thanks to Mary Sinclair for the long hours on the wordprocessor and for
strong support over the long haul; for valuable support and checking Ted
Thompson, Ken Douglas and Graham Kelly; for the title Angela Foulkes.
Thanks also to those who helped in many ways during the writing: Lyn
Bruce and Don Swan, Rona Ensor and Ryan Small, Stephanie and John
Kirby, Charles Chauvel and Dave Hollander, Ian and Diane Grant,
Charlie and Nancy Baldwin, Ray Stewart and my many friends here and
abroad.

Random House New Zealand Ltd
(An imprint of the Random House Group)

18 Poland Road
Glenfield
Auckland 10
NEW ZEALAND

Sydney   New York   Toronto
London   Auckland   Johannesburg
and agencies throughout the world

© Sonja Davies 1997
The moral rights of the Author have been asserted.

Printed in Auckland by Publishing Press Limited
ISBN 1 86941 296 6

All rights reserved. No part of this publication may be reproduced or transmitted in
any form or by any means, electronic or mechanical, including photocopying, record-
ing, storage in any information retrieval system or otherwise, without the written
permission of the publisher.

Contents

Introduction

Look, the winter is past
And the rains are over and done with
Flowers have begun to appear on the earth
The time of the singing birds has come
And the voice of the turtle dove
Shall be heard in the land.

1996 was the year when influenza in its various guises swept through the country, when the winter was interminable, and when it seemed that the steady stream of rain would never stop. It was also the year of this country's first MMP election.

All of these affected me, and the flu and the bleak winter were certainly major contributory factors to my state of mind. For the previous two years I hadn't had a flu injection or flu, but this year I decided to play safe and presented myself to my doctor for a shot. It was unfortunate that I should then fall victim to one of the most virulent types of flu, which kept me bed- or house-bound for most of the winter. Fortunately, I had stocked up on food supplies, though in the beginning food was irrelevant.

I lay in bed, looking out at the rain and the sodden and often flooded garden. It has been said that in winter the bare bones of a garden predominate and it is possible for the gardener to see design mistakes. I found that to be true, and perhaps the same observation can be applied to one's life as well.

It seemed to me in my flu-ridden state that the winter and the flu would never end. At halfway point, I told myself I needed to brace up, get out of bed and get on with life. I showered and dressed, hooked up the vacuum cleaner, blacked out and collapsed on the kitchen floor. Coming round, I realised that two of my cats, Abbie and Clawdia, were involved in a fight on my chest to establish who was to sit there and keep me warm.

I wouldn't let friends and neighbours near me as long as I felt I was a threat to their health. I didn't want anyone to catch this horrible bug. People were wonderful, rang often and left soup and other goodies on my doorstep. My friend Mary took over the cooking at weekends. We have been friends since I first met her through the Women's Movement in the early 70s, and over the years we have worked and lived together. At this time she was working very hard for her boss, Chris Carter, in the run-up to the election, and I was concerned that, in her tired state, she might inherit my flu — but fortunately that didn't happen.

As I write this, the winter is indeed past, the rains over and done with, and flowers — daffodils, tulips, clematis, kowhai — and blossom have begun to appear. Now that spring is here, I have to admit that the wet winter has resulted in phenomenal growth, and many trees planted some time ago are now vigorously growing up and out. So much of life seems to be about holding out for the spring.

After Bread and Roses was published and the film, which dealt with my life until I was 33 years old, appeared in theatres and on television, people all over the country and around the world started asking me, 'What happened next?'

The book *Bread and Roses* finished in 1978 with the death of my son Mark. As I start writing this sequel, it is now 1996. The years between have been traumatic and action-packed, and some of that is not easy to write about. New Zealand has gone through a period of unprecedented change in almost every facet of society, and, as with the first volume, my problem is not what should be included but what should be left out. I have travelled round the world several times during this period, but I'm not writing a travel book; I've become a passionate gardener, but I'm not writing a gardening book; I've been a parliamentarian during a very dramatic period, but I'm not writing a political treatise. What I write will be an amalgam of all that has happened.

In writing this second volume, I want to keep faith with the many people who have urged, cajoled and even bullied me to continue the story, and the people in the supermarket who say to me, 'Why are you doing your own shopping? You should be home writing your book.'

Sonja Davies
Rangiiti, 1997

Part One

The Second Beginning

Con

In the months after Mark died, I flung myself into work. For the first year I was angry about the loss of a special 20-year-old who many of us felt had much to contribute to his country. I felt bitter when I read media reports of young men his age who had been arrested for rape, arson and violence, and asked why Mark should have been picked out. Now I realise that this was the beginning of the grief process that continued for two years; at the end of which I had gone on to be philosophically grateful for the 20 years that I had been privileged to share with him.

During that time, I kept feeling he was somewhere around, and on several occasions thought I saw glimpses of him. Once, when my trade union boss Graham Kelly and I were driving to a meeting in Napier, I was certain I saw him riding his bike across the bridge that spans the Ngaruro River at Clive. There was this tall blond boy in Mark's black-and-green checked bush-shirt who turned and smiled reassuringly at me. I called to Graham to look at him, but he had disappeared.

My friend Con Foot kept tabs on me from her home in Epuni in Lower Hutt. She became very concerned about my state of mind and rang me often, sometimes late at night. She finally convinced me that I should stay with her at the weekends for a while. Con and I had been friends for 35 years, since the day we fronted up as eighteen-year-olds at the Kilbirnie Nurses' Home. Because we had lived in different parts of the country, we sometimes didn't see each other for long stretches of time, but we still kept in touch, and when either of us was going through a rough patch, we telephoned and wrote long letters to each other. Once during my years fighting TB I desperately needed her, and she came with her husband Bill to help me; and once when her marriage had struck a bad patch, she sent for me, and I drove her to her parents' place, 'Newington', in Stratford. Our husbands, Charlie and Bill, knew that our friendship was a pivotal factor in our lives; they knew also that although we would not leave our families and other responsibilities lightly, there would be rare times when we just had to be together, to talk and to share whatever was worrying us. Bill was a workaholic, he developed cardiac problems and ultimately retired early. He and Con had several loving years before he died, far too young.

When I first met Con, even at the age of eighteen, it was obvious to me, who was much more mercurial and politically motivated, that here was a person who possessed the virtues of absolute integrity and a code of honour that would never change all through the years of our friendship. Con became one of the most important lynchpins of my life. One of her best attributes was that she was absolutely non-judgmental: she may not always have approved of or even understood my actions in the trade union movement or in politics, but she always supported me. When Con established a close friendship, let no one rend it asunder.

People often wondered how we could be such friends. Her background, like mine, was conservative, but I had jettisoned mine. One of her brothers, David, was a Cabinet minister in the National Government. He was Minister of Defence when many of us were fighting for a nuclear-free New Zealand, which he and his Government absolutely opposed. The young National MP Marilyn Waring was seriously at odds with him on this issue. But on family occasions with Con, David and I temporarily transcended these major political differences and found issues about which we could have a reasonable and rational conversation. I have to say, though, that I'm glad that Con was not Rob Muldoon's sister. That might have taxed me beyond endurance.

Between working for the Wellington Shop Employees Union and being an Executive member and ultimately vice-president of the Federation of Labour (FOL), my weeks in the early 1980s were action-packed. There were meetings and negotiations with members right around our area, which took in the lower half of the North Island across to New Plymouth in the west, to Waiouru in the centre of the island and north through Hawkes Bay to Wairoa in the east. The FOL was involved in many complicated issues, including the tripartite wage talks with the Muldoon Government, the long-running Mangere Bridge dispute in Auckland and the Kinleith dispute in Tokoroa, which are discussed later. There was a great deal of travelling and stress, but it was, of course, all incredibly interesting. As for other FOL Executive members, balancing the competing demands of union work and time with the FOL was a constant problem.

I often arrived at Con's house in Fairfield Avenue early on Friday evening feeling like a piece of chewed string. Con would be waiting at the kitchen table with a gin, tonic and grapefruit juice, the Concert Programme or a record playing in the background, and wonderful smells coming from the oven. If the weather was fine, we would walk around the garden and she would show me what had happened during the week.

After dinner in her cosy sitting room, we'd listen to music, talk, and catch up with each other's lives. It was a complete contrast to the week I'd just spent and a real lifesaver. When I went up to the comfortable bed in one of the attic bedrooms, Con would sometimes play the piano, and often went through the sheet music she had kept since we used to sing around the piano at Wellington Nurses' Home. It was great to drift off to sleep with those well-loved tunes washing over me.

I was totally spoilt on those weekends. It was Con's way of helping me. Breakfast in bed, no pressures, absolute peace. Con was a crossword addict and on Sunday mornings she liked to listen to the Concert Programme and grapple with the current crossword — the more difficult, the better. I as always brought books with me.

Con and I started going to Stratford at Labour Weekend to stay with Con's youngest brother Hugh, who lives in the family home, Newington, and, in and around his legal work, keeps the garden in shape. We invariably set out late on Friday afternoon and arrived mid-evening, to find a warm welcome, food and drink and a roaring fire. I slept in the double bed where Con and I had shared flu when we were nineteen and nursing; and Con slept in her parents' bedroom. We spent a lot of time exploring that wonderful garden, visiting Gwen Masters, a farmer's widow who has a famous garden on the other side of the town, or going to the rhododendron gardens at Pukeiti. Newington is a delightful old house: it was, and still is, a healing place. On Saturday evenings, Hugh invited some of his many friends for dinner, and over the years I met some amazing people there.

Hugh is very much a creature of habit and never more happy than when at home. He and Con were the two youngest members of their family and were great friends. She persuaded him to come to Lower Hutt to her home each Christmas, and it became an annual visit. My daughter Penny and her husband Mick did not celebrate Christmas because it has become too commercialised, so I would join Con and Hugh for their celebrations, then visit my daughter afterwards.

At one point during these years, Con went to Europe, explored the Greek Islands and came back determined to return there during her retirement. She and I had often talked about what I would do when I retired. I loved my little cottage in Brooklyn, where I was then living, but as I grew older, my susceptibility to colds and 'flu, and the effects on my damaged lungs, convinced me that I should move somewhere warmer. One Friday evening after dinner, Con said she had something she wanted to discuss with me. We sat at the kitchen table and she told me she wanted me to be able to buy a property where I would be secure, comfortable and happy. I said that although I would have some superannuation when I left the union, it wouldn't be enough to buy a house.

Con took out her chequebook and before my horrified eyes started writing a cheque. She told me I was not to refuse what she was giving me: she had discussed it with her children, who were in agreement. When she handed me the cheque, I was stunned at the amount; but she said it was something she really wanted to do, could afford and it would make her very unhappy if I turned it down. Money has never meant a great deal to me but I must confess that I'd wished I had enough to buy a property without a large mortgage that I couldn't service. What Con did was to make this possible. She said she never wanted to discuss it again — ever; any attempt I made to thank her for her incredible generosity was brushed aside and I was asked to talk about something else.

One day, Con and I went to one of the Wellington Hospital Nurses' reunions. The hospital itself had exploded in every direction and was rapidly occupying every inch of space on its grounds. We met old friends we hadn't seen for years — former senior staff, now quite elderly; and, best of all, caught up with the 'Gang', who had been our special friends throughout our training. All were married and, apart from one who lived in Auckland, were settled in various parts of Wellington and the Hutt Valley. We all sat on the verandah of the old three-storeyed red brick nurses' home and caught up with each other's lives.

Like most professions, nursing has gone through some major changes — in training, and in attitudes towards authority — which have broken down hierarchical bureaucracies. People are now hospitalised for much shorter periods; day surgery is common; mothers coming to give birth are sent home sometimes after only 24 hours, which doesn't give either mother or child necessary time to develop a satisfactory breast-feding routine. At the same time there have been dramatic changes in administration, which have swept away elected people who represented the public and replaced them with business people who are there to administer a diminishing amount of money.

When we were training in the 1940s, we studied the theory of nursing and care in two-week block courses at intervals during the year, slotted in and around our daily work-shifts. We knew this wasn't ideal and that there would have to be changes — and of course there were. It was decided to greatly increase the theoretical content of nurses' training in courses at polytechnic colleges around the country to explain about new techniques, drugs and other developments.

Sitting there on that verandah at the reunion, we had no idea of what was ahead for nursing and the health service. But one thing we did agree on was that we had been lucky to be in training when nurses lived in: it had meant we could develop the friendships that have endured for 50 years. Nurses today are quite likely to share a flat with a computer analyst, a researcher and a management consultant who are perhaps less understanding of the events, some of them traumatic, that are still part and parcel of nurses' daily lives. It was very therapeutic for us, coming off duty late at night, to drink cocoa with friends and talk things out. I suspect that the need for this, given present tensions and uncertainties, is still there.

By Christmas of 1985 I had become concerned about Con's health, her weight loss, her cough which she insisted was a 'smoker's cough and nothing more', and the fact that she who had always had boundless energy now tired easily. Her children and I started pressing her to see a doctor but she kept insisting she was just a bit run-down. Finally, early in 1986, she consulted her doctor, who referred her to a specialist at Hutt Hospital. I discovered when the appointment was and went to meet her as she came out. To my look of enquiry, she said, 'I have lung cancer, quite well advanced. If I have chemotherapy, I could live for a year. If not, I could be dead in six months.'

To say that I was shattered was an understatement, but I knew I mustn't show that, so I said as calmly as I could that I would drive her home and we could discuss the options. Con's initial reaction was to veto chemotherapy. I said of course it was her decision entirely and we should think about the things she had always wanted to do and draw up an itinerary.

I had to travel to Auckland that night, so left to catch my plane. Con had the sad task of telling her family. By the time I came back, she had decided to undergo chemotherapy straight away. Her family all had luxuriant wavy hair, inherited from their mother, and of course Con's disappeared and she entered the wig world.

Con asked me if I could spare ten days to take her to the South Island. She had never seen Collingwood, about which I had talked so much, at the tip of Golden Bay. She wanted to go to the West Coast, across to Christchurch and to Akaroa, which she thought sounded delightful. She knew it was too late to make the return trip to Greece, but there were other places she was determined to see.

We took the car over on the ferry and drove to wonderful Nelson, where I showed her the house in which Charlie and I had lived in Atmore Terrace. It was early autumn and, as usual, the deciduous trees were beautiful. Indeed, as we travelled to Lower Moutere to see my old friend Merle Hyland at Riverside Community on our way to Golden Bay, it seemed to me that nature was turning on a special display for Con. Merle has a charming garden, always of great interest. We stayed in a motel in Collingwood which Con loved, walked on the beach and saw the oyster-catchers and the godwits which were about to embark on their annual

Con with Merle Hyland at Riverside Community during the South Island tour

migration to the northern hemisphere. On down through the Buller Gorge; we stopped at Westport and Greymouth, and then drove across to Christchurch. I tried not to do too much each day, or to overtire Con. Her first action at day's end was to shed her wig, which she said felt the same as tight shoes. We stayed in Christchurch and pottered a bit because it truly is a garden city and offers so much to see in spring and autumn.

Con enjoyed Akaroa's uniqueness and atmosphere. Residents have retained the environment introduced by the original French settlers and new houses or alterations are carried out very carefully. On the way back via the east coast, we stayed overnight at a very pleasant hotel in Hanmer Springs and had a crayfish lunch in Kaikoura. Coming back on the ferry, a tired Con said that she was really glad we'd made the trip.

1986 was the United Nations International Year of Peace, and as the New Zealand convenor of a large, stroppy, opinionated and truly wonderful committee, I was fully occupied. We were all absolutely dedicated to peace: our only point of disagreement was the means of obtaining it. I travelled all over the country, had frequent meetings in small remote towns where the enthusiasm was heartwarming. In and around all this, I saw Con as often as possible. It was so sad to watch the inevitable deterioration of her body. Her children and grandchildren were often by her side.

In April I received a letter from Ray Stewart, a New Zealander who was the executive officer of the World Peace Council based in Helsinki. He told me that he wanted me to go to Dublin in May, to a meeting to consider the social and economic aspects of disarmament. I will talk about that meeting elsewhere, but it was a subject that interested me greatly. I would be away ten days as I needed to come back via Moscow to talk to the Soviet Women's Committee. I discussed this with Con. She was very anxious that I should go because she knew that I felt that people who worked in armament factories around the world would resist peace because of the threat to their jobs. She said she was going through a good phase in her treatment. The wonderful caring nurses from Te Omanga Hospice and her neighbour Phyllis Argue would also be around. I told her that I expected her to be there when I got back and she said, 'Of course.' I went off on my long journey with a very troubled mind, but she had given her word and I comforted myself that she had never let me down.

I arrived back in Auckland, rather exhausted, to attend a two-day meeting of the Pacific Trade Union Forum. These were always very interesting meetings, at which it was possible to observe the dynamics of the politics of the Pacific, about which I had been abysmally ignorant until a few years before. When I reached the hotel, Graham Kelly, who was also attending the meeting, came to see me. From his face I knew that what he had to tell me was not good. He said that Con had died two days before, and that Mary Sinclair would be ringing me to give me more details. Con's daughter Carol had rung Mary to find out when I would be coming home. Mary, who had been in touch with Con while I was away, had had no inkling that the end was near. Carol told her that her mother's condition had deteriorated that week and that she and her small son Russell had come to be with her. Con was experiencing a lot of pain and was given morphine to try to diminish this. Her doctor and the hospice nurses visited daily. On the day she died, she received a postcard from me, sent from Dublin, had a cup of tea with her doctor, talked with Carol and Russell, and at day's end went to sleep for the last time.

Carol said that the family had arranged for the funeral to be held on Monday, that everything was under control and that they would talk to me and see me before then. I was absolutely desolated, but despite that, I had to be glad that, for Con, there would be no more pain. I rang Carol and learned more: we agreed that it was good for Con that the end came fast. She said she would see me at Con's home on Monday. I presume I participated in the meeting but it was all rather a blur.

The funeral was to be held in the Presbyterian Church in Waiwhetu Road. Con had not been a regular churchgoer. Bill had been raised a Catholic and I had always assumed that because of their disparate religious upbringings, they had decided not to play an active part in religious life. So the Presbyterian minister didn't know Con well. At the church, surrounded by Con's immediate family, her brothers, cousins, nieces and nephews, the Gang and friends, I felt a growing conviction that the routine church service was not enough for this wonderful friend. I went to the front and spoke, looking out on this sad and grieving congregation, talked about Con and her life, how much we all loved and valued her, how much her family had meant to her, and how one of her great sadnesses since her cancer was diagnosed was that she would not see her beloved grandchildren grow up.

With brother David, sister Beverley and sister-in-law Lyn, sitting on Con's sofa for the last time, the day after her funeral

It was a shattering time. Like all bereaved people, we had to get on with our lives, but Con's death created a major gap, and for me the adjustment was difficult. I had lost my immediate family, my husband Charlie, my son Mark, all of whom I loved dearly. I felt bleak at this new loss of someone who had been my friend for 44 years. This sense of loss remains to this day.

A week later Mary rang me and said that a group of my friends who knew I was feeling sad wanted me to have dinner with them the next evening. She knew that Graham and I were going to Palmerston North to work for the day, so said I should put a nice dress in my bag. I was inclined to be a bit stroppy and told her that my friends could put up with me in my working suit, but she was adamant. She also said that she had asked Graham to drive me to her house when we got back from Palmerston North. I thought that rather odd and said so, but she said that with such a large crowd an early booking had been made at a favourite restaurant.

I was busy preparing for the next day's work in Palmerston North so dismissed the whole idea. In the morning, I was some way along the road when I remembered the dress, rushed back and grabbed the first one I saw, then went into town to meet Graham. We were to end the day with a large meeting of union members, and during a busy day of negotiations and the meeting, there wasn't time to think about anything else.

After the meeting I was talking to members and then came out onto the street to find Graham and the car. I saw him talking to a man who didn't look to me like a union member, but then other people came up and talked to me and I forgot the incident. In the car I remarked to Graham that I suddenly felt very tired and would rather have scrambled eggs and an early night instead of even an early dinner in a restaurant. I was amazed at Graham's reaction: he said that I couldn't do that, I had to go to the dinner. I was about to argue the point but then noticed that he was constantly looking in his rear mirror and asked if we were being followed. He said he had thought that one of our colleagues was behind us but had been mistaken.

At Mary's house in Worser Bay, I was hustled to press my dress and get changed. She said that Graham would take me to the restaurant and she would follow in her car. I asked as we drove along which restaurant we were going to and was told I would see. I soon realised that we were going to my favourite, Pierre's, at the top of Bowen Street. Beside the restaurant there was an off-street parking space that was not usually available for diners but Graham drove into it and, over my protests, hustled me inside.

There was just one long table set up in the restaurant, and at it sat many of my friends. I had never seen Pierre's Restaurant other than filled with diners. There was an empty chair closest to the door next to Naomi Trigg, who looked rather nervous, and I was told that this was for me. By now I had many questions whirling around in my head. Someone handed me a glass of wine and I had hardly taken the first sip when the door of the restaurant burst open and in came a man in evening dress: Television New Zealand's Bob Parker. He came up to me, handed me a large red book and asked me to read its title. He then said, 'Sonja Davies, this is your life. We have a wonderful programme arranged for you and I want you to come to Avalon with me now.'

My initial reaction, which endured for some time, was pure anger that someone — my friend or friends — had organised this without any consultation with me. How could people I loved do this to me? I recalled thinking, the last time I had seen a *This Is Your Life* programme on television, 'Thank God that's never going to happen to me!' Mary told me later that when, as my friend, she was approached by TV One, her initial reaction was that I would not want to do it. She rang Con, expecting her to agree, but Con said, 'People (ie, the public) don't know her as she really is. They see her as a tough radical working in a man's world. This will give thousands of people the chance to see her as we know her.' Mary was rather daunted by this reaction, but she thought that if Con believed it was the right thing to do, then maybe they should go ahead. Con told her that as I would want the Gang to be there, she would organise to contact them all. In a conversation the week before she died, she told Mary that she was going out to buy a new dress for the event. However, I knew nothing of this the night the programme was going to air, and continued to feel very aggrieved.

At Avalon, Bob hurried me along to makeup, still protesting, and then shut me in with a member of his staff. He said that people had travelled a long way to be with me that night and I couldn't disappoint them — people I'd be delighted to see. Reluctantly, I decided I'd better go along with it.

When I stepped onto the set and looked out to the audience, I saw my erstwhile dinner-party friends and a lot of other people I knew, and was angry all over again, but Bob was already starting on the programme. It would have been churlish in the extreme not to have been swept along and participated in the events that followed. First of all, Bob called Mary Sinclair, Sue Kedgley and Graham Kelly, all of whom he said had been of great help with the organisation of the programme. Graham said that he'd just gone through the worst 24 hours of subterfuge he'd ever experienced and that he'd been afraid that I would realise that the car following us from Palmerston North was in fact there in case his car broke down. Mary said that she hoped our friendship would survive this experience and I replied that it was a bit shaky right then. Sue, with whom I had shared many experiences here and overseas, talked about those and some of the things I'd done.

Then came the Gang — all of them, even Paddy from Auckland. Bob talked about Con, who only ten days earlier had provided his researchers with the Gang's names and where they could be found. For me it was heartwarming to have them all there together. The next person to appear was my daughter Penny. I looked at the video of this programme recently and saw how wonderful, fit and well she looked. She was then teaching at Porirua College, and when Bob asked her how she had coped with my protracted absences in hospital when she was a child, she told him that we had a pact that at a particular time each day we would be together regardless of the distances and that had helped enormously.

To my astonishment, next to appear was Dr John MacKay, who I believed had saved my life after I'd had two major haemorrhages. He looked just the same — older, of course, but still an impressive figure. He said that it was not he who was responsible for my recovery, but the drug company which had developed the drug; but I said the drug had only been part of it and that the main influence had been his telling me I could now get well — after describing my haemorrhages as 'spitting a bit of blood'! — which had put everything into perspective. I was adamant that his faith in me had saved me. He replied that my determination was a major factor, that I had been a very determined woman then and he suspected I still was.

The This Is Your Life *gang: (front from left) Sylvia Oliver, Ronnie Coles, Dr John McKay, Ruth Page, Sonja, Bob Parker, Graham Kelly, Sally Raymond, Penny; (back from left) Paddy Zonneveld, Joy Aislabie, Helene Kearns, Betty Sutton, Tipene O'Regan, Erena Pucher, Wendy Dear, brother David, sister Beverley, Davina Whitehouse, Sue Kedgley, Mary Sinclair, Stan Stables, Dougal Dickson*

Right after that, a small bundle of 81-year-old energy bounced into view. It was Ruth Page, who had led the Nelson Railway protest. She was marvellous and almost stole the show, as indomitable as always. She was fascinated with the whole process, caught sight of herself in the TV monitor and said, 'Goodness, is that me?' Hard on her heels came the two policemen who had arrested me at Kiwi, Dougal Dickson and Stan Stables. I had then, and still have, the utmost respect for these two, who really agreed with our attempt to prevent the demolition of the railway (which they confirmed again on the programme) but when Prime Minister Syd Holland ordered our arrest, they carried it out competently and calmly. They were part of a very tense situation that day. I hadn't seen them since the 1960s, so it was a real joy to have them there.

I had hardly recovered from all this when Bob called on my brother David. I couldn't believe he had actually allowed himself to become involved in this sort of thing — but there he was, tall, solid, understated, one of my very favourite people and very dear. He was followed by a well-known voice speaking in Maori — my kinsman Tipene O'Regan, who is always an impressive presence. When Bob asked him about my Ngai Tahu connections and how they affected me, he said that, like many New Zealanders, I valued that part of me that was Ngai Tahu, that I was a tani-wha in my own right and had fire in my belly. I was naturally very taken with this.

I had no time to wonder who on earth would come next, because off-screen I heard my sister Beverley's Canadian-accented voice talking to me — and there she was, all the way from Vancouver. We hadn't seen each other for years and both realised we had a lot of catching up to do. Beverley had, some years before, become a charismatic Christian and had thrown herself into that with her usual thoroughness. Naturally, my lifestyle, trade union and peace activities did not fit well with her beliefs. I was sorry about that because during my first two visits to Vancouver to stay with her, before her conversion, it had seemed to me that we could be really good friends. The second time I visited her, she was going through a very bad patch following the breakup of her marriage. I told her I thought she needed to find a new direction. Well, she did, and the fact that it was one I could not embrace was not my business. So here we were, on this rather traumatic night, both building bridges, and I was very glad to see her.

No time to dwell on all that, because the next thing I heard was the voice of Davina Whitehouse, actress, gallant and enduring and a good friend. She had jettisoned a Christchurch commitment to be with me and was her usual warm, special self. I couldn't even imagine what would happen next, but suddenly there was Sally Raymond, who had led the battle for equal pay for meatpackers when she was in the butchery unit at Woolworths in Upper Hutt. She had been down to the depths and fought her way up on a number of occasions. She has survived it all, and is doing well: she is now at Whangarei Polytechnic, succeeding in her studies. I was so glad to see her that night. When asked what I meant to her, she said that no matter what she had done over the years, I had never turned my back on her and was always there for her. Those of you who have read *Bread and Roses* will see how well she has done.

And then there, before my amazed gaze by satellite from Sydney, was Cath Tizard, who at that time was Mayor of Auckland. She was over there to speak at a conference, and said she was very angry not to be with me. Cath was as supportive as she always has been, and I was delighted to have her as part of the programme. Then she said there was someone else I'd love to see . . . and there was my splendid eldest grandson Tony, who had flown from Brisbane. He was obviously rather overwhelmed by this whole experience, but told me he loved me and said there were not many times he wanted to be back in New Zealand, but this was one of them.

After that, I thought nothing else could happen, but suddenly there was the loved voice of an old dear friend, Wendy James from London. I simply couldn't believe it. There she was, part of my London family with whom I'd shared so much and, long-distance, still do. She talked about my contribution to her garden, how I had pruned her roses and, while she was away and on the eve of my journey to Israel, had renewed the soil in her windowboxes and planted spring bulbs which bloomed long after I'd gone home. She looked so vibrant, a successful editor in London, her wonderful Titian hair as luxuriant as ever. I had been very put out when I rang her from Dublin three weeks before to touch base, only to be told by her children that she was out of the country. She said that, because she knew she was about to make the long journey to participate in the programme, she had had to tell her children to lie to me.

Mary, knowing how much I would like it, had asked TV One to bring my good friend Maya Toydze from Moscow to be on the programme. She was then a film editor; she now has her own studio and produces films with her second husband. However, in those days the vestiges of the Cold War still lingered and TV One didn't think it was appropriate.

I was quite overwhelmed by all this, and at the dinner party that followed the programme, tried to express some of this. I learned how many of the people involved had been accommodated at the Angus Inn in Lower Hutt some days prior to the programme. I think I came to terms with Bob Parker and even thanked him warmly, though I have a sneaking idea that he never really forgave my intransigence.

I had to go to Auckland the next day, so I made arrangements to meet up with people when I returned that evening. When I approached the air hostesses standing at the front of the aircraft, I learned the consequences of being the central person on *This Is Your Life*. They and a good number of the passengers had seen the show and I had a very busy journey. In Auckland I was to take part in a television interview as an FOL representative and a radio interview with Ewing Stevens. As I had an hour to fill in before my first interview, I decided to find a coffee bar in lower Queen Street, but I had quite underestimated how slow progress along the street would be. Dozens of people wanted to talk to me and I was only rescued by my TV interview.

Back in Wellington I had dinner with Wendy and Mary. Beverley had another appointment with an old school chum and would join me in the morning. I learned of the trauma of trying to find appropriate photographs and information for the programme. Wendy was going to Australia, her home country, to visit her mother and family in Bowral. The next day we went to Con's home in Fairfield Avenue, where her children were packing up and allocating her belongings according to her instructions. We sat in Con's sitting room on her leather settee and I felt that I had come to the end of a very important part of my life.

The FOL

In early 1981, Mary applied successfully for a position with the Commonwealth Secretariat in London. She was to be the Senior Documentalist in the Women In Development Programme and would travel to Commonwealth countries around the world to talk to women, run seminars and training sessions and do the developmental work that was her passion. It was a wonderful opportunity and all her friends were delighted for her.

Her contract with the Secretariat was for two years so it was necessary for her to find a tenant for her house in Apuka Street in Brooklyn, not far from where I lived. Before she could leave, apart from packing for an extended stay, she wanted to move some of her best furniture, china and other personal effects to the lockup shed at the rear of her garden and also paint the interior of the house. Of course, all those available were pressed into this service and we became quite frantic as the day of her departure approached. On that day, Mary had planned a farewell party which simply added to the ambience of the occasion. People could be seen balancing a glass of wine, French bread and pâté and a paintbrush, while in the kitchen a self-appointed and very much appreciated crew kept the glasses, coffee cups and plates washed and stacked away so that the tenants would find the kitchen as they would wish.

Daring friends helped Mary stack more and more things in her shed. I was painting the bathroom so thankfully was not involved in that exercise. But at last, with paint still drying and the kitchen in pristine condition, we went off with Mary and heavy suitcases to Wellington Airport, where I and our close friends Mary Strang, Simon Walker and Olivia Weekley had a farewell drink with her.

I didn't have much time to dwell on Mary's departure as both the union and the Federation of Labour were engaged in major activities. I hurtled from one airport to another, drove hundreds of miles and attended many meetings in the next few weeks. The FOL Executive had decided that I would go with the president, Jim Knox, to the International Labour Organisation (ILO) Conference in Geneva that year. As it happened, both

Jim and I needed to work hard right up to the minute we left. I learned that we were flying to Zurich via America and then on to Geneva.

It occurred to me that when I had finished my old passport and obtained a new one, I had burned the old one and with it my permanent American visa, and had not since tried to renew it. I rang the American Embassy and asked whether I would need a US visa in order to spend two hours in Los Angeles Airport on the way to Europe. They said no, so I stopped worrying and decided to apply for a new American visa when I returned from Europe.

Shortly before I left, I received the agenda and papers for the ILO Conference and realised how much study I needed to do before arriving in Geneva. Jim would of course give the workers' keynote speech for New Zealand and that was being wordsmithed by FOL researchers and Ken Douglas. But in the brief time I had to study the ILO papers, I realised that what I was about to experience would be pretty amazing.

The day of our departure dawned and Jim and I met at the airport. The competent, unflappable FOL vice-president, Ted Thompson, was to hold the fort in Jim's absence and he and Ken Douglas showed every wish for us to get on with the task ahead of us in Geneva. I had written to Mary as soon as I knew about the conference, and she had rung and suggested that I come back via London and stay with her. She would ask for leave and we could go down to Cornwall in her Citroën Deux Chevaux, Henrietta. There were a number of things I wanted to do in London, not least of which was to touch base with Wendy and Ian Dear and their children in Wimbledon.

In Auckland, we boarded our Air New Zealand jet and flew direct to Los Angeles. Jim was in business class as befitted his status and I was in economy which reflected mine, so we met up in the immigration queue. Jim was ahead of me, so he had gone through to Customs by the time I presented my passport, and knew I was in terrible trouble. 'You don't have a US visa,' said the immigration officer accusingly. I explained that I was in transit, and that the US Embassy in Wellington had told me I didn't need a visa for a two-hour stay. At that, he curled his lip disdainfully and told me to stand aside and someone would deal with me.

I didn't like the sound of that, and stood waiting beside my briefcase with its essential papers and pristine block of notepaper, clutching my travel documents. I'd hoped to spend the time in transit working on the conference papers, a hope that dwindled as time ticked by. Ultimately, an airport bureaucrat came and whisked me away. Today, transit passengers go to the transit desk, are processed and directed to the departure lounge. But then, the Cold War mentality still lingered, and I found myself being regarded with some suspicion. My explanations were swept aside and I was taken to a locked room which was empty apart from a couple of chairs. My briefcase was taken from me despite my offering to show the official its contents.

I was assured I would get them back when it was time to board my Lufthansa flight. Jim was being met by friends of his from the American Federation of Labor and Congress of Industrial Organisation (AFL-CIO), but somewhere during their warm greetings he realised that I was missing, made enquiries and was enraged to find out what had happened. I heard raised voices outside my locked door, the loudest of which was Jim's. But in spite of the combined efforts of the leader of the New Zealand trade union movement and the AFL-CIO, they couldn't shake the opinion of the airport authorities that I was an undesirable.

Once airborne on the Lufthansa flight, Jim came to see me. I had been taken aboard by yet another official, given my belongings ahead of other passengers, and was not a happy person, but I saw no point in flogging a dead horse and told Jim that I was fine and would see him at the Zurich Airport. Once there, he told me he hadn't believed I wasn't upset and had come to see me during the night but had found me sound asleep.

In Geneva, we were met by the car that was used each year by the New Zealand delegation and driven by a Briton, Graeme, who came over every year to perform this service. He took us to the Hôtel Angleterre, which Jim knew very well. It was modest but very comfortable and was handy to shops and restaurants and to the Palais des Nations where the ILO Conference is held. That first day, we settled in and unpacked, and met the rest of the New Zealand delegation with the exception of Jim Bolger (then Minister of Labour), who was staying elsewhere.

We had a free evening so Jim said he would take me to his favourite restaurant — the British Café — which was within easy walking distance from the hotel. Once I read the menu, I knew why he liked it so much: the fare consisted of good, basic, English cooking produced by the English couple who owned the place. Home-made beef, chicken and veal pies, fish and chips, bacon, eggs and chips, all at a reasonable price. The owners came out to welcome Jim, who had patronised this place over the years.

Each day thereafter, Graeme arrived at eight-thirty a.m. to drive us to the conference. I usually sat in the back between the Labour Department representative who came from Hamilton and the president of the Employers Federation, Jim Rowe. It was not an easy situation. Jim Knox couldn't stand Jim Rowe, and as time went on, he became infuriated by what he and Jim Bolger had said in their keynote speeches and attacked them all the way. Jim Knox sat in the front seat because, he said, his old rugby league knee injury made this necessary. Jim Rowe didn't accept this excuse and each morning there was a race to be the first in the car. If Jim Knox lost out, he would sit beside me, fuming and using very colourful language, telling the Employers' chief what he thought of him and his policies.

Jim's speech that year was a very strong one, attacking the Muldoon Government's policies and the disastrous effects they were having on the lives of working people, and lambasting the Employers Federation support for those policies. The speech was not well received by either Jim Bolger or Jim Rowe, who were vocal in their condemnation; though I have to add that it was appreciated by many delegates. The more his detractors tackled Jim Knox, the more vigorously he retaliated. Our route to the conference took us past the Soviet Embassy, a massive building behind secure fences. Grasping my shoulder, Jim said, 'That's where you and I wrote that speech, isn't it, Sonja?'

Jim Knox was in his element in the international environment. His many journeys around the world, his links with trade unionists, peace and human-rights activists, and his unswerving support for the principles involved, made him a much appreciated person.

Each morning on our arrival, we went to our locker and found piles of invitations to diplomatic and other functions; we attended several each evening, as well as luncheons. The conference was held in a huge chamber and although I should have known better from my experiences at international peace and trade union meetings, I was overwhelmed by the great preponderance of male delegates. Of course there were committee meetings going on at the same time as the plenary session in various parts of the building, so there was seldom a large group in the plenary. Only when an important delegate or speaker was to take the floor was there a good muster. As always at international fora, the discussions that took place behind the scenes were the most satisfying.

The ILO section of the Palais had seemingly endless marble corridors and dozens of committee rooms. I walked miles each day and sometimes arrived at the wrong committee, only realising this when I had clamped the headphones to my ears and turned the knob to the English translation.

Representatives of women working for ILO came to see me. They said they had heard about me and had a copy of the Working Women's Charter, which I had brought back from Australia in 1978 and introduced at an FOL conference some time later. The ILO representatives were unhappy about the status and treatment of women in the ILO and in the United Nations generally. They invited me to a meeting later in the week. As I had had similar meetings with women at the United Nations in New York, I was very interested to hear what they had to say. Afterwards I reflected that a great deal of effort and hard work had to happen before any

The New Zealand delegation to the ILO Conference in Geneva: Jim Bolger, at extreme right, was then Minister of Labour

improvement could take place. Like many male-dominated organisations at that time, sexism, sexual harassment and lack of equal opportunity were real problems. The women were interested in the efforts that women at the United Nations were making to deal with these. I gave them some names and addresses of UN women, and they said they'd contact them and, I hoped, would exchange useful information.

As I hurtled around Geneva from embassy to embassy, I was aware of what an attractive city it was, with the lake, the stunning backdrop of the mountains, the sparkling cleanliness everywhere, the homes of the rich and famous around the lake, the huge and very expensive apartment houses, and the shops with their watches, cuckoo clocks and delicious Swiss chocolate.

On the third weekend in Geneva, the whole delegation went to France for lunch on the Sunday. We set out on a wonderful summer's day. Jim was not very enthusiastic — it was not his sort of happening — but I was keen to see something of the country, and I knew we would be going up Mont Blanc in a funicular. We arrived at the restaurant to find lunch spread outside at a long table with a snowy starched tablecloth, placed between stone columns covered by climbing roses in bloom. The sparkling crystal, silverware and beautiful crockery didn't impress Jim, who I knew would rather be back at the British Café. The waiters hovered with the menus, and as it happened, Jim was the last to make his choice. 'I want fish and chips,' he told the startled waiter, who said, 'Feesh and cheeps?' 'Well,' said Jim, 'this is France, isn't it? Don't tell me you've never heard of French fries!' The delegation dissolved with laughter, but Jim was not amused.

It was an idyllic setting and the food was wonderful. Later I went off to board the funicular. Jim wouldn't come, said he had done it before and would stay below. As it happened, I was put with an English couple and unfortunately, once we got underway, the wife developed a severe case of claustrophobia and became very agitated. When we reached the top and I was taking in the fabulous views, she said firmly that she would not go back in 'that thing'. Fortunately she was persuaded to do so.

I had observed with some alarm that Jim's temper was increasingly at flashpoint — and even I was not spared. On several occasions he would attack me out of the blue for some imagined wrong. One morning when he was taking our mail out of the locker, the man who had the one above ours opened his. It had sharp edges and Jim, who had been stooping, stood up and connected with it. As a result he received quite a deep cut which began to bleed profusely. Jim was infuriated and yelled at the offending delegate, accusing him of acting deliberately. I thought he was going to hit him and tried to pour oil on stormy waters. I found some tissues to stem the flow of blood pouring down from Jim's vulnerable bald head, but he thrust me aside and continued with the altercation. Somehow things were eventually resolved, the delegate sidled off muttering, and I found some Elastoplast and applied it. Then I saw that Jim's newly drycleaned suit was stained with blood. I had to persuade him to let me try to blot the worst of it off with a sponge. Later, when one of his suits came back from the drycleaner with a slight scorch mark, Jim took it out on the concierge at the desk, blaming him and making a really nasty scene.

All this was so out of character with his usual self. If I had only known of his diabetes and his refusal to take medication or eat and drink sensibly for that disease, I would have understood; but I was never told. It was like being with a naughty preschooler at times. But worse was to follow.

The following week, we went to dinner at the home of the New Zealand deputy ambassador. He had gathered together some very interesting people to meet us. We were having pre-dinner drinks when out of the blue Jim attacked me with a stream of amazing accusations which grew wilder each minute. What he said was so untrue and so vicious that I was absolutely devastated and, rather than cry in front of my host and the other guests, hurried from the room. I found Graeme and asked him to take me back to the hotel. The residence staff could not help but hear what Jim had said and were shocked. Graeme was very kind and very angry on my behalf, but of course, I had to be loyal to Jim. It was a bad time.

The next morning in the car, Jim said to me, 'What on earth made you go home and miss dinner last night?' I looked at him in amazement and so did Graeme. I decided to tread very carefully for the rest of the conference, but even that didn't help. After any outburst, Jim was always his warm friendly self. It was all very puzzling. Somehow we survived to the end of the conference, and as he left to visit several countries on his way home, Jim wished me a good visit in England.

Mary was at Heathrow to meet me in Henrietta, and took me to her rather splendid flat in St John's Wood in North London. It had been part of a lovely family home and had high ceilings and a view of the rear garden. The flat was round the corner from the Abbey Road studios where the Beatles had recorded their famous hits. Each time we came or went home we passed over the well-known zebra crossing.

For the first week, while Mary was at work I recovered from a very busy month in Geneva, working on my report and telephoning and visiting friends. Mary worked at Marlborough House and one day I went to meet her and talked with my old friend Chris Laidlaw, who was then personal assistant to the secretary-general of the Commonwealth Secretariat (he much later became the Member of Parliament for Wellington Central).

Mary and I had discussed our proposed journey to Cornwall and had decided to go down to Land's End, where my friend May Davis and her husband Harry had had a pottery studio before they came to Nelson to establish their pottery there. May had told me how unique and beautiful Cornwall was, but nothing had really prepared me for the impact of that historic, colourful landscape. It was the quality of the light that first struck me, quite different from anywhere else that I've been. I think that the east coast of the North Island, particularly north of Gisborne, comes closest. I could tell why so many artists chose to paint in Cornwall.

By the time we got there, though, the individual towns had become commercialised to appeal to tourists, with huge carparks, electronic games and jukeboxes in historic pubs, old houses too large for single families converted into hotels, their gardens now carparks — but in spite of all this, there was still a lot of magic around. Small towns like Mousehole and Truro were a delight. At Land's End, we were photographed under the famous signpost pointing the way to so many countries. We travelled down through Broadmoor where the well-known prison is, a brooding, windswept landscape. On the way back we stopped off at Bath, which was quite something, still with many old buildings, including the Bathhouse and the wonderful crescent of Wren houses.

Back in London, it was time to prepare for my journey home. I had known before I left on my trip that the Springbok Tour of New Zealand, which had been the subject of so much protest, would have begun before I got back. On my last day, Mary drove me through London on our return from visiting Wendy and Ian in Wimbledon. Two days before, appalled citizens had watched the Brixton riots, in which police response had been particularly violent and much property had been smashed as well as the bones and bodies of black people. We drove through Brixton, which looked like a deserted battleground with boarded-up shop fronts, piles of rubble and scorched houses. I said somewhat smugly that such things couldn't happen back home where the police were civilised. Famous last words.

The Springbok Tour

For many years prior to 1981, New Zealand had a strong anti-apartheid movement. I was in Nelson in the 1960s when there was to be an All Black tour of South Africa. The New Zealand Rugby Union was told that because of the apartheid regime firmly in place in that country, no Maori should be included in the New Zealand team. This enraged thousands of New Zealanders, who didn't want the team to go anyway and felt that the ban on Maori rugby players was quite untenable. A No Maoris No Tour campaign sprang up and gathered momentum.

Nelson was no exception. We went door to door with a petition to the Rugby Union arguing the case against the tour. As always, the passions for and against were clear-cut. Our local Labour Representation Committee (LRC) debated the issue and in that body too, opinions were divided: there were those who wanted the All Blacks to go to South Africa and genuinely believed (wrongly, as it later transpired) that politics and sport didn't mix; and there were those who felt that South Africa's racist policies towards the black majority of their own population was unacceptable to New Zealand.

Our campaign in Nelson culminated in a large meeting on Church Steps in Trafalgar Street, below the Cathedral. I was saddened and frustrated, though not surprised, to see our own Labour Member of Parliament, Stan Whitehead, and the LRC president, Eric Pearce, marching along to the steps with the tour supporters. We had God on our side in the person of Bishop Hulme Moir, who stood beneath the cathedral in his ecclesiastical purple vest, his gold crucifix gleaming in the autumn sunshine, and delivered an eloquent and compelling speech about the horrors of apartheid, spelling out what was happening to black and coloured people in South Africa and why we should not give the tour any support whatsoever. In Nelson anyway, it was the first time that rugby tour supporters were made aware that those who opposed the tour were not a bunch of mad radicals but a real cross-section of their community.

By 1973, the New Zealand Rugby Union was preparing to welcome a Springbok team for a tour of the country. Norman Kirk was Prime

Minister at the time. He had a real ability to tap the mood of the electorate at large and knew from Labour Party conference debates on this issue what the majority of us thought. He had strong views on matters of racial prejudice and exploitation, and after careful consideration and discussion with his Cabinet, he instructed the Rugby Union to cancel the tour. At the time he said, 'A Springbok Tour would engender the greatest eruption of violence that this country has ever known,' and that such a tour would tarnish New Zealand's image as a multi-racial country. Leader of the Opposition Robert Muldoon was incensed at the cancellation of the tour and said that a National Government would welcome a Springbok Tour even if there were threats of violence and civil strife. At that time the police were gearing up for confrontation should the tour go ahead and were amassing what they saw as the necessary armoury — which would be used in 1981.

By 1981, a National Government was in power, and when they were told that a Springbok Tour was imminent, they didn't discourage it. It was known that several Cabinet ministers welcomed a tour. Prime Minister Muldoon said that he thought it would be a disaster. He nevertheless allocated $2.7 million for police protection of the Springboks as they travelled around the country. The tour was a watershed for New Zealanders, who were forced to grapple with some hard truths.

I arrived back in Wellington from London late afternoon to traditionally dull winter weather. Calling in to the office to pick up my car, I was told that at that moment a protest group was preparing to march up Molesworth Street to the South African Embassy and that my daughter Penny and her partner were to be part of that protest. I drove to Lambton Quay but the march was already underway and I crossed to the main gates leading to Parliament so that Penny and Mick could see me. I knew that in my jetlagged state, I wouldn't exactly be an asset to the protest, but decided to wait until all the marchers had passed. By now it was getting dark. Above me I saw the stars tentatively appearing.

What followed was a scenario that I had never witnessed in my life before. Marching for peace, for a nuclear-free New Zealand, I had been told by bystanders to go back to Moscow where I belonged (not that the hecklers had ever been there). But I had never experienced the violence I was about to see.

I was in a strategic position to observe the horrible events that followed. The marchers moved up Molesworth Street with linked arms towards the first intersection. In the front row, people wore crash helmets and had obviously padded their shoulders and chests. Suddenly, to my astonishment, I saw a squad of police in riot gear carrying what we later learned were the lethal Monadnock PR24 long batons. They peeled back the front rows and began whacking the heads and shoulders of the fourth row. There was quite a long line of protestors and those who were further down the line couldn't see what was happening and kept on walking forward, which exerted pressure further up front.

The police appeared to take this as provocation and the whole situation became very ugly. My old friend Rona Bailey, then in her mid-sixties and in the fourth row, slipped in the crush and, as she did, a baton caught her on the side of the head. She later said it had not hit her full force because she wasn't upright, but hard enough to draw blood. I went across the road to get her away and, with help, took her over to Parliament gates and sat her down while someone went to get her son-in-law, Ted Sheehan, who then worked as a television journalist in the parliamentary press gallery. As we waited there, a senior police officer came and asked me if there was anything he could do. I told him he should go home and beat up his own grandmother. Not exactly polite but I was so enraged by what I'd seen that police were low on my list. When Ted came to take Rona home, I tried to find Penny and Mick but many people were milling around. I saw my friends' daughter with blood running down her face.

The next morning the *Dominion* had a photo of her like that and I was again filled with disgust. The terrible thing was that these were not violent people. It was a peaceful protest met by police violence. As I had been away, I didn't know what had happened elsewhere. When Penny and Mick got home, they rang and filled me in, telling me about the progress of the protests so far. Back at work, Graham had kept all the relevant newspaper cuttings and from them I read about the first game in Gisborne and the match in Hamilton where the protestors actually got onto the playing field and the game was stopped.

I discovered that the anti-tour movement in Wellington was superbly organised, a fact grudgingly acknowledged by the police. The marshalls and protestors met weekly and planned for the week ahead. During the week, protestors were directed to various points on Wellington's motorways and intersections, blocking traffic and stretching police resources. It was at one of these points that I realised that protestors came from all sectors of our society, and all age groups — even women in twinset-and-pearls from Khandallah and Karori like the ones who told me how angry they were about the Springbok Tour, the Government's role and the police activities. Many turned out to be well-informed about events in South Africa under the apartheid regime.

The marshalls divided up the protestors into squads: Yellow, White, Pink, Orange, Blue, Green and Brown. We were allocated a colour and were told each week where to assemble, though not what we would be doing. That wasn't revealed until the Saturday, when we assembled in our allotted place. I gave up going to the weekly meetings partly because of work commitments and partly because I found the male dominance and treatment of women at meetings difficult to deal with. While I never doubted the organisers' skills and abilities, I knew that I would be a better protestor if someone else reported to me where I was to go each weekday or Saturday. I trusted their judgement absolutely and no matter what they proposed on Saturdays, I co-operated.

A lot of key people were masterminding the protest: people like Pauline McKay who was chairperson of Halt All Racist Tours (HART). John Minto in Auckland was the North Island organiser, attacked and reviled by people who had never met him or known him. Dick Cuthbert in Auckland resigned his job with Social Welfare to work fulltime on protest organisation. Trevor Richards and a whole raft of others masterminded the tight, well-organised activities in Wellington. In Christchurch, where the anti-apartheid movement was particularly strong, Steve Bayliss was the organiser.

Graham Kelly, his wife Jeanette and their children were in a different-coloured squad from me, as were Penny and Mick. On Sundays, we all compared notes and experiences. On weekdays on the motorways and on Saturdays, there were always people I knew in my squad and I also met many new people. This was the first time most of them had ever been involved in anything like this. From London, Mary reported that she had demonstrated against the tour and apartheid with a very respectable number of expatriate New Zealanders outside New Zealand House.

By this time, the Wellington game of the tour was fast approaching. I was by now quite skilled at padding my chest and shoulders and on the day of the match, I set out wearing Mark's crash helmet from Rangipo as well, with a real sense of foreboding. I always left my car in the union carpark where it would be safe, and walked to where the squad was gathering. This time we were not told where we were going, only that we should watch the marshalls closely. I must say that with my limited lung power, I found climbing up the steep hill of the Town Belt rather taxing. We came out of the trees and saw below us McAllister Park, opposite Athletic Park where the game was to be played. By now the police had co-opted the army, who had set huge piles of barbed wire in place on the edge of the park to stop us from getting over to Athletic Park. The marshalls had had a tip-off about this and provided large grappling hooks for us to demolish the barbed wire; and a number of protestors clawed at the wire with these.

Graham's squad was in Rintoul Street where the plan was to block access by rugby enthusiasts to the game. They sat down in a solid mass so they couldn't be pushed aside and police waded in with batons. Some people were pushed through a plate-glass shop window. Things were becoming very fraught. At that time, the press reported that their polls told them that 52 per cent opposed the tour and 48 per cent were in favour. This was later amended to 60/40, which gives some idea of the situation.

By then, the game was in progress. Onto McAllister Park came police in full riot gear — metal helmets, long thick navy overcoats, riot shields and long batons. The protestors were now assembled in several rows right across the park and the police positioned themselves in front of us, eyeball to eyeball so to speak, although they stared straight ahead. It had rained during the night and my shoes sank into the turf. I hoped I wasn't going to have to leave in a hurry. Next to me was a Chilean refugee friend, Victor, who had come to New Zealand to escape the excesses of the Pinochet regime. Remembering that in Chile, thousands had been murdered in and around stadiums, I said to him, 'Do you have a sense of déjà vu?' and he said that he did, but of course in Chile one would be taken round the back of the stadium and shot.

It was a tense encounter. Ken Douglas appeared. He said, 'Go home, Sonja, you've made your point. You'll get hurt.' I looked along the line and saw Joanna Kelly, Graham and Jeanette's daughter, and knew I couldn't leave. Not long before the match ended, the police decided that, in order to avoid a major after-match confrontation, they would move us out and off down the road. The Springboks had spent the night under the stadium at Athletic Park and feelings were running high. We finally hit the road and started back to town. On the way we passed a pub where rugby fans who hadn't been able to get into the park had been watching the match on television. They poured out of the pub and assailed us, threw beer cans, and a young Maori spat in my face. Someone saw a man he knew behind me and lashed out with a punch. Unfortunately he missed and punched me very hard, catching me below my padding.

I walked back to my car and went home, feeling rather strange. When I got home, Penny phoned. Her squad had gone out to the airport when the Springboks arrived, had got onto the tarmac, been arrested and she and Mick had spent a very uncomfortable night in police cells. They were charged and released until their case came up in court. When I woke in the morning, I realised that I was in great pain and real trouble. I rang Graham, who said he would take me to see my doctor, Carol Shand. She had me x-rayed and reported that I had two cracked ribs and three broken ones. I should rest as much as possible and not do anything strenuous! Chance would be a fine thing, I thought.

I went to work each day for as long as I could cope and at night, as I couldn't lie in bed, I sat up with a sheepskin in my chair, reading a very catholic collection of books. On fine mornings I saw the sun come up over the Orongorongo ranges behind Eastbourne.

Throughout the tour, the protestors had always had impressed on them that ours was to be a peaceful and tightly disciplined protest. And in all that I took part in, that's the way it was. I was told that there were some protestors who retaliated in Auckland at the end of the tour, but by and large it was a peaceful protest, despite severe police provocation. The press generally and National politicians continually spread the word that protestors were destroying property and being violent. It was just not true.

The tour changed New Zealanders' perception of each other. For the first time, very deep divisions developed within families, in workplaces, in the churches (though most played a major role against the tour), the armed forces, and in fact between married couples, and young adults and their parents. Mealtimes became very fraught. I knew a couple who were on opposite sides. He was a policeman and she a real estate agent. Every Saturday morning, he would pad her shoulders and chest, make sure her crash helmet was firmly in place, then go off to climb into his riot gear. They went their separate ways, not knowing whether they would meet up later in the day in a confrontational situation.

The Saturday after the Springboks left, I found myself automatically climbing into my protest gear. I was halfway through padding up before I realised that it was all over. I wondered first what I would do with my Saturdays (something that didn't turn out to be a problem) and then I hoped that I would never again have to be involved in such activities.

The activities of the protest were not lost on the people of South Africa. White South Africans at the game in Hamilton, for instance, watched with astonishment and amazement as the protestors poured onto the playing field. They saw the game abandoned and were surprised at the strength of the opposition to what the Springboks represented. When Nelson Mandela was in New Zealand in 1995, he explained just how much support black South Africans had felt when they saw on the screen, in a country half a world away, people going to such lengths to oppose apartheid. He conveyed his Government's thanks to all who had protested. I have been amazed at how Prime Minister Bolger has become a born-again anti-apartheid supporter, even using his meeting with Nelson Mandela as part of the 1996 National Party conference election video.

Things were not easy in the cities during the tour, but the real heroes were those brave and gallant people who demonstrated in small numbers in rural towns against the tour. Most rural towns have passionate rugby supporters and protestors were often assaulted with eggs, tomatoes and other unmentionable objects, as well as much verbal and sometimes physical abuse from enraged fans.

I wish I had known that the future for South Africa would change so dramatically and that the total sports boycott imposed by the international community would play such a major role in the destruction of apartheid. I have been to South Africa since the Government of Reconciliation took power. Wherever I went, I was asked if I knew Jonah Lomu, who is a real hero over there. How things change.

The Trade Union Movement

There is not the space, neither is this the appropriate place to write a history of the trade union movement between 1980 and 1996. In *Bread and Roses* I wrote about my election as first woman to the Executive of the New Zealand Federation of Labour. I had seen many changes in the years since I was sixteen and first joined a union in Auckland.

From the beginning, because I was a woman, I was very much in the public eye, both here and abroad. Jim took a jaundiced view of this. He found me quite difficult. At that time, all I wanted to be was a useful contributing member of the Executive. It's never easy breaching the barriers of a long-term male power organisation. I'd done it before and was prepared for that. When colleagues told Jim Napier, then secretary of the Waterside Workers Union, that I had been elected to the FOL Executive, he said enthusiastically, 'How wonderful. We always need good typists!' It took a little time to be accepted as a real person. Not that anyone on the Executive treated me with anything but care and concern. That was why, warts and all, I cared for them so much and went to bat for each or all of them.

By the time I was elected, Tom Skinner was president and the FOL had its own custom-built premises in Lukes Lane. It even had an apartment at the top which the president could use when he was in Wellington. But Tom preferred what was then known as the Airport Inn in Kilbirnie. Tom had followed the very colourful, ruthless and tough Finton Patrick Walsh, and was a very different character. An Auckland trade unionist, he was a pragmatist, a natty dresser and one who could mix confidently with politicians and captains of industry.

At this time, Jim Knox was secretary of the FOL. When I first came into the room where the Executive met and took my place as the new chum at the very bottom of the table, I remembered the stories that my husband Charlie had told me about what he had been told about the 'old days' when the Executive met in Trades Hall in the secretary's office. Ken Baxter, who was secretary at that time, was a man of strong principle, who saw everything in black and white. He was dedicated to the working people of the country. I had seen his office with its curling linoleum flooring, its plastic bucket for washing the dishes.

Charlie told me that then, the Executive members, who met at least once a month and came from all around the country, did not have any lunch. One day, they asked Ken Baxter why they couldn't send out for some lunch and he was scandalised. One would have thought it strange that people who spent so much time working to ensure that workers had lunch and tea breaks should not have any themselves. But that's how it was. The members insisted, and reluctantly Ken sent the office staff out to buy some food. When they came back, the Executive members saw that Ken had ordered pies. He is said to have taken each pie, cut it in half and handed half to each member. Ken of course did not join them.

By the time I arrived, at least we had rolls and sandwiches but we didn't stop work to eat them. At that time, there were still some of the old-style unionists around, men like Toby Hill, Jim Knox and Frank Thorn, who had been scarred during the 1951 lockout on the waterfronts of New Zealand. They were a particular breed, absolutely principled, tough, outspoken and uncompromising. During my years as an FOL Executive member, we grappled with a number of major and lengthy disputes.

Demarcation — that is, the right of a union to represent workers in a particular industry and to resist the onslaught of another union — was an ever-present problem. Already, breezes of change were permeating the workplace. The waterfront industry was an example. Waterside workers were a special type, much maligned by the media and the public who had little idea of the work they did. Their union was strong and its officials were very knowledgable about the industry. But the industry was about to change dramatically with the arrival at the ports of the first containers. When Ted (EG) Thompson, a Waterside Workers Union official, saw what was happening, he had the common sense to initiate discussion with the port employers about the effects containerised shipping would have on his members and their future employment. It was obvious that container ships would transport the cargo of the future, and that these containers would need to be unloaded by cranes and not by waterside workers. From the 1970s, unions involved with handling cargo had been meeting to discuss a wide range of issues, each of course concerned with the interests of their own members: drivers, storemen packers, dairyworkers and waterside workers. Reading through the minutes of one of these meetings chaired by Ted Thompson in 1981 takes one back to a world that has disappeared. It gives the lie to anti-trade union advocates who contend that unions ignored technological change.

Ted Thompson was an intelligent man. Thanks to his foresight and skill at the negotiating table, when containerisation started to make inroads into the jobs of watersiders, he had created a fund with financial co-operation from the port employers which made it possible for the workers who were being laid off to receive a sum of money which would enable them to train and establish a new life. Redundancy arguments and industrial action were not necessary. I often felt it was a shame that the meat industry unions and employers, who were also facing technological changes and problems with aging and outdated plants, could not have made a similar accommodation.

When Tom Skinner retired, Jim Knox became president and Ken Douglas secretary of the FOL. Ken tells me that he certainly wasn't Jim's first choice, and initially I think there was a strain between them, but Ken was to be an incredibly loyal supporter of the president — sometimes, I felt, excessively so. Jim grew up in the then working-class suburb of Freemans Bay. His oldest and closest friend, Johnny Mitchell, had been sent to mine coal at the age of twelve. They shared strong working-class principles and Jim always kept in touch. While Jim believed that employers were the enemy and that asking for higher wages was seen as taking profit from employers, Ken was from another generation and realised that free wage-bargaining was only possible in times of full employment.

Jim was an Aucklander by birth and by long experience, but he realised when he was elected president that it would be sensible to live in Wellington, so he prised his Auckland-based wife away and bought a nice home in Churton Park. It was a classic situation. She had been taken away from her family and friends, given a nice home, and realised early that much of her time would be spent alone in a strange environment. Jim worked long hours, had evening meetings and travelled extensively. It was a recipe for failure. Jim was a very private person and it took the Executive some time to realise that things in the Knox domestic situation were not well. His wife returned to Auckland and ultimately they were divorced. My impression was that he was genuinely unable to understand why — 'I gave her a nice home. What more did she want?' was the only comment he made to me.

When Ken took over as secretary, he soon realised that Jim had not been a good administrator. There was no filing system, and when Ken moved a safe, he found a pile of old unanswered letters. My opinion is that Jim should have been president much earlier, in a different environment. Tom Skinner had a good relationship with Rob Muldoon and rumour had it that they met on Sundays in the suburb where they both lived; but Jim never really coped on equal terms with Muldoon and often said, 'The only good politician is a dead one.'

Jim Knox is very much a part of working-class history in this country. My grandmother would have said of him, 'He's all wool and a yard wide,' which was her way of saying that someone was worth considering. I knew, early on, that he trusted very few people, but for those he did trust, his loyalty was boundless. One he trusted very much was Ashley Russ, then national secretary of the New Zealand Carpenters Union, who played a positive role on the FOL Executive, knowing more than most of us about Jim's intentions. Jim was paranoid, but that was the nature of the trade union movement at that time. He felt that information was power but he couldn't or wouldn't share it. He was instinctively perceptive about working-class issues such as racism and peace and was very much respected at international meetings.

I have explained elsewhere about Jim's untreated diabetes and his behaviour when his blood-sugar level was low. As an ex-nurse, I would have understood that, but because of his extreme privacy about his personal life, I was never told, and that was to have very serious consequences. He was an extremely generous person to those he loved and to people overseas, and when he retired we realised just how much he had given of himself.

At the beginning of the 1980s, the Executive realised that the separate entities of the private and public sectors of the trade union movement should not continue in the climate we were entering and, in 1981, after lengthy and sometimes acrimonious debate, a New Zealand Combined Trade Unions (CTU) Working Party was set up. The opposition came mainly from the blue-collar unions who were very suspicious of state unions and felt that the movement would be weakened by uniting with them. It said much for the calibre of Ted Thompson, representing tough blue-collar workers, that he saw clearly the benefits for workers of a united public and private sector union movement; and he made some very useful contributions to the CTU debate. I know that the PSA had members who had real doubts about joining with that FOL lot, so we all came to the negotiating table with a certain amount of baggage.

Ted Thompson was now vice-president of the FOL and a rock of common sense and calm. He was, I believe, the most skilful person in either the FOL or Parliament, who could quickly summarise a debate and come up with a resolution with which the majority of the Executive could agree. The FOL was much involved in the formation of credit unions, welfare societies, building societies, trust banks, industry training boards, apprenticeship schemes and training and, later, superannuation funds. We supported and worked with the Health Department in many areas of safety promotion, eye protection, safety footwear and clothing on work-sites, hearing protection (at that time boilermakers working in small, enclosed areas with loud implements went deaf). We were very involved with the education of workers on matters of safety in the workplace.

It was through these endeavours that I met Tord Kjelstrom and Adrienne Taylor, who were spearheading industrial health and safety for Auckland unions and who came to Wellington to talk to the FOL about those issues. They were to become two of my nearest and dearest friends.

The Executive was very concerned that we should set in place a super-annuation scheme for Jim. We knew that he had always existed on a limited wage, and that the salary that we paid him didn't allow for retire-ment, and that in any case he was not good at looking after himself. When we presented the super package to him, he behaved as though we had offered something completely unpalatable. He was just like Ken Baxter and the lunch pies, and wouldn't even consider it. He said that all his life he had paid taxes and that some of those were earmarked for retirement superannuation. He would exist on that. He didn't want any workers' money used on him. We argued with him that he didn't trust politicians and said that any government could decrease or do away with superannu-ation, but he was immovable. He said, 'They wouldn't dare!' Over the years, we tried to get him to change his mind but he was adamant.

The Executive decided that Jim and I should go to Australia to talk to the Australian Council of Trade Unions about this combined state and private sector union organisation and find out how it worked over there. This was very useful and reinforced our belief that over here, we were doing the right thing. We went out for a celebratory dinner and, as we began, he launched into an attack on me out of the blue, accusing me of wanting his job, of being constantly disloyal and a whole raft of other alle-gations which were also unfounded. I understand now that Jim's blood-sugar level must have been low (we'd been too busy to have lunch) but I was devastated at the time. As Jim ate his dinner and mine tasted like sawdust in my mouth, he suddenly relaxed and became his old friendly, funny self. It was obvious to me the next morning that he didn't remem-ber anything of his outburst. At a lunch with the ACTU, he said what a great support to him I was and how good it was to have a woman on the Executive. I couldn't have been more confused.

For me, Jim's finest efforts were during the Kinleith dispute over different pay rates being given by different mills. I had gone to Tokoroa at the invitation of the wives of trade unionists involved in the bitter dispute. Their husbands couldn't or wouldn't tell them what it was all about. We had a very frank discussion and during it I asked that the male leaders of the dispute explain the situation to the women. When the men finally did this, a magnificent woman stood up and said, 'You stupid bastards, why didn't you tell us sooner? Being without money and trying to feed the kids would be easier if we understood why you were on strike.'

At the end of the meeting, a resolution was unanimously passed which said that in any future dispute, wives and partners should be involved. It was important for the unions to recognise and overcome the gender divisions they had often fostered in the past, and with my appointment and resolutions such as this they were gradually making advancements.

When Jim went to Tokoroa, I reminded him of this and he really took it on board. Women were absolutely involved during that dispute, arranged food and sustenance for strikers' families and for the strikers themselves and received support from far and wide. At the end of the dispute, I stood with Jim at an outdoor meeting of unionists and their families, toddlers in pushchairs, babies in prams, and saw Jim in his finest hour telling them of the final agreement with the employers. With hindsight, this is when he should have retired.

There was much change in the air. Young people who were university-educated were coming to work in the union movement as researchers, and the election of people like Rob Campbell and Rex Jones to the Executive brought a new dimension. Ted Thompson has told me about the protracted procedure that extended through three general elections and four governments to establish tripartite wage talks with the Muldoon Government. These were the successors of the Industrial Relations Council of the 1970s. At these tripartite talks were the unions, including representatives from both state and private sectors, the Employers Federation and Government ministers. Over the years, the players changed but not the battle lines.

For Jim, this was alien territory. He simply didn't enjoy these meetings and I'm sure that he realised that he was going into uncharted country where his skills were not applicable. In such circumstances, he tended to strike out. We had some memorable meetings. At the end of these, the media were there en masse. I tried very hard to persuade Jim not to go out of the meeting angry, but to tell the journalists that he would meet them in the Beehive foyer when he had had time to draw breath, but he always brushed me aside and interviews were never productive. If I had known the journalists then as well as I did later, I would have talked to them before the meetings and we would at least have had a coherent and useful result. I participated in those meetings during the Muldoon regime and after 1984 and felt that they should have been scripted better.

My brother David rang me and told me that his son Robin was marrying Linda, a young woman of Tuwharetoa descent and wanted me to come to the wedding. Because it was at the end of an FOL conference, I didn't think I could be there. FOL conferences were bracing and I usually spent the weekend after them recovering. On the last day of the conference,

Ken Douglas asked to see me. He said that the Soviet trade union delegate and his interpreter wanted to go to Rotorua by car and asked me to take them. My heart plummeted. I was exhausted but Ken said that he would provide me with a comfortable and reliable automatic car and book accommodation for us in Rotorua. The Soviet colleagues wanted to see the country, walk in the New Zealand bush and then go over to the east coast and put their feet in the ocean at Hawkes Bay. So of course I said yes. At that time the last vestiges of the Cold War were still around. I rang David and told him that I could come to the wedding but would be going on to Rotorua and that I would be bringing two Russians with me. It says much for my relationship with my brother that, after a discernible pause, he said that would be fine.

As it was, the Soviet delegate slept like a baby, but the interpreter who sat beside me said, 'I can't believe that I am sitting beside Sonja Davies, who came to Moscow with a trade union delegation and met my wife Maya Toydze and when we had our son, sent her a mohair rug which we call the Sonja rug.' It was one of those moments.

At that time, David and Lyn had a house on the main road into Taupo. I always loved that house, though they soon bought elsewhere. It looked out over the lake and left to the mountains and had a marvellous heated mineral pool. We arrived after the wedding but in time for the celebrations. Robin's wife Linda had numbers of her whanau there, one of whom had a definite moko. The Russians were riveted. They really enjoyed the festivities and had a swim in the heated pool. We went to Rotorua that evening, and in the morning went back to Taupo to go over the Taupo–Napier road. We had lunch with David and Lyn and the Russians provided recipes for preserving mushrooms. Lyn gave them each a chunk of wedding cake. On the way over to Napier, we stopped for them to walk, and when we got there, they were like children, dipping their feet in the cool autumn surf. And then to Wellington where I delivered happy people to their hotel, returned the rental car, picked up my own at the union office, and went home to collapse.

When Ted Thompson retired as secretary of the Waterside Workers Union and as vice-president of the FOL, I knew that I would miss him, and wondered who would take his place. I was approached by many people who asked me to nominate for the vice-presidential position. I was amazed but warmed by their support. When the nominations were announced, it was obvious that there were only two contenders, Ernie Ball, a senior official of the Engineers Union, and me. The media kept saying that Ernie would be the successful candidate. They talked about the clout of the Engineers Union and my minimal support from a predominantly female union. I was reasonably ambivalent about all this and, as time went by, geared myself not to succeed. But I had strong support. Executive member Rob Campbell came out positively for me and important unions came with him. At that time, Rob was a real influence in the trade union movement, but the media persuaded me that I didn't have a chance.

So I went to the FOL Conference with the media predictions ringing in my ears. I had got up early and written what I felt was a generous defeat speech. At the conference, when the voting was in progress, the atmosphere was electric. I looked at Ernie Ball, surrounded by his Engineers Union delegates, and wondered what sort of a vice-president he would make. I was so convinced that he would be the victor that when Rob Campbell came and hugged me and said 'Congratulations!', I couldn't believe that it had happened. What I thought of was that I was succeeding very competent people and I had a big responsibility.

Shortly after my election, Jim left for Geneva and the ILO Conference. He had been dropping hints about a 'lovely little lady', but wouldn't be drawn further. However, we could tell that whoever it was, he was very smitten. It was some time before we met Elizabeth, who was to become his second wife.

I had long been concerned about Ken's health. He worked punishing hours, and ate too much fast food, usually on the run. I had watched him trying to diet but it never lasted more than a few weeks. It seemed to me that it was time the Executive paused in its work and ate lunch in a more leisurely fashion. I talked to the staff to see how they would react to this suggestion, because they were the ones who obtained the food and made the tea and coffee. They were enthusiastic and later showed me the lunchroom they had created on the mezzanine floor above the Executive room. When I reported this to the Executive, they were agreeable and lunch upstairs became the norm.

Jim was away for several weeks as he had meetings to attend in several countries. At the last meeting before he returned, the Executive suggested to me that I should explain the changes we had made to him. Jim came back to a very busy period. We were all involved in different directions and I didn't have a chance to talk with him about minor matters such as lunch before the meeting. At the next meeting, we were called upstairs and told that lunch was ready. Jim asked if it was someone's birthday, and I replied that we had decided to have a break at lunchtime and eat upstairs. The Executive held its collective breath. 'What a good idea', said Jim. Later, as we sat in the lunchroom with the sun pouring in, I could tell that this decision wouldn't be reversed. Sadly, it didn't help Ken who used the break to catch up on work in his office, taking his lunch with him.

The National Executive of the New Zealand Federation of Labour, 1986/87; Jim Knox as President, and me as Vice-President

Linda Sissons came to work with Ken at the FOL. I had known her for some time and had heard of the excellent work she did at Waikato University. She and her husband had young children, and she was pregnant again. Linda sat in on Executive meetings. When her baby was born, her husband would bring him in to be breastfed right there at the Executive table — and no one ever commented. I felt we had moved on since the acceptance of the Working Women's Charter.

Several times a year we had meetings of the National Council of the FOL, a rather large, unwieldy body of trade unionists from many parts of New Zealand. These were the representatives of the working people and provided a chance for an exchange of views on the many issues of the day. When Labour was Government, appropriate Cabinet ministers came and spoke to the Council, and when they were in Opposition, spokespeople came. These were two-day meetings and as ever the things we learned in the evenings outside the meetings were very useful. Many of the councillors were people I had known for years, and sometimes there were one or two women present. I was still anxious to have a better gender balance in all union activity. We now had a Women's Advisory Council chaired by Therese O'Connell. She was great fun, witty, irreverent about male power figures, and dedicated to promoting the interests of working women. She was a very popular figure and did a lot of good work.

When Tom Skinner was president, he would see politicians either alone or with Jim. Jim announced early in his presidency that he wanted as many Executive members as possible to accompany him to such meetings, so that we would know what took place. We were all very busy in our own unions, so sometimes this was difficult, but it's fair to say that Jim was seldom if ever alone with politicians. Towards the end of an Executive meeting, Jim suddenly said that he had to go out for a minute, and asked me to take the chair. A short time later, the door opened and Jim came in with a small, slight person, whom he introduced to us as Elizabeth. Jim and Elizabeth were eventually married at a delightful service and it was a very happy occasion. He was genuinely in love with her and as I sat and watched them, I hoped he wouldn't be difficult or unkind.

Jim had a tendency to keep disputes as his province. He and Ashley Russ saw each other socially so, as Jim didn't have outside interests, I presumed they discussed disputes. As far as I was concerned, Jim only told me as much as he wanted me to know. He had decided that when I was acting president when he was absent, I was not to make any press statements. This was very difficult because the media wanted to know what was happening about disputes or arguments with Government. When I talked to Jim about this, he said it was none of their business and wouldn't budge.

One morning I arrived at the Executive meeting to find that Jim wouldn't be there. I had been away with Graham Kelly doing a series of meetings with our members in Hawkes Bay, so had had no contact with Jim for at least a week. Ken reported that he had some problem with one of his legs and was not able to walk very well. As the meeting progressed, one of the members asked me for a progress report on a dispute that Jim had been dealing with and of which I was not aware. I told them that Jim hadn't discussed the matter with me, so they asked me to ring him and get a report. When I rang him, Jim was absolutely furious and shouted at me, telling me that it was not my business, that he was dealing with the matter and would report to the Executive when he saw fit. The Executive had heard the shouting and I relayed to them what Jim had said. They were very angry and said they wanted me to see Jim and get the information they sought. Because Jim trusted Ashley, they suggested that he accompany me. We set out for Lyall Bay where Jim and Elizabeth lived, with some trepidation. Elizabeth sensibly said she was going for a walk and we had a very lively half hour, during which Jim called me scheming and conniving and accused me of trying to take his place and a whole raft of other things. But in the end he gave me the information I needed.

A crunchy conversation with Jim Knox at a 1980s FOL conference

Speaking as FOL Vice-President at a Trade Union rally in Hamilton in mid 1980s

*Maya, young Tim and I in my hotel room after she had
redeployed my bandages around my broken ribs*

I travelled a great deal representing the FOL: a number of times to the
Pacific, to Asia and to the USSR. I made strong links with the Soviet
Women's Committee and the Soviet Peace Movement. I seldom stayed for
more than a few days but usually managed to get to the fabulous ballet or
an opera. It wasn't always enjoyable, though. Somehow, whenever I went
to the USSR, it was winter and freezing outside. Once, when I was visiting a hospital some distance from what was then Leningrad, I slipped on
sheet ice and broke several ribs. I was taken to a hospital in Leningrad and
doctors bound me up and had me taken to the train to go back to Moscow.
I was in a lot of pain and had been given no medication. I asked my interpreter to ring my friend and colleague Maya and tell her what had
happened. She arrived in my room a couple of hours later with hot soup
and a bottle of red wine. She and one of the women staff members on my
floor undid my bandages and redid them so that I was more comfortable.
We had a long talk and she said she would find some painkillers for me to
have on my long journey home. She was and is a good friend.

Joyce Hawe of the Clothing Workers Union was elected to the FOL
Executive in the early 1980s, so I was pleased not to be the only woman. We
were still in endless discussion on the CTU, and ultimately came to a point
where it became a possibility. When I retired in 1986, the plans to merge the
two sectors were in place and after Jim retired, the CTU became a reality.

The International Year of Peace

1986 was something of a watershed for me. I retired from the Shop Employees Union and from the vice-presidency of the New Zealand Federation of Labour and became the chairperson of the United Nations International Year of Peace New Zealand National Committee, operating out of what became known as Peace House in what is now Kate Sheppard Street, behind the Backbencher Bar and Restaurant. Just across the road from Parliament and adjacent to government departments, we were admirably placed for lobbying purposes. The house itself was a lovely old two-storeyed colonial structure and belonged to the Ministry of Works, which intended to remove or demolish it and replace it with a courthouse or government department building. They leased it to us from June 1985 to December 1986 for a rental of $10,000.

The house had a reasonably large meeting room which we used when the IYP Committee came to Wellington, and as a place to talk to the many visitors from around New Zealand and from overseas. We leased a good-sized upstairs office to the organisation Peace Movement Aotearoa; and the Wellington Peace Forum and the Wellington IYP Committee also operated out of these premises.

New Zealand was one of only 28 countries in which the government supported an IYP national committee. The fact that the UN member governments had unanimously designated 1986 the International Year of Peace, yet so few countries responded, was a matter of concern to peace activists around the world. They were disappointed at the sparse funding given to the UN Secretariat for IYP. At this time the UN was becoming financially strapped because some countries — sadly (and still) including the US — failed to pay their annual dues; but we still felt that as peace was an integral part of the founding UN Charter, they could and should have done better.

In New Zealand, during 1985/86, the Ministry of Foreign Affairs allocated $97,000 for administration purposes for the national committee and for 24 IYP committees around the country. The New Zealand Lottery Board allocated $50,000 for projects, which had to meet stipulated criteria. From the Department of Maori Affairs came a contribution of $1000. The Ministry of Works and Development leased us Peace House. The Ministry of Social Welfare agreed to second and pay one of its senior advisory officers, Barbara Holt, as executive officer for the Year of Peace.

Throughout New Zealand, eight IYP committees were given the services of eight full-time workers under employment schemes administered by government departments. At Peace House, we were loaned a photocopier and an electric typewriter and given access to word-processing machines at the Government Computing Service. From August 1985 a monthly newsletter, *Peacemeal*, produced by June Melser, kept IYP committees around the country in touch with what was happening.

The committee decided it needed a logo and we asked one of New Zealand's most famous cartoonists, Murray Ball in Gisborne, if he would submit a design. The result was Oi Oi, a fur seal, so named and chosen, said Murray, because, like humans, he was an endangered species. He produced this endearing little creature in a variety of moods and poses, on posters, T-shirts, cards and stickers, and he became well known throughout the country. Thirty thousand brochures outlining the committee's aims for the Year of Peace were printed; these also featured Oi Oi. They were very popular here and overseas, and we always ran out at the international peace conferences we attended.

In Peace House, Barbara had an upstairs front office and I had a charming attic-type one at the rear. Lyn Belt of Eastbourne joined us as secretary to the committee. We all worked hard and a great deal was achieved in that year. The committee itself was made up mostly of strong-minded peace activists from various parts of the country. There were seventeen of us: May Bass (Hamilton), Kate Boanas (Christchurch), Jim Chapple (Auckland), Neil Cherry (Christchurch), Kevin Clements (Christchurch), Ngahiti Faulkner (Wellington), Lewis Holden (Wellington), Georgina Kirby (Auckland), Peter Matheson (Dunedin), Joan Morrell (Wellington), Wiremu Parker (Wellington), Ian Prior (Wellington), Grace Robertson (Auckland), Laurie Salas (Wellington), Pauline Thurston (Auckland), Rinny Westra (Auckland) and myself.

As always with new governmental organisations with finite budgets, everyone had a strong opinion as to how and where that money should be spent. We had some very lively weekend meetings, but we were, and in many cases still are, good friends. During the year, there was widespread activity around the country — peace festivals, concerts, essays and special contests, seminars, hui, conferences, speech contests, art exhibitions and peace poster displays. Peace parks and gardens were established in a number of places. Books and other publications were printed to commemorate the year. Several original songs and plays were produced and from Wanganui came young people to present *The Peace Child* at Parliament, and at the Wellington College of Education. Churches of many denominations played a major role in the activities of the year, particularly in provincial cities and small towns. In Wellington, the Rev John Murray arranged a number of peace activities at St Andrews on the Terrace. The WEA and community colleges also got involved: for example, Waikato University's Continuing Education Department ran peace courses in Hamilton, Tokoroa and Gisborne and invited me to speak at them, and also at public meetings in Thames and Coromandel. All these were very well attended.

Meanwhile, in Parliament the National Opposition was saying that the people of New Zealand were angry that the Labour Government's anti-nuclear legislation was threatening ANZUS and its future. I was prepared for spirited debate on the issue, particularly in conservative small towns, but in the end there was little interest.

A considerable number of schools invited me to speak to their senior students. One Monday, I visited a school and found that some of the male students were sporting limbs in plaster and bruised faces. I asked if there had been a fight and was told that there had been a rough game of rugby with a neighbouring school the previous Saturday. As it happened, I was to speak at that school later in the day, and when I did, I talked about the fact that peace really had to begin at home, and peacefully negotiated decisions had to be part of everyday life. I told them about a secondary school in Dunedin during my schooldays where there was a splendid coach who called the rugby teams together just before the rugby season started and told them that he expected the skills he had taught them to play a major role in their winning; but that he would not tolerate violence of any sort, and anyone indulging in that would be sent off and barred from the team for the rest of the season. At that time this was an unusual concept, but it was accepted.

In the event, to everyone's horror, in the second game of the season, the captain of the First Fifteen behaved very violently, breaking his opponent's shinbone. He was a popular figure and people held their breaths. He was sent off and told later that he was out for the season. There was a great outcry about this but the coach was adamant. He said that the captain of the team is a role model. He had thought the captain had taken his no-violence policy on board, but obviously he hadn't. A couple of days later, the principal called the coach to his office. He explained that he was in a very difficult position as the banned player's father, who was a successful businessman and at present a very angry one, had told him that he had intended to make a major contribution to the proposed gymnasium, but in the light of the coach's treatment of his son, this was now highly unlikely. The principal wondered if the coach would reconsider the decision, give the lad a second chance and smooth things down. The coach said that this issue was one he felt strongly about and that if the principal really wanted him to reverse his decision, he would resign. In the end the coach remained, and under his guidance, the teams played exciting and non-violent rugby.

While I was speaking, I could tell by the young men's body language that they had got the message, but I also saw that one of the male teachers was very angry. Later in the staffroom at afternoon break, I asked about this man. I was told he was the sports master, a blood-and-guts man, and the only teacher in the school still using corporal punishment.

On the night that I spoke in Thames, there was a very good audience. I had been told that the National Party selection was taking place. The incumbent MP had died and his son, John Luxton, was one of the aspirants. From time to time someone would come in and encourage people from the audience to vote.

During the year the slogan became 'Work locally, act nationally, think globally.' Most IYP Committee members undertook speaking engagements. I was fascinated to find that, in places where peace issues had not previously been debated, there were splendid meetings. As a person who had been reviled and spat on when marching for a nuclear-free New Zealand, I found a very different response to peace issues in 1986.

I went to Geneva at the beginning of the year to attend the Non-Governmental Organisations (NGO) Conference to mark the beginning of the International Year of Peace. There I met the keynote speaker, Margarita Papandreou, who at that time was still married to the former Greek President. She was a clear, concise and skilled speaker with a challenging message for peace. She bravely attacked the machismo of militarism and said that systems of militarism on the one hand and sexism on the other so complemented each other as to be interdependent, and that in addressing the causes of militarism and the alternatives, one must address the causes of sexism or we wouldn't find the means of transcending either. I wanted to cheer!

My next overseas trip was to Dublin to a conference on the socio-economic aspects of disarmament, and then to New York to the United Nations as part of an Eminent Persons Group to consider the social and economic crises facing the UN. By this time, my passport was full and I needed a new one. I applied to the US Embassy in Wellington for a visa to enter the country. I gave the reasons for my visit, and despite the fact that I had had a permanent visa, there seemed to be a problem. Jim Knox was again in Geneva at another ILO Conference and I was very busy with IYP and the FOL. I kept ringing the embassy and being put off. They kept telling me that my visa was being processed. Finally, I decided to enlist the assistance of my old friend Bill Rowling, who was at that time the New Zealand ambassador in Washington. I rang him and explained what I wanted to do and the difficulty I was having with the embassy in Wellington. They had finally told me that my application had been sent to Washington for processing, which I found quite incredible. I asked Bill if he could make some enquiries. He said that he was not exactly flavour of the month because he was trying to convince Americans that our nuclear-free legislation was not specifically anti-US but opposed to all countries with nuclear capacity. He said he would give it his best shot.

A couple of weeks later I was chairing an FOL Executive meeting, having almost given up hope of going to the UN, when the phone rang and it was Bill. He told me that he had been informed that my application had been lost in a mass of paperwork. I should go to the embassy tomorrow and my visa would be ready. Because I was so busy, I didn't understand that my visa had been given a special political status.

When I fronted up in Honolulu, the entry port for New Zealanders, I was part of a long queue with many of my countrypeople behind me. The immigration officer looked at my visa and said in a loud voice, 'And how long have you been a card-carrying Communist?' I was enraged, and said, 'Regardless of what your embassy has provided me with in the way of a visa, I am a long-term member of the New Zealand Labour Party. I am coming here on a mission of peace. So I can only assume that for Americans, peace is a dirty word.' He crossly stamped my entry card and I swept past. When I got to the transit lounge I discovered that many Kiwis who had heard the exchange were also very angry about it.

The visit to the UN, the meetings with general secretaries and ambassadors were fascinating but depressing. If key countries didn't pay their dues, the crucial work of the UN couldn't be carried out. It seemed to me that the UN was a bureaucratic nightmare, and that there were many and varied reasons for this.

In July, I went to Japan to open and speak at exhibitions on the effects of nuclear war in Osaka and Kyoto, both attended by thousands of people. With me I took our nuclear-free legislation, IYP brochures and photos of the Peace Squadron out in New Zealand's harbours opposing ships that wouldn't declare whether they were nuclear-powered or carried nuclear weapons. I had about ten speeches to make each day, and in a city like Osaka where the traffic is wall-to-wall, getting from one venue to another was never easy.

After a couple of days, I realised that there had been no women at all

*At the Kiyomizu Temple, Kyoto, with Mr Fukuoka, a
senior Buddhist priest.*

at the meetings and asked why. At first I was told that women just weren't interested, but when I said that I didn't believe that, I was taken to a co-operative where I met lots of lively and intelligent women, dedicated to pure food and peace and equality. They held rallies and ran seminars.

It was on this visit that I met a young woman called Ritsko Kondo, who was assigned to me part-time as an interpreter. She was the editor of the Japan Free Press Organisation, and very bright. She was married, and has had three children over the time I have known her. As I write, I'm hoping that she will come this rugby season to interpret for a Japanese team, and will also bring her children. It is a bonus of my overseas trips to make such lasting friends, who also keep me in touch with events in their countries.

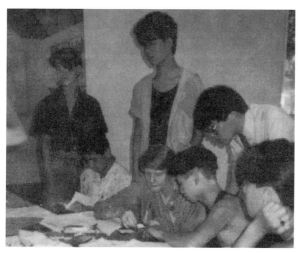

*Learning to make origami peace cranes, with young
people in Osaka in 1986*

The deputy chair of the IYP national committee, Laurie Salas, also went abroad to attend conferences: the Women's International League for Peace and Freedom Conference in the Netherlands; and the Asian and Pacific Regional Seminar in Tashkent. Committee member Ian Prior, a charming and dedicated doctor working through the International Physicians for Prevention of Nuclear Warfare (IPPNW), went to the IYP Conference in Nadi, Fiji and the 6th World Congress of IPPNW in Cologne. Ngahiti Faulkner, Maori Chair of IYP, went to Bangkok to a World Council of Churches Peace Conference. Kevin Clements, also a deputy chair, went to an IYP Conference in Tashkent; Georgina Kirby went to Samoa to help establish a Commonwealth liaison unit; Pauline Thurston had a series of peace meetings in Japan and Katie Boanas (who was later to play a major international role in the World Court Project) went to Australia to visit peace educators, peace education being her specialty. From these meetings, we established a network of international peace activists. These links have been very useful for us and for people overseas, particularly those interested in our nuclear legislation and who wanted to know how it was achieved.

With all the to-ing and fro-ing of IYP National Committee members, we always had plenty to report to each other. During the year, we presented submissions to the Defence Committee of Inquiry and the Parliamentary Select Committee on the New Zealand Nuclear-Free and Arms Control Bill and the Select Committee on Violence. We also partic, ipated in events such as the First Earth Run and A Million Minutes for Peace.

Within New Zealand, the courageous Alyn Ware was travelling around schools in his Peace Van to talk about peace education. Alyn was a trailblazer in this and much criticised by anti-peace people. He later went to New York to work for the International Lawyers for Peace; there he played a major role in lobbying endlessly at the UN for support for the World Court Project, which sought to have the International Court of Justice in the Hague rule on the legal status of nuclear weapons. The World Court Project was instigated by Harold Evans, a retired Christchurch judge and much work has been done to promote it. After several years, the UN together with the World Health Organisation succeeded in bringing a hearing at the International Court of Justice on the status of nuclear weapons. It finally took place at the end of 1995, and 44 governments and the World Health Organisation made submissions and 22 governments made oral statements. During the hearing, members of the World Court Project presented 3.3 million signatures as a declaration of Public Conscience from all over the world, and the court accepted them as citizens' evidence. The court, in its 34-page opinion, decided that

In the Beehive, on the occasion of the launch of the Million Minutes for Peace; David Lange is on my right

'a threat or use of nuclear weapons would generally be contrary to the rules of international law applicable in armed conflict and in particular the principles of humanitarian law'. It was, however, unable to conclude definitively whether the threat or use of nuclear weapons would be unlawful in an extreme circumstance of self-defence. Finally, the judges unanimously agreed that 'there exists an obligation to pursue in good faith and bring to conclusion negotiations leading to nuclear disarmament in all its aspects under strict and effective international control'. Alyn and his colleagues are examples of the many dedicated, hard-working people in the New Zealand peace movement who have made a substantial contribution to peace here and abroad. It's people and movements like this that give me hope for the country's future.

Back in 1986, though, the whole question of peace education seemed to send the National Opposition into flights of frenzy: some called it Communist-inspired! When we ultimately called it conflict resolution, it suddenly became respectable. Within three months of becoming Minister of Education in the Fourth Labour Government, Russell Marshall had instructed his departmental officials to bring people together to discuss the introduction of peace education at all levels in our schools. The IYP Committee, spearheaded by Jim Chapple and Katie Boanas, made peace education one of our major goals for the year. We wanted it to be an integral part of the school curriculum.

I have to say that in the early 1960s, when we were campaigning for peace, it was mainly the intellectuals, trade unionists and many, many women doing the work. Our detractors called us the 'crochet and sandal brigade'. The whole debate about nuclear-free legislation, plus, I am sure,

David Lange's debate at the Oxford Union with Jerry Falwell, the emergence of the IPPNW and Lawyers and Architects for Peace, helped people to understand that peace was sought not only by what they considered to be fringe groups: it had suddenly become respectable.

The National Opposition took a long time to recognise this development. I could have told them that in the conservative heartland, people wanted to talk about peace. As I write, it is Anzac Day, and in the speeches reported on radio and television, church leaders, RSA presidents and veterans have all spoken about remembering the dead of the two wars, and also about peace, so that their sacrifice hasn't been in vain. One of two remaining Diggers from Gallipoli, Doug Dibley, now 100 years old, said from his retirement home that 'Anzac Day is not to glorify war but to honour all those young men who didn't come back.' We have come a long way.

One of the most spectacular events of the year was the Peace Ribbon Project. Based on an American example, peace banners were made by thousands of people from all over the country, particularly from small towns and rural areas. At meetings, on radio and television, I explained that we wanted to join these ribbons and take them across Wellington from the US Embassy to the Soviet Embassy on Messines Road, as a gentle reminder to the two superpowers that we expected positive results from the upcoming summit meeting.

The idea really caught on. In *Peacemeal*, instructions were given as to how the banners should be constructed so that they would be of uniform depth. Peace workers visited schools and organisations and explained the proposal. When I was in Japan, I talked about our project at meetings and on television and the result was amazing: the Japanese were fascinated by the idea and soon exquisite and innovative ribbons arrived at Peace House in great numbers from Japan, along with a large number of origami cranes, the symbol for peace in that country.

In New Zealand, Girl Guides, church groups, schools, peace groups and individuals worked for months on banners of the required size. Embroiderers produced stunning ribbons and all were very welcome. The committee was not sure how many ribbons we would end up with and there were some anxious moments. In the days preceding 19 October, the day designated for the ribbon event, contributions streamed into Peace House.

On 19 October, Barbara Holt led a contingent of people stringing ribbons, starting at both the US Embassy in Fitzherbert Terrace in Thorndon and the Soviet Embassy in Karori. It had been decided to present a statement to each ambassador and we had publicised this, but sadly at the US Embassy we were told that there was no one to receive it.

With a Japanese Peace delegation and members of the New Zealand Peace Council in 1986.

We had better luck with the Soviets, who accepted our statement and one of the two peace ribbons, each quite exquisite, that we had allocated to the ambassadors.

In all it was a dramatic event, the work of thousands of people. This made the media's scanty reportage of the event all the more disappointing — but to them peace was not a high priority at that time. I have to say that one of the greatest frustrations of the IYP national committee was the refusal of the media to treat our activities as newsworthy. This was not so evident in the provinces, where daily newspapers and local radio stations were happy to record the many peace initiatives, but, in the cities, newspaper editors considered peace activities to be 'soft news'. Just as the 1985 End of Decade UN Conference for Women in Nairobi, Kenya, was not considered to be of sufficient importance for New Zealand to send a TV crew, despite even male chauvinistic Australia's presence, the New Zealand media treated the UNIYP as a big yawn.

We decided that until the hearts and minds of the decisionmakers in the media changed drastically, peace would have to be promoted by word of mouth. The Year of Peace took place against the backdrop of the Reyjavik and Geneva Peace Summits, and the continuing negotiations in Geneva for ending the Cold War. That there was no agreement on a moratorium on disarmament was a matter of serious concern. Gorbachev made some proposals in his early days of power but the West disregarded them and had no counter-proposals to offer. We took comfort in the news that far-reaching proposals for nuclear arms reduction had been mooted at the latest summit.

In October, I led a delegation of 20 New Zealand delegates, peace workers, trade unionists, scientists and youth peace supporters to the World Congress devoted to the principles of the IYP in Copenhagen. We walked into a fraught and, to us, totally incomprehensible situation. It was good to travel with people that I knew and trusted, but we were astounded to find that this conference was opposed by some well-heeled and powerful opponents. From the beginning, expensive posters opposing the congress were pasted on every powerpole en route to the conference venue. Back in New Zealand, we had been told that the congress was sponsored by the Women's International League for Peace and Freedom, the Women's International Democratic League, the World Council of Churches, the World Federationist Movement, the International Union of Students, the World Peace Council and the United Nations Council of Youth. In the months prior to our arrival, a preparatory committee had been working hard in Copenhagen to ensure the success of the congress. So the open hostility of a fairly large group of people puzzled us.

On the second day of the proceedings, a group stormed into the huge auditorium and onto the stage, in an attempt to stop proceedings. Who were these people? What was their reason for behaving this way? No one could tell us. We decided that we had come a long way to participate and were determined to do just that. We set up our display stall and all took turns of duty. There were other delegations from all round the world, including at least 20 different Japanese ones. There was a lot of interest in our delegation and always plenty of questions to answer.

At this distance, I can't remember all those who were part of our delegation, but I do know that May Bass came from Hamilton. For years, she produced the peace magazine, *Peacelink*, on a very thin shoestring. Graham Kelly represented the trade union movement, Joan Thurston came from Auckland, Wayne Hennessy from Wellington and a very intellegent secondary school student from Takaka.

Our nuclear-free legislation was of particular interest to other delegates. Ray Stewart from the World Peace Council in Helsinki spent a lot of time with us. On our last day in Copenhagen, artists, potters, actors, sculptors and other arts representatives held a meeting in the city square. They asked me to speak at this rally. It was teeming with rain but the square was packed. Just as we started, music blasted from an upstairs window across the road, amplified to such an extent that it drowned us out. We struggled on regardless.

Most of the New Zealand delegation to the conference in Copenhagen, 1986

Years later, I was at a garden party at Government House in honour of the Queen of Denmark. When I was introduced to her, she looked at me intently and asked if I had ever been to Denmark. When I told her I had, and the circumstances, she said she remembered me speaking in the square against the noise. She and her husband had been in the crowd.

As the members of the delegation were travelling at their own cost, we were of necessity booked in low-cost hotels. Graham Kelly and I found we were close to the red-light district. This didn't concern us greatly as we were perpetually at conference and associated activities, but on our final night in Copenhagen we found ourselves without responsibilities and with few funds. We went out to find somewhere cheap to eat. We loved Copenhagen, which was colourful, exciting and foreign to us. But the red-light district was something else. As we walked around, Graham blenched at the phallic symbols in the sex shops and I found the approaches of the prostitutes disturbing, and wanted to talk to them about why they were there and what other options they had in this supposedly affluent country. Graham was horrified and hurried me on.

In Copenhagen, all restaurants had billboards outside showing their menus and prices. We closely scrutinised these and finally chose one that we could afford. When we entered, a very unsavoury, brawny and pock-marked man seemed quite astonished to see us. He took our coats (at a cost) and directed us to a table. We looked around and had the distinct impression that we were in a rather unusual situation. For one thing, at the bar there were only attractive young women. At a large table near us were what we took to be young businessmen, who were showing photos of their wives and children to more young women. A waitress finally arrived

— an older woman, who asked what we wanted to eat. Then she leaned over and whispered into Graham's ear. His face turned puce. When she left, I asked what she had said. He told me she had asked him whether we realised that we had come to eat in a brothel! Graham was all for leaving, but I said, 'We've ordered our meal, it's the cheapest around for whatever reason, and we should stay and eat.' I went up to the bar and asked if anyone spoke English. Two of them did, so I talked to them about their pay rates and conditions. Graham was sure that I would have us both thrown out, but it was a very satisfactory sisterly exchange. When we got back to the hotel, we berated the concierge and asked why she hadn't warned us that there were brothels nearby. She said with a curling lip that everyone of sense knew that.

Being conferred with the Honorary Doctorate in Law by Vice-Chancellor Holborow at the Victoria University Wellington graduation ceremony, 30 April 1987

Years later, when Ray Stewart retired from the World Peace Council and returned to New Zealand, he told me that he had stayed on in Copenhagen and had learned something of what the opposition had been about. It appears that groups in Europe and the US were angry that the peace movements, and in particular the World Peace Council, had not opposed the invasion of Afghanistan by the Soviet Union; and others were angry that the US was supplying arms to Pakistan and thereby encouraging extreme Muslim fundamentalists. Why they couldn't have sent a delegation to the congress and had the two issues debated, I have no idea — they might have been surprised at what emerged.

Back in New Zealand it was obvious that, in spite of our lack of funds, the Year of Peace had generated a wide variety of activities right throughout the country, in places like Gore in Southland, Takaka in Golden Bay, Taranaki and the Wairarapa — just everywhere, and all of it faithfully reported in *Peacemeal* by June Melser and in *Peacelink* by May Bass.

At Peace House, visitors continued to stream in, testing our small and inadequate kitchen to capacity. In the PMA offices upstairs, Owen Wilkes, Kevin Hackwell and Nicky Hager were joined regularly by seven volunteers, and they too had many visitors. Often these people came to see both organisations and, at times, Peace House really throbbed with activity. As the year closed, we realised that there was still a great deal more to be done. We liked to think that IYP had been a catalyst for changing people's hearts and minds. For me, working with the IYP Committee had been at times frustrating, but mostly a warm and inspirational experience, and I remember that whole year with much pleasure.

Although these kind of endeavours may be invisible to the media, I was overwhelmed and honoured when, early in 1987, the Vice-Chancellor of Victoria University, Professor Holborow, wrote to me telling me that the University Council wanted to bestow on me an honorary Doctorate of Law in recognition of the work that I had done for this country. Graduation ceremonies are always colourful affairs, with senior academics in colouful gowns and many young high achievers there to receive their reward for hard work. Professor Holborow read a very generous citation before presenting me with my honorary degree. I sat there thinking of all the things that had happened to me since I was sixteen and a student at Victoria University.

Pencarrow Selection

One Saturday afternoon early in 1987, I was sitting in my rear apartment at Marina Court in Eastbourne, turning over the possibilities of the year ahead. Several days before, I had noted in the *Evening Post* that Fraser Colman, who had served the Pencarrow electorate for over 20 years, was retiring from Parliament, and wondered idly who would replace him. I had agreed to go to a World Peace Council meeting in Venezuela in June and was scheduled to go to Scandinavia in July to discuss the possibility of nuclear-free zones in Europe. Now that I was officially retired, I had really begun to want a real garden and somewhere I could sit outside on sunny afternoons.

I was just reviewing my finances and thinking that I would need to rent rather than buy some disused farm cottage, when there was a knock on my door. When I opened it, I found Rex Jones, the general secretary of the Engineers Union. He and his wife Cathy lived in the village of Eastbourne. In his usual fashion, he came straight to the point. He said that a number of people, both within the electorate and outside it, were anxious that I should nominate for selection to replace Fraser as MP for Pencarrow. I told him not to be ridiculous, that I was too old. 'Nonsense', he said firmly. I was by no means convinced by the time he left.

In the next week, there was a steady stream of people calling on me to persuade me to put my name forward. They felt it was time Pencarrow was represented by a woman — someone strong who could ensure that the Government implemented the second part of its programme; for having seen the economic changes, they now wanted the health and social needs of the community addressed. They were concerned that no one else who was nominating would do that.

I began to feel rather beleaguered. Then Helen Clark rang me. She was at her most persuasive: to my statement that I was too old, she said that I would only need to be there for two terms. 'Just be a little back-bencher,' she said. I was to remind her of that often in the future.

The Eastbourne Women's Branch came to see me and were most persistent. The Labour Party president, Margaret Wilson, rang me and said I should at least put my name forward. She had heard of my reluctance and said I would have to take my chances along with the other candidates, but my experience would be of value to the Party in Parliament.

And then I had a visit from Simon Walker. For some time, I had been rather concerned about his political direction, and it saddened me. He said he had lived in the electorate for longer than me and felt he had more right to represent it. He had really come to persuade me not to put my name forward and said he didn't want us to be in opposition.

More and more it had seemed to me that Simon was in agreement with the direction that Roger Douglas was taking. He was closely in touch with Roger and had angered David Lange early in June when he sent a newsletter to the clients of his PR firm prior to the presentation of the Budget, forecasting what would be in it. Things like increasing GST to 15 per cent, a move to user-pays health services, a capital gains tax.

I knew that already several of the 'dry' ministers were appalled at the idea that not one but four trade unionists, Graham Kelly, Liz Tennet, Larry Sutherland and I might be successful in safe Labour seats. The media caught up with all this and began the fiction that affiliated unions would bus in union delegates from outside the electorates to support us. I told Simon that I still hadn't made up my mind, but that if I did decide to go for it, we should simply each do the best we could and let others make the choice.

After he had gone, my resolve strengthened and I rang Rex and told him of my decision to stand for selection. When the nominations became public, the fact that Liz was nominating in Island Bay, Graham in Porirua and I in Pencarrow caused the supporters of a market-driven economy to be very vocal in their opposition. I attended preselection meetings with the other hopefuls and visited as many electors as I could.

On the night of the selection, I believed that anything could happen. I was extremely nervous and not at all convinced that I would be successful. There were ten candidates so the speeches took a long time. Then we had the straw vote which took two hours, before the selection committee retired to debate and make their selection. It was very late when the committee came back into the Wainuiomata Community Hall where the selection was taking place. The decision was announced by Labour Party President Margaret Wilson, who told the large crowd present that I would be the candidate.

I was quite overwhelmed. About a dozen of the people who had opposed me in those preselection days stood up and walked out. I was very aware that I had some electorate fences to mend. However, there were a lot of people there who were very pleased with their new candidate. The previous week, Graham Kelly had been selected as the candidate for Porirua, a choice which anti-trade unionists said was part of a planned union takeover bid for safe seats. His opponents were also very vocal and were already demanding a reselection, saying that the constitution had been breached. I suspected I was in for a rough ride. However, on the night I was hustled away to celebrate with a crowd of supporters.

As I left, I passed Simon outside and realised he was very upset. Later, after the selection of all four ex-trade unionists, he sent another newsletter to his clients to reassure them that we wouldn't have any clout anyway. He said that the Cabinet minister and undersecretaries would close ranks and outvote us, and that in any case the really important policies were not decided in caucus. (Sadly, in this he was right.) His newsletter also included comments about me which were less than complimentary, some of which appeared in the press.

In the days following the selection the small group of opponents to my selection, mainly from Wainuiomata, began making a series of accusations against me — about my party membership, the selection procedures, anything they could raise to try to discredit me. They wrote to the Party Executive lodging a formal complaint, and consulted a solicitor from a well-known Wellington firm.

The Party decided to follow the constitutional disputes procedures and appoint a member of the New Zealand Council of the Party to act as a conciliator. The General Secretary, Tony Timms, wrote to the group's solicitor advising him of this and inviting the group to meet with the conciliator. They declined this invitation and said they would take the matter to the High Court.

I had opened a campaign office in Wainuiomata and set up a campaign committee. In the local press, the opposition by a vociferous group against me continued unabated. I went to Wainuiomata every day, and each morning when I arrived, I had to soak notices off the windows, notices that said things like: 'Union Jackboots Crush Out Grassroots'. I decided not to respond to the accusations, and to prove to them by my presence that I didn't have horns or a forked tail, nor was I accompanied by the busloads of union members they attributed to me.

I had had some rough times during my FOL years, but this was worse. I was accused of being an abortionist, of not being a family person, of being a Communist. I got on with my campaign. I knew that if the Pencarrow Labour Reselection Trust, as they called themselves, went to the High Court, the case would probably be heard prior to the election. I was not in any way concerned about the outcome because I was convinced that nothing wrong had occurred. Of course I wasn't privy to the discussion of the selection panel, but I was convinced of their absolute integrity.

I had known Tony Timms and Margaret Wilson for years and knew they were always dedicated to keeping strictly within the Party's constitution. The group canvassed Labour Party members for funds to cover legal costs, which made a lot of loyal Party members angry. Over in Porirua, Graham was experiencing similar problems, as was Liz Tennet in Island Bay.

What the people in the Reselection Trust did was to create a real feeling of mistrust about me, mainly in Wainuiomata, and all sorts of people got into the act. People outside the Party who didn't really know me made a number of accusations in the local press. I was accused of having acquired a list of members from the Shop Employees Union, which was affiliated to the Labour Party, so that I could ensure a large turnout. But the only Union members present were some of those who lived in the electorate, which was perfectly legitimate.

When Larry Sutherland, our trade union colleague, was selected for Avon, things really took off. However, at this point, thoughtful journalists such as Colin James, Patricia Herbert and Tim Pankhurst started examining the issues in the national press, and appeared to be of the opinion that the whole fabric of our society would not be rent asunder if we were elected to Parliament; that we would no doubt fight for the principles we espoused, but that our lives in the trade union world had of necessity often been ones of compromise. What was noted was that we were all strongly in favour of government-funded social services.

With hindsight, I should have realised that after 22 years with the same much-loved MP and his wife, who had lived in Wainuiomata, I was a complete change: my social agenda was thought too liberal by conservative sections in that community. I knew I would have to prove myself. It took all of three years there. Everywhere else I found much support and embarked on candidate meetings, cottage meetings (held in private homes), and meetings with organisations. Groups in Eastbourne and the Bays, in Epuni and Waiwhetu gave me incredible support and continued to do so for all the six years that I served the electorate.

Then, towards the end of July, the Reselection Trust revealed to the media that they were not proceeding with their court action, and instead were supporting their own candidate, Dr Ian Greig, who had a local medical practice. On 29 July, President Margaret Wilson wrote to all Labour Party members in Pencarrow, advising them that, under the terms of the constitution, people who publicly campaign against the Labour Party must lose their Party membership for six years. She included with this letter a summary of the complaints to the National Executive, and outlined the actions the Party had taken to investigate each complaint, none of which was found to have any validity.

I had known that former trade unionists would not be welcomed by Cabinet ministers such as Roger Douglas, Richard Prebble or Michael Bassett, but there would be others in Parliament I could happily work with. And the unions, knowing about the orchestrated campaign against trade union MPs, showed their support by arranging a function for Graham, Liz and I at the Hotel Workers Union. Supporters came from all over Wellington.

Simon and his wife, Mary Strang, decided to move to Europe to work for a while. I felt really sad that my candidacy had meant the loss of a valued friendship; but in any case, Simon and I were increasingly heading in different directions. He eventually became the personal assistant to the then British Tory Prime Minister, John Major. This whole political process, as a result of Rogernomics, caused former colleagues to change their allegiance. In addition to Simon, Rob Campbell and Alf Kirk of FOL days became advocates of Rogernomics, while Peter Dunne, the MP for Ohario, left Labour and formed the United Party and ultimately became a National Cabinet Minister.

I had a month to campaign. I met as many people as possible: I visited worksites wherever the management would permit it, participated in candidate meetings and the large inter-church meetings in Waiwhetu, and talked with the Maori, Pacific Island and Indian communities. In Brooklyn, my son Mark and I had become friends with the Indian couple, Vinoo and Kamala Patel, who had the dairy at the foot of Todman Street, and their replacements when they left. I came to know them and their extended families, and through them and their customers I had an additional means of keeping in touch with grassroots feelings and thoughts.

Anyone who has been involved in an election campaign knows that there are never enough hours for the candidate to do what needs to be done. Sleep becomes an absolute luxury. At campaign meetings we plotted strategies for election day. We planned to have the election-day headquarters at Te Kokiri in Wainuiomata, which was where New Zealand's first kohanga reo (Maori language preschool) was established. During my six-year term, the local tangata whenua were a large part of my life.

At meetings, there were always questions about the dramatic changes that had taken place during the 1984–87 period. I talked to my audiences about the parlous state of the economy when the Fourth Labour Government was elected in 1984. I told them that I knew things had to change: we had virtually lost our main market when Britain joined the Common Market; and the comfortable gravy train we had occupied (give or take a few glitches such as externally created recessions) was now permanently parked at the station and in the present climate would be done away with.

But I told them I was not convinced that the speed and the nature of the changes, or the way they were being carried out, was the right way to go. I told them I was dedicated to free, quality health and education systems and housing that people could afford. I said that I would do everything I could to ensure that the second part of Labour's programme, which dealt with social issues, was implemented.

I had dozens of cottage meetings throughout the electorate and these were very special. All through the month of the campaign, people helped in a wide variety of ways, from inside and outside the electorate. With a limited election budget (still only $5000 in 1987), there was not a great deal of fat to do things such as erect hoardings to make people familiar with my name, and aware of the Party flag. My wonderful helpers had a signwriter produce the hoardings, then nailed them to sturdy timber structures and erected them where the local council permitted. This required trucks and trailers and strong people. I realised how much things had changed since I organised three of Stan Whitehead's campaigns in Nelson and my own in Hastings in 1966. In 1987, hoardings were vandalised time and time again — and not just mine. I ask myself now, 'Do we need them? Why can't we have a central area in every electorate where all candidates can display their hoardings high above the reach of graffiti artists, well-lit, where people can see them?' For the campaign worker, having to go out, wet or fine, and resuscitate the hoardings was a real bind, particularly when there were other crucial campaign duties to get on with.

Election Day dawned, scary, hopeful, and yet of concern because of the Wainuiomata factor. Dear Fraser, the outgoing member, had endorsed me in my election pamphlet, but what effect would that have? Naturally, I had been assailed in the press and elsewhere by Ian Greig (Local Labour), Ossie Renata (Independent) and Andrew Harvey (National), who kept saying that I hadn't been seen in the electorate since I was selected — but that was all par for the course. It was in the lap of the gods.

All day, there were many people at the Kokiri, helpers from all over the electorate and the hospitable Maori community providing cups of tea, food and friendship. All sorts of people helped by driving voters to the polling booths.

After the polls had closed, we watched the television. When we saw that Pencarrow was won by Labour, it was a great moment. The facts finally emerged: I had won by 1735 votes, which the media said was a reduced majority, although they didn't explain why. Because of the atmosphere created before the election, the local Wainuiomata paper was not at all supportive of me and printed whatever people claimed as gospel against me, Ian Greig was a well-known doctor, so he attracted local support. I refused to get into a slanging match with any of them. It would have been a miracle if I hadn't had a reduced majority. We had a wonderful celebration, and when I was deposited at Marina Court in Eastbourne, the phone was ringing. It was after midnight, but a friend from the Japanese press said that many people there wanted to congratulate me. Looking out over the wonderful exotic beauty of Wellington at night, I wondered what was in store.

I fell into bed and woke up to a whole new world, one that I had no idea would be so traumatic.

Part Two

In the Belly of the Beast

The Class of '87

Labour Party MPs, 1987: (from back left) Jeff Grant, John Carter, Ross Robertson, John Luxton, David Robinson, Harry Duynhoven, Larry Sutherland, Maurice Williamson, Robert Anderson, Jenny Kirk, Peter Simpson, Graham Kelly, Murray McCully, Ross Meurant, Warren Kyd, Liz Tennet, Jenny Shipley, Rob Munro, and me. Tom Scott

Jousting with Juggernauts

When I walked into Parliament as an MP for the first time in August 1987, I foolishly imagined that now that I was part of the Government, I would be welcomed, given instructions about parliamentary procedure, told what legislation was coming up and given briefing papers on what the Cabinet was planning and why. What a silly bunny I was. We were flung into the major change and massive legislating that would rearrange the lives of New Zealand people forever — and for which I would be held responsible in my electorate.

Nowadays when I hear the new MMP list MPs talking about what a breeze it is, I think back to those days. To begin with, I didn't seem to have an office. Jenny Kirk, Graham Kelly, Peter Simpson and Larry Sutherland had offices in the prefabricated building at the rear of the main Parliament, and had been allotted secretaries. (This building was known as Siberia, and in winter I knew why.) I was then told that Jim Anderton, who had the last easterly office on this, the ground, floor, had been relocated to the second storey of the complex and that I had been allocated his office with a non-connecting office next door for whoever would be my secretary. Jonathan Hunt sent me a message to say that they wanted a pro-active political secretary for me and it might be a little time before that person could be found.

Up to the 1987 election, Mary had been doing part-time work for Helen Clark, researching and writing speech notes — mostly in the evenings, as she was also working for Amnesty International. When Helen became part of Cabinet and moved over to the Beehive building where Cabinet ministers hang out, there wasn't a place for Mary. I had told her that I might not have a secretary for some weeks. She said that if Jonathan agreed, she would take on the job until they found me a suitable one. When I retired six years later, she was still there and went on for another three years as executive secretary to New Zealand's first openly gay MP, Chris Carter.

The new intake of MPs soon realised that a 'them and us' situation existed between the Cabinet, its undersecretaries and backbench MPs.

There were, of course, free-market supporters in the body of the caucus. Our first Thursday caucus was an eye-opener — even then, I realised I'd got myself into a very difficult environment. It didn't take long to sense the underlying and irreconcilable ideological differences among the participants, and that strengthened as time went on. Ironically, the Rogernomics supporters, who favoured the free market, diminished state responsibility and user pays, always sat on the left of that caucus room and, equally strangely, Jim Anderton sat on the end of a side row on the right. We occupied the centre group facing the top table, where David Lange sat, along with his deputy, Geoffrey Palmer, the Chief Whip Margaret Austin and her deputy, Trevor Mallard, and the caucus secretary Peter Dunne.

Although Cabinet ministers were obliged to present their proposals to caucus to have them debated and voted on, the debate was always heavily weighted on the side of Rogernomics and even mildly dissenting contributions were met with impatience and even open contempt. This was no climate for consensus or any sort of negotiation.

After our first caucus, Graham and I negotiated the stairs, corridors and more stairs back to Siberia. We agreed that we wanted to be better prepared for caucuses in the future. We decided to see Richard Northey, who had been elected MP for Eden in 1984. He had three years' experience under his belt. I had known Richard since he was a student at Auckland University; he and other young members of the Campaign for Nuclear Disarmament (CND) had taken part in a week's activity on Tahunanui Beach in Nelson, to promote a nuclear-free New Zealand. As the local CND secretary, I was very involved in this and forged a friendship with Richard which still exists. I knew we could trust him.

We told him how unhappy and frustrated we were; and we straightaway saw that he understood what we were talking about. We decided to approach other MPs who might want to discuss agendas and how we could achieve them in caucus. We ended up with a group of a dozen MPs, sometimes fifteen, who met every Wednesday night before caucus and tried to anticipate what the ministers would be planning to sell off next, what effects that would have, particularly on low-paid people, and whether we could do anything to deflect or stop it. The numbers of the group dropped to ten as people realised their membership compromised their chances of entering Cabinet and they had to make decisions about which to sacrifice.

Since 1990, MPs entering the House for the first time are given briefing sessions, on the Labour side anyway, and I suspect it is now a general policy for all parties. They are told about procedures in the House and select committees, and representatives or executive secretaries talk to them about the relationship between MPs and their staff and how their parliamentary offices work. In effect, they go into the House much better prepared than us — we were literally thrown in at the deep end, and for the first weeks, didn't know which way was up.

We had joined a Government engaged in far-reaching legislative change. At 6.00 every morning as I stood in the shower with *Morning Report* on the radio balanced on the handbasin, it seemed that I kept hearing yet another minister talking about the imminent sale of yet another state asset, and I would leap out, bruising my shin, filled with rage because this was the first I had heard of it. It seemed that there were two levels of operation, and anyone who wasn't smart (or self-interested) enough to get on the side of the 'progressive change guys' wasn't even given the time of day. For the first six months that we were there, the Rogernomes didn't speak to the trade union MPs directly, and unless making derogatory remarks about us simply ignored us.

People in my electorate quite naturally wondered what on earth I was doing to stop all this. We knew that Jim Anderton was deeply concerned, but he was a loner, and it was difficult to work with him. We asked him to be part of our group and initially he seemed interested, but it didn't work out. He certainly didn't tell us that he was going to jump ship and form the New Labour Party, where he would be in control. I had known Jim for many years and worked with him as a Labour Party activist. He was a good Labour Party president who reorganised the Party and the finances. In 1978 I had doubts about him when he produced the red book at the Timaru Labour Conference, which advocated distancing the Labour Party from the union movement. He didn't succeed, but it began a downward spiral between the unions and the Party that was to fester on. More and more academics became Labour MPs: doctors, teachers, lawyers, none of whom had a real understanding of industrial relations or how unions worked; nor did they try to find out. The sort of anti-union mutterings that I heard from those people between 1987 and 1990 came back to haunt me when the National Government of 1990 launched an all-out campaign against unions. The National Government had even less understanding, and that led to the Employment Contracts Act. Unions had to change, that was obvious, and they were in fact in the process of doing so, but whatever they did would never satisfy the National Government, which simply wanted them gone. Processes such as 'consultation' and 'consensus' — words which now so freely trip from National politicians' lips — were obviously never considered.

Meanwhile, back in 1987, we new chums tried to come to grips with the task ahead, to wade through Treasury papers which were often facile and full of new terminology for practically everything, and to try to find the underlying purpose. Then there were the select committees to which we had been assigned. I mainly enjoyed those. Initially I was assigned to the Education and Science and the Foreign Affairs and Defence Select Committees. We also had our own Government caucus committees: I was assigned to the Social Welfare and Foreign Affairs Caucus Committees, and later was a member of the Maori Affairs and Education Caucus Committees. All of these met weekly, and frequently more often depending on oncoming upcoming legislation.

Not long after I was sworn in at Parliament, I was invited by the Wainuiomata Council to attend a function in their council chambers, which were just over the road from my electorate office. I obtained permission from the Whips to absent myself from the House and set out in my car. At the foot of a hill on the way up to Wainuiomata there is a short tunnel. In the middle of this the car died and I couldn't get it going again. I looked at the fuel gauge and saw that I was out of gas. This was awful. My first official function in Wainuiomata, of all places, and I was going to be late. There was a car behind me and suddenly I heard a tap on the window. I opened it and saw two very large Black Power gang members with their patches and prominent tattoos. My blood froze. They smiled pleasantly and asked what the problem was. I told them what had happened, who I was and where I was supposed to be going. They told me not to worry, went off to their car boot and extracted a can of petrol and poured it into my tank. They said this would get me to my meeting, and that there was a service station in Wainuiomata which was open late — I could fill my tank there after the meeting. They waited beside me until the car started up, waving away my thanks and my offer to refill their can. I arrived at the meeting on time and with a nice warm glow.

Maybe it was a portent. The Council showed itself to be pragmatic and, whatever their personal misgivings, welcomed me with reasonable warmth. I began a relationship with them that I valued, and which only foundered ultimately when Michael Bassett's local government reforms forced them to amalgamate with Lower Hutt, which enraged them.

Straight after the election, I established an electorate office in the one I had used for the campaign. I heard that Shona Robb, who lived in Wainuiomata and had worked as a secretary for Parliament for MPs Gerald Wall and John Terris and then in the Whips' Office, was interested in working for me. Now she had two small boys just beginning primary school. Shona, her husband Graeme who had worked for New Zealand Railways since he was a lad, and their two sons became an integral part of my life.

In the beginning, wonderful Eastbourne friends came over with me each Saturday morning to my Wainuiomata clinic. Shona soon came to grips with the work of the electorate office. I took her to meet the people she would be contacting in government departments in Lower Hutt, and with them we discussed how we could work together. Those were the days, of course, before restructuring of government departments had really reached its worst gutting phase, when many experienced and skilled state employees simply disappeared — given early retirement or simply made redundant. It was still possible then to create networks in order to help my constituents in trouble.

As the electorate work expanded, I realised that I shouldn't be asking women friends, all of whom worked outside as well as at home, to give up several hours on Saturday mornings to the clinic. That was the day they did their shopping and caught up with family and housework. On the other hand, having someone else there, particularly when there was a queue of people waiting, often with small children, was very helpful. And there were many people who urgently needed assistance and others who could only come on Saturdays. Given these circumstances, Shona said she felt she was the one who needed to be with me and so, give or take sick leave, holidays or family emergencies, she always was.

To cater for constituents on the Wellington side of the hill, I initially opened an office in Lower Hutt, sharing it with John Terris, who was then MP for Western Hutt, Chairman of Committees and Deputy Speaker in Parliament. I was lucky enough to find Katie Hawley, a potter, part-time worker at the Family Planning Clinic in Lower Hutt and an intelligent, warm and caring woman. After her marriage fell apart, she had to raise young children alone and was doing fine. Today she is married to John Terris who is currently Mayor of Lower Hutt.

After a while, we decided that for solo parents and the elderly in the electorate, we needed to have an office closer to where the action was, so we hired a room once a week in the community hall in Moera, and Katie staffed that office for me. For the people in the Eastern Bays, I was available in the Drop-In Centre at Eastbourne once or twice a month. Mary, Shona and Katie kept in touch, particularly as the lines between electorate and Parliament became blurred and they needed to sort out schedules for me.

Back in Parliament our small group continued to meet each Wednesday evening in Richard Northey's office to review the week and discuss what we knew would be the topics at the next day's caucus. We were invited to submit subjects for inclusion on the caucus agenda. In the beginning the group consisted of Richard, Peter Simpson (MP for Lyttelton), Jenny Kirk (Birkenhead), Liz Tennet (Island Bay), Dave Robinson (Manawatu), Fran Wilde (Wellington Central), Clive Matthewson (Dunedin Central), Annette King (Horowhenua), Graham and I, and now and then, Larry Sutherland (Avon) and Harry Duynhoven (New Plymouth and my benchmate).

Harry was an ebullient young man of Dutch descent who had wrested New Plymouth back from National in the 1987 election. He sometimes drove me mad as a benchmate as he constantly interjected loudly when the Opposition was speaking. I used to take him aside and say, 'Look, Harry, we're in Government, not Opposition. If you feel you can support a particular policy being debated, get on the speaking list.' But he just couldn't help himself. It was rather like sitting beside an angry gnat. There was no doubt that his heart was in the right place, but he was basically a conservative, and while he understood why we were meeting, it seemed to me that we made him uneasy. One could say he was more often of us than with us.

As a group, we were very aware that all was not well between David Lange and Roger Douglas. I remember both Walter Nash and Bill Rowling telling me that being the head of Government is a very lonely experience at times, and I'm sure it was no different for David. We used to talk about how we could let him know that we supported him and what we could do to help him. We decided to try to arrange a meeting with him early in the New Year. Richard, who was an Auckland MP, undertook to talk to David about this during the parliamentary recess.

We discovered that many areas of state operations were being studied by Treasury and consultants, and soon reports began to surface. We knew that Treasury had education in its sights and was hell-bent on reform. That had been made crystal clear in the second volume of its study, *Government Management*. So we viewed the Picot Report with some suspicion when it emerged. This report recommended doing away with education boards and other central structures and the establishment of boards of trustees with elected parent representatives as well as some teacher input. It sounded democratic and simple but it was a massive change. In the Education Caucus Committee we spent hours and hours debating the proposals and listening to endless submissions from interest groups within the education sector, often till late at night. Late in 1987, we had a three-day caucus meeting in Ashburton, and here we talked to the ministers about their intentions, told them that the information we were being given in Parliament was inadequate, and came away with assurances that there would be more consultation and better quality information. Pigs can fly too!

This was just after the sharemarket crash. I had been amazed at the number of people who had become involved in stocks and shares that year, in cities and small towns all over the country. A lot of them were badly seared by the effects of the crash. And then, on 17 December, Roger Douglas produced his flat tax proposal, parts of which had been foreshadowed by Simon Walker in his newsletter to clients earlier in the year. Douglas's flat tax meant that everyone regardless of income paid the same tax, so there would be less revenue for health, education and social services. I saw it as a back-door method to privatise these services.

I was punch-drunk. So much was happening and all of it at once, it seemed. I felt as though I was in the path of a juggernaut and in danger of being obliterated. At that time, the mutterings about the closure of post offices added yet another dimension, and my constituents started gathering signatures on petitions against the closures in various parts of the electorate. In my earliest developed area, the oldest part of Wainuiomata, was a village which had a post office. Many young mums and elderly folk lived there. We had been assured by Jonathan Hunt when he was postmaster-general that there was no Government intention to sell post offices. He no longer held that portfolio and here we were closing post offices all round the country. People were destabilised, and the pity was that Roger Douglas didn't believe it. He operated on a different plateau. The Rogernomics ministers had different terminology: they stressed the need for a level playing field, but never explained what that meant in their terms. When I talked to Roger about what was happening to forestry workers and many others whose workplaces were being restructured with loss of jobs, careers and homes, and asked why we couldn't carry out some pilot schemes to assess what effect the policy would have on schools, shops and health services in the area, he said there was just no time for that.

The aim of his programme was to proceed ahead with no pauses. To be fair to Roger, he really did (and in fact still does) believe that what he was doing was absolutely right, and couldn't accept that people's lives were being dislocated in an unacceptable way. 'Short-term pain for long-term gain' and 'the light at the end of the tunnel' were phrases we came to find very suspect. The theory that people at the top in financial terms would let their wealth trickle down to the low-paid was never one that impressed me.

So it was in a spirit of anger that I set off with Mary and her wonderful mother Mabel on the ferry to Picton at the end of the year, on our way to spend the Christmas break at a friend's house in the Moutere Valley. We had lunch in Picton and found the town absolutely crowded. The café proprietor told us that many of the people were from the Russian cruise ship, the *Michael Lermontov*. We saw it later, steaming off down the spectacular sounds, and were stunned to learn on the six o'clock news that the ship had sunk with some lives lost.

The whole question of the flat tax gnawed away at me, and three days into January, I wrote to David and told him I simply couldn't accept a proposal that would benefit the well-heeled and harm the poor. I asked what would happen to health and education if we had a flat tax? I learned later that others had done the same. In the event, David's own concerns led him to spend the month of January consulting a wide range of people and, in particular, economists outside of Treasury. What he learned caused him to, as he put it, 'draw a line in the sand and pause for a cup of tea', and that was to cause major disruption in Cabinet.

Lines in the Sand

Prior to the 1987 election, the Government had shed half of its assets and thousands of workers were flung on the scrapheap. Many of the government departments it had done away with had provided jobs in small towns and cities. People had worked in those departments since they left school: some of them had remained in semi-skilled jobs; others had moved upwards, studying for exams and reaching top ranks. There was a social climate built around those jobs — sports days, picnics, socials. The whole family felt a part of Dad's job. The Post Office Association, for example, built basic but comfortable holiday homes in well-known areas, and workers went into a ballot each year to win a family holiday that they could afford. Wages paid by those departments were modest but adequate; but the real benefit was that there was stability of employment.

In a number of these departments, young people were able to learn a wide variety of trades, and many of them went out into private enterprise as electricians, plumbers, painters, printers and mechanics with a training that was the envy of other countries.

The effect on these people of the gutting of their departments was traumatic. It was useless for Roger and his gang to parrot 'short-term pain for long-term gain'. Instead it was long-term pain, with any long-term gain being the proverbial 'light at the end of a long tunnel'. Many of those who worked for a department like Forestry, Electricity or Railways, and had for years, were living in departmental houses at modest rentals which were part of their wages, in places like Gisborne, Hokitika, Wanganui, or in the huge forestry operation based on Tapawera in Nelson province. When they found themselves suddenly out of work and with no savings because their wages provided only for the family's immediate needs, it was extremely difficult for them to pick themselves up and forge ahead into the uncertain and insecure new world of the free market.

I just happened to have speaking engagements in Hokitika and Gisborne days after Judith Aitken, then working for the State Services Commission, had the unpalatable task of telling the forestry workers that only a third of their jobs would survive, and that they should spend the

75

weekend applying for those positions. In Hokitika, the locals took me to meet some of these people in their homes. It was a very unhappy experience. In one home, the senior forester's wife asked me if I would go into the other room and speak to her husband, who was in shock and hadn't talked to his family for two days. I went in and found him with his head in his hands. He told me that he had spent all his life in forestry and was just reaching the spot where he could become the Deputy Conservator of Forests for his area. He and his wife had hoped that the extra salary boost would help them send their teenage children to university.

Later, I asked people what support services had been provided. They said they were told if they had family problems, they should consult Marriage Guidance. When I got back to Wellington, I rang Marriage Guidance and asked whether they had been consulted by Government and given any extra funding and they said 'No'. It was obscene.

The closure of post offices went on and it became obvious that for people living in remote areas in small villages, the central core of their daily lives had disappeared. Beneficiaries of all sorts came to the post office to collect their benefits and then did their shopping at the local store. The disappearance of the post office meant a journey to another town. With little or no public transport available, people had to save and buy an old car or rely on a neighbour with one. And they did their shopping where they cashed their benefit.

When I raised this issue in caucus, Richard Prebble said they'd have to get on with it and use chequebooks or plastic cards. He didn't know or understand that most of these people mistrusted cheques, and plastic cards were not part of their lives.

Attending a public meeting of my constituents in Waiwhetu, I knew that it was clear that the Rogernomes were into selling every state asset the country had. After I had spoken about local issues, a constituent stood up and said that he believed that Roger Douglas would sell his grandmother's underclothes if he could get a good price for them. I told him I had worked with Roger's mother and father, Norman and Jenny, and knew about his grandparents, the Andertons of homeopathic reputation, and said that Roger's grandmother was not the sort of person to let anyone sell her underwear — she was a strong and determined woman with a will equal to Roger's. But I knew what my constituent felt.

Just before the 1987 Christmas break, I had a phone call from a young woman in Tapawera in the Nelson province, who was organising an event to commemorate the loss of their part of the Nelson Railway. She asked me to be part of the programme. Tapawera had been adversely affected first by the closure and destruction of the railway and then by the restruc-

Tapawera Railway Station re-enactment of Nelson Railway incident

turing of the state forestry industry. There had been a large modern boarding hostel for young single forestry cadets and houses for married workers. Then a supermarket arrived to challenge the old general store. The store was the type which appeals to the romantics — a long wooden counter, large covered bins of flour, sugar and other basic supplies, strings of onions attached to the roof — all those things that have been swept aside by plastic and fast foods. It was no match for the supermarket.

When I arrived there on a clear sunny Nelson day early in January, I found that the locals had laid a small section of track and recreated the railway station. They had arranged for me to sit on the rails (as I had at Kiwi in 1956) and to be 'arrested' by a couple of policemen. Later, as I spoke to them, I realised that the anger and resentment about the railway had not gone away. The man who had driven the train on the day we were arrested all those years before was there, and I learned the 'cab's eye' view of our protest. It was a nostalgic and pleasant day, and as I drank a cuppa in the old general store which now sold crafts, I thought of how people's lives can be drastically changed by political policies devised by people miles away who have no idea what those policies will mean to families.

Back in Wellington, select committee meetings began again early in February. I had decided, when I had come to grips with what seemed to be key essentials of Tomorrow's Schools, that I would visit all the schools in the Pencarrow electorate, meet the new boards of trustees (BOTs) and listen to what they had to say. Leave from Parliament when the House was sitting was not easy to come by despite our large majority, so in the beginning, I had only Monday nights free to do this as BOTs didn't meet on my only other free night, Friday. Later, I wheedled other week nights.

Discussing policies with the BOTs was a fascinating experience and I was able to give the Education Caucus Committee the actual concerns as well as aspirations of Pencarrow trustees. Each BOT was different, reflecting the area the school was in. But regardless of where they were, there were general concerns. To begin with, a number of trustees didn't feel comfortable making decisions that would affect teachers as well as students. They were overwhelmed by the responsibility of dealing with so much money. There should have been good training sessions right at the beginning to let trustees know what their rights and responsibilities were. Most of them had spent many more hours working on issues than they had envisaged.

I met many interesting people, all concerned with achieving quality education for their children. Principals found they were meant to become businesspeople overnight. Another issue was a lack of trustees to represent Maori and Pacific Island children in each community. When told of this, David Lange said that boards should co-opt them, but I could see that there were probably cultural reasons for this lack of representation. Maori people in particular were really wanting to establish their own schools. This has happened since those days, and now, as well as more Kohanga Reo, Kura Kaupapa schools have sprung up for older pupils.

It also became clear that establishing BOTs in areas where family incomes were low was very difficult. Often, of necessity, both parents worked outside the home and were unable to put in the time required of trustees. When I had visited all the schools and relayed their problems to David Lange and Phil Goff, I decided to wait for six months and then repeat the visits. Getting to know teachers, trustees and students was one of the most enjoyable aspects of my job.

Just before the Christmas recess, the State Sector Bill was introduced in the House. It was concerned with changes in the work of those employed by the state and was to cause massive resentment among unionists, many of whom marched to Parliament to protest. Graham and I, who both shared union concerns and had worked with Trevor Mallard to try to amend the Bill, went out to speak to the crowd. It was a salutary lesson for us because it was clear that we were now part of 'them', the enemy. When we tried to speak we were hissed and booed and spat at. Obviously people felt we should have stopped the introduction of the Bill. Just how we could have done that wasn't clear.

In 1988, Graham and I made the first of two approaches to the general secretary of the Labour Party, Tony Timms, and the president, Margaret Wilson, and asked them if the Party would support us if we voted against any further privatisation of state assets. They turned us down. Recently I talked to someone who was a member of the New Zealand Council of the

Labour Party at the time. He said that the majority view then was that our request should be declined, but with hindsight he felt we should have been supported.

When it came to the debate over the sale of the Bank of New Zealand, our small group of ten MPs collectively walked out of the House as the bells were ringing for the vote. We decided we would issue a press statement opposing the sale. We went down to Graham's office, locked the door and started on the press release. Some time later there was an urgent rapping on the door. It was Senior Whip Margaret Austin. She asked us what we were doing and we told her. She said, 'The Prime Minister has asked me to tell you that you're to come back into the House immediately.' We told her to tell him we would not come back, and we added, 'Tell him we may never come back.' We spent the rest of the evening wondering what on earth we could do to stem the tide.

In the end we decided once again to consult Labour people in our electorates. The advice of my people was that I should hang in there, and Graham received pretty much the same advice. But it was an uneasy period. I think that part of the problem was that everything in our society was being changed at the same time. Schools, health, the sale of what people called 'the family silver', restructuring of government departments, closure of post offices — in fact, everything that people depended on. We had earlier been assured by Roger Douglas, Richard Prebble and David Lange that government departments that were or had recently been corporatised would not subsequently be privatised. Telecom was just one example where the legislation went through very quickly, without going to a select committee.

Unemployment soared, family violence increased as men lost their careers. But a number of people at the top were doing very nicely, thank you, and it was to these people that Roger, Richard et al. were talking often, in Auckland where the big commercial players operated. None of us was saying that change wasn't necessary, but the Rogernomics solutions were too brutal, too arbitrary and totally lacking in awareness of the adverse effects on people.

In March 1988, because Jim Anderton was publicly opposing Government economic policies, David Lange decided to remove him from his chairmanship of the Foreign Affairs and Defence Select Committee. I was confused about this as my understanding was that the committee usually elected its own chair, but frustration often causes people to do strange things.

At the end of a select committee meeting, I was the last to leave and was sorting out my papers when the phone rang. It was Fran Wilde asking for me. She told me that a number of people had been discussing who should replace Jim as chair of the committee, and they thought I should be that person. I was absolutely astounded and said that, as a first-term MP, I was just coming to grips with the committee's work, but she was quite positive that I could do it. And so, after reflection, I did.

It had become obvious that Jim Anderton was rapidly reaching the point where he would sever his ties with the Labour Party. He had stopped eating at Bellamy's some time ago, and was becoming a lone shadowy figure; we saw him only in caucus, where he appeared very unhappy. And then he was gone, and in May formed the New Labour Party.

Many people asked at the time why we didn't go too. In today's MMP environment, changing parties seems to be acceptable, though I doubt that I could do it. In any case, the Labour Party had been part of my life for many years. We didn't have the numbers both inside Cabinet and in caucus to turn the tide, and we lacked an organised leader. David Lange was and is a brilliant man and we shall not see his like again, but in my opinion he couldn't organise himself out of a paper bag. When we finally got to see him on several occasions, we tried to get our concerns across to him, without success. He was not a team person. When we were with him, he always seemed to be on the way to somewhere else. When I spoke to a former Cabinet minister recently, I learned that their group supporting David, or trying to, had the same experience. He had very competent people working for him, but he just didn't pick up the ball and run with it. He needed to, because his opponents were so absolutely certain they were right.

Some good things did emerge from all this. Considering they were working in a climate where at every turn state responsibility was being eroded, ministers such as Helen Clark, who had the Housing portfolio, managed to put in place some very innovative plans for housing Maori, women, women's refuges and the disabled. Margaret Shields, working with good people like Lynne Bruce, put childcare and early childhood education on the map. Michael Cullen, who was Minister of Social Welfare, increased support for women's refuges, and the building blocks for Pay Equity legislation were laid by Helen Clark.

From the minute I came into the House, several Opposition members referred to me as a union dinosaur. However, two people from the Opposition who did impress me because they were bright, intelligent and forthright were Jenny Shipley and Ruth Richardson. I noted that they would in the future be people to reckon with.

The ideology of asset sales was well and truly underway. Value and cost had become terms solely for money — people had become irrelevant. But even dollar value was squandered: the sale of the Government Printing Office being one of many, many examples.

On a wall of the Government Printing Office in Wellington was a statement which declared its original raison d'être. It read:

THIS IS
A PRINTING OFFICE
CROSSROADS OF CIVILISATION
REFUGE OF ALL THE ARTS
AGAINST THE RAVAGES OF TIME.
ARMOURY OF FEARLESS TRUTH
AGAINST WHISPERING RUMOUR
INCESSANT TRUMPET OF TRADE
FROM THIS PLACE WORDS MAY FLY ABROAD
NOT TO PERISH ON WAVES OF SOUND
NOT TO VARY WITH THE WRITER'S HAND
BUT FIXED IN TIME HAVING BEEN VERIFIED IN PROOF
FRIEND, YOU STAND ON SACRED GROUND
THIS IS A PRINTING OFFICE.

For over 100 years, the Government Printing Office (GPO) had a proud reputation for excellence, for efficiency, and for the way it conducted its business. But by the early 1980s it was recognised that it needed to change to meet the demands of a changing environment. Reconstruction took place in 1981, and efficiencies were put in place.

By December 1987, Richard Prebble had the GPO in his sights, first as a state-owned enterprise (SOE) but ultimately for sale. The first mention of the sale was in the 1988 Budget and then, without establishing an SOE, Richard Prebble authorised the sale in June of that year. The Labour Government was fixated on substantially reducing the huge public debt bequeathed to it by the Muldoon Government. None of the Rogernomics ministers considered whether the GPO could be made profitable. An article in the Wellington *Evening Post* on 7 March 1992 makes interesting reading: it reports that the share price of Rank, the company which had bought the GPO, had risen meteorically since the GPO sale. Valued at less that $1 per share when the sale was announced, Rank's shares had jumped to $7.15 by September, rising to $10.15, at which point Rank bought Whitcoulls for $7.21 million. The Rank Group had made an after-tax profit of $5.6 million.

Were our Rogernomics ministers so inept that they couldn't devise a system where the state could do what Rank did and put that $5.6 million profit into health, social welfare or reduction of debt? But of course, by then our group of concerned MPs realised that the free-market philosophy was set firmly in place and that meant that state involvement in any government departments was to be removed.

State-owned Enterprise Minister Richard Prebble created a steering committee and gave it three months to report on the feasibility of selling the GPO. He appointed my old colleague and one-time friend Rob Campbell to chair the committee. On top of all that was happening, it was a matter of considerable concern to me. I think that the real anguish was that people like Simon Walker, Rob Campbell and Alf Kirk jumped ship and went to jobs where they were supporting free-market policies.

The sales criteria for state assets stated that:

(a)   The Government must receive more from the sale of the business than it would from retaining ownership, bearing in mind the risk attached to continued ownership; and

(b)   The sale of the business must not impede the Government's economic goals and must contribute to them.

As far as I can establish, Rob talked to the Government Printer, Rex Ward, but not to other staff members, a process which he would have despised in his FOL days. The staff had the distinct impression that Rob began this exercise with his mind already made up about the sale of the GPO. On 5 June 1988, he submitted his report to Cabinet, and the majority accepted his recommendation that the GPO sale should proceed.

The Chief Parliamentary Counsel, Walter Eyles, had very serious concerns about what would happen to Crown copyright if the GPO was sold to private enterprise. Rob Campbell was appointed as a one-person advisory board. Staff morale was quite understandably at an all-time low. The Government enlisted Jardens and Fay, Richwhite in the second stage of the sale. It took two years to coordinate the sale, and during that time, loss of jobs and low morale took a toll on the workings of the GPO. I have been told that Fay Richwhite and Jardens jointly received $12 million in consultancy fees.

The Public Service Association (PSA) was adamantly opposed to the sale. In the *Evening Post* on 17 May 1988, the PSA said it had not been consulted in the steering committee deliberations, nor was it consulted before the Government announcement of the sale of the GPO. The PSA also said that the report did not dispassionately examine the alternatives faced by the GPO and merely produced the recommendation that the Government had said it wanted. They said that Government's report took little account of longer-term development goals or returns, non-commercial goals, quality of service, conditions of employment in the state, public wealth versus private profit or other broader public-interest issues.

Rob Campbell had recommended in his report that if the GPO was not sold by October 1988, it should be turned into an SOE; but that recommendation was not implemented. The PSA further said that, at the time of sale, the Government's report itself showed that the GPO's present returns compared favourably with private sector counterparts and that the department had a sound commercial infrastructure.

At the end of the sale process, the Government received $9.6 million net for the GPO. The GPO building was sold to Internal Affairs which brought the figure up to $23 million. The PSA assessed the value of the GPO at between $85 and $125 million, and Fay Richwhite assessed it at $71 million.

What all this did to the GPO staff, who were mainly skilled tradespeople, should not be underestimated. They were part of a generation which had served an apprenticeship and had been encouraged to believe that as long as they acquitted themselves competently, they would be employed. This sale was the first of many which ushered in a climate of short-term controls and no certainty about the future.

I wonder if it ever occurred to Richard Prebble what the end result of his policies would do to families. He was so intent on destroying state control of departments that, in the end, the human result became lost in the exercise. The GPO not only printed all Government legislation; it printed Hansard reports of Parliamentary debates, books and a wide variety of other publications. All that was going to be contracted out.

In 1991, the new Bolger Government's Select Committee on Government Administration, chaired by Christine Fletcher, instituted an inquiry into the sale of the GPO. They did this, of course, not because they opposed the sale but because they thought the GPO had been sold at bargain-basement price. By then, the new Government had picked up Rogernomics at speed. But their report only highlighted the ineptitude of the sale, and how the sale was so drawn out that in the end the GPO seemed worthless.

The Dismantling of Labour

When I became chair of the Foreign Affairs and Defence Select Committee, one of the tasks I inherited from Jim Anderton was a commitment to review this country's Overseas Aid and Development programme, to discover whether the right people were being consulted in each country where we had projects set up, the usefulness of these projects to the people they were meant to assist — in fact, all aspects of this work. For some time, people had been expressing concern about the modest financial commitment of successive New Zealand governments to aid and development.

The committee had called for submissions on all these issues and these had begun to pour in. I knew that our Australian counterparts were carrying out a similar study and their chair had told me that their Labor Government had sanctioned two visits of their committee to the Pacific Islands, which was where the bulk of their aid money went. I discussed this idea with our committee, and we agreed that I should write to the Prime Minister seeking his agreement for the committee to visit New Zealand's aid projects. The answer came back very promptly. The Government, he said, did not have the resources to finance such a project. So, for the time being, that was that and we carried on hearing submissions and talking to officials of the then Department of Foreign Affairs, now the Ministry of Foreign Affairs and Trade.

In Australia there was a separate department which dealt with aid and development, and we discussed the merits and disadvantages of this system with a wide range of people. Later, the committee was told that the New Zealand and Australian Governments had decided to hold exchange visits of select committees and that ours was chosen as the first exchange. We were given the date when the Australian committee would visit us, a couple of months ahead.

Of course, I received a number of letters from people who wanted to know why, when so many displaced people were hurting here, I was bothering myself with strangers overseas. I understood where they were coming from but told them that we needed to have concern for people both here and overseas, especially in the Pacific, of which our country was part. When I talked in the House about our need to realise that we were no longer an outpost of Britain but part of the Pacific and Asia and that was where our future markets would be, Opposition MPs were very scornful and laughed at me. In the National Government of 1990–96, more and more National MPs and ministers promoted the Asia–Pacific idea, and today there is no question about where we are placed, and where our trade and other interests lie.

The Labour Caucus elected me to represent them at a meeting of the Asian Committee on Population and Development, which was holding a meeting in Kuala Lumpur. It was the beginning of my relationship with this group, some of whom I came to know well. Two women in particular I liked very much. They were both Chinese: Hu Yamei, professor of paediatrics at Beijing Hospital, and Hao Yichun, professor of palaeontology at the China University of Geosciences. Hao was also vice-president of the All China Women's Federation. But most of the delegates to this committee were men.

Because MPs feel, quite understandably, that everyone should have the chance to attend international fora, it is rare to achieve continuity, which is so helpful towards making a useful contribution. I was very fortunate that the caucus sent me to meetings of this organisation four times during my time in Parliament. I learned so much about the lives and cultures of the participants. They were mainly from countries where males are dominant, and this was reflected in their attitude to population control. Some of the women reacted angrily to reports of research which showed that men were more often the determinant of the sex of a child. But there were also men there who were aware that both men and women had to participate in population control if future generations were to be healthy and live better lives.

Back at Parliament, I found colleagues studying the Rogernomics proposal for taxi deregulation, a proposal to contract out the parliamentary cleaning services to private contractors, and a raft of other issues. I became immersed in meetings. Taxi drivers were outraged about plans for deregulation and told me so in great detail. I knew the parliamentary cleaners' group well — when I worked for the PSA, cleaners, most of whom worked at night, were my responsibility in Wellington and Hutt Valley government departments. Many were Pacific Island women who could only work outside the home at night. Often when the House was in urgency and we were there until midnight or later, we met them coming on duty.

It was becoming very obvious that the Rogernomes considered all state services inefficient and in need of commercialisation. In April 1987, Roger

Douglas sent MPs a Special Economic Newsletter which was headed, 'Questions and Answers on State-Owned Enterprises', with a subtitle, 'Why is Corporatisation Necessary?', in which he said that the creation of state-owned corporations was part of the Government's response to New Zealand's deep economic problems. He talked about how it was possible 20 years ago for our economy to sustain a considerable amount of waste and inefficiency because our trade with the rest of the world was healthy, but today we couldn't afford that waste because of the high balance of payments deficit, larger than desirable budget deficits, poor terms of trade, persistently high inflation and falling real standards of living for some years.

Nowhere in the document did he examine any possibility of the future Minister of State-owned Enterprises being given the task of working with the State Services Commission, the PSA and its members to transform state services into efficient modern structures able to operate in a rapidly changing world.

Roger also said in his paper that the savings from corporatisation would be potentially huge and would grow over time because they would come from basic changes in the way things were done, rather than specific cuts for particular activities. This, he said, was the Government's approach to controlling spending — improving the quality of government spending rather than just the quantity.

He said that at present the state trading investments were returning nothing to the taxpayer, and that the taxpayer was subsidising the consumer; and he asked if that was fair. He said that corporatisation was different from privatisation and would keep assets paid for by the taxpayer in the taxpayers' hands.

By 1988 we were well aware that state-owned enterprises were simply the means to ready the services for privatisation. This perception was confirmed by Terry Hall, the *Dominion*'s business editor, who said in an article on 19 March 1990, headed, 'Mad Rush to Sell Telecom before National Victory', that the sale of Telecom would temporarily ease the Government's potential embarrassment over its inability to cut its own spending, which was the reason that New Zealand was headed for a massive blowout in the internal deficit. He also said that it would be a temporary respite, as the Government flogged off the silver to pay for the housekeeping and set out to confuse the people with talk of the need to pay off the debt — soon there would be nothing left to sell. He gave a list of state asset sales and asked his readers to tell him one that was well-handled or didn't arouse criticism that it had been sold too cheaply; and he said that the list also showed how active the Government had been in disposing of state assets, some of which it had promised not to sell:

° The Rural Bank
° Petrocorp (these two, sold to Fletcher Challenge, provided a big share of
  FCL's latest profits)
° The National Film Unit
° The Shipping Corporation
° Government Print
° Postbank (which turned into a significant contributor to the ANZ's
  otherwise lacklustre result)
° Synfuels and Maui Gas
° The Bank of New Zealand
  Controversy surrounds other state selloffs such as:
° DFC (which left egg over the Government's, Treasury's, Mr Caygill's and
  the NPF's faces besides causing international embarrassment)
° New Zealand Steel
° Air New Zealand
° Health Computing Services
° Communicate New Zealand
  Among assets still to go are State Forests (any day now it seems), THC
(ditto), Railways, Coalcorp and the Tourist Department's travel offices.
  Further down the track are Electricorp, Landcorp (the property market is
too depressed), and New Zealand Post.
  Treasury have been busy little boys, have they not, helped by compliant
ministers like Stan Rodger and Richard Prebble.
  When National is elected, there won't be much left. It'll have the difficult
task of trying to balance budgets without contributions from asset sales, or
the dividends organisations like Telecom have been delivering.

Out in the electorate and as I travelled round the country, people were
appalled at what was happening. This was nowhere more obvious than
within Labour Party circles, where disillusionment was rife. There was the
rise of the Backbone Club, a right-wing organisation based mainly in
Auckland but with small groups in Miramar and Pencarrow. Labour Party
conferences became fraught with dissent. The Backbone Club concen-
trated quite feverishly on increasing its influence in branches. In
Pencarrow, the Women's Branch in Wainuiomata found it suddenly had a
very inflated membership. We sent that list to National Office, which
discovered that most of the new members did not reside in Wainuiomata
but lived outside the electorate, a number of them in Auckland. As the
number of members in each branch determines the number of delegates
to conference, it was obvious what was happening. Never did the
Backbone Club have the numbers to dominate conferences and Labour
electorate committees, but they did cause considerable disruption and
disillusionment among members, who simply withdrew en masse.
  In 1987 Margaret Wilson had stepped down as president of the Party

and Rex Jones was elected in her place. Margaret is a highly principled, able and intelligent woman who had led the Party through some extremely difficult times, had worked for and supported David Lange wherever possible, and had for me been a breath of sanity in a divided caucus. In her book, *Labour in Government 1984–1987*, she said that the tensions that had become apparent within Government and the Labour Party were obvious during the first three years of the Fourth Labour Government, and had their roots in the period prior to 1984; and that one of the reasons she was handing over the job to Rex Jones at the end of 1987 was that she could no longer see how she could assist with the reconciliation of these differences. She felt there was a total unwillingness on the part of the key people within the parliamentary Party to compromise, and that this had become very apparent at the 1987 annual conference, where the level of delegates' frustration was expressed in an unwillingness to permit people with a contrary view to be heard. In such an intolerant environment, she said, it was difficult to see how the differences could be resolved internally.

Rex Jones was a different kettle of fish, as my grandmother would have said. Never one to suffer fools gladly, he was a forthright and strong man. Tact was not one of his foremost attributes, but he was good for the Party at that time. During his term of office, he kept close to what was happening in Parliament, as Margaret had. How he did it I can't imagine, because his job as general secretary of one of the country's biggest unions was very demanding. He travelled literally thousands of kilometres each year. He had very definite ideas (not always shared by other unionists) about what unions had to do to survive and serve their members in this challenging new environment. The Engineers Union traditionally confined its activities to the wages and conditions of its members and did not become involved in the wider issues dealt with by other unions such as anti-apartheid, anti-Vietnam War, anti-Pinochet activites. At caucuses he often looked very frustrated at what was happening.

So I had the president of the Party as my Labour Electorate Committee (LEC) chair, though I knew that his time in that position was limited. In addition to his union responsibilities, he had to visit branches and LECs and try to persuade them that their world wasn't coming to an end. In the meantime, Ruth Dyson, the senior vice-president, also travelled far and wide, getting to know the people she was representing. In 1988, Ruth was a contender for the presidency, narrowly defeating Jim Anderton. Prior to this election, a statement of intent was set down by the Cabinet and Ruth Dyson that future asset sales would be considered individually, each on its merits. I was quite cynical about this because I had seen so many things reversed.

The seeds of the dismantling of the Labour Party had been sown long before, and it was not until 1996 that I would attend a Labour Party conference with which I felt comfortable. There are now some wonderful young people coming into the Party, lots more activists, and some who had defected in the 1980s. But, back then, the Party was ripping itself apart.

In 1988, Richard Prebble decided to seek a High Court ruling on the role of union membership in the Party. It was an unprecedented move and a measure of the parlous state the Party was in. The Labour Party was founded by the unions, but their historic relationship with the Party had got out of kilter in the 1960s when Finton Patrick Walsh, then president of the New Zealand Federation of Labour, encouraged unions to block vote on issues such as compulsory military training. I felt it should have been possible to talk to the unions about their role, but conciliation and negotiation were not part of the Rogernomics agenda. Richard Prebble sought to limit union influence in Party deliberations, and made his attack while Rex Jones was president, so he was in effect attacking his union members.

Richard projected a holier-than-thou attitude about the fact that unions paid only $1 per affiliated member, whereas other Party members had to pay $11 each per year. This so-called high moral ground was very strange when one considered how the Treasury ministers had reversed Labour Party manifesto promises. David Lange in principle favoured a change to limit union power over the Party at electorate level so that delegates voting on Party matters should be members of the Party. But he felt that negotiations with the union movement should be conducted amicably. He also said that neither he nor a court had the power to change the constitution of the Labour Party; and that any changes were a matter for the Party. He was, of course, right.

Against this backdrop of dissent, MPs tried to get on with the job they had been elected to do. On Mondays and Fridays, when the House wasn't sitting, I got to know the organisations and people of my electorate better, in Wainuiomata, Eastbourne and Moera. As policies affected more and more people, attendance at my clinics escalated. I did what I could to help and was often able to suggest ways to alleviate difficulties. Outwardly, I wasn't disloyal but I didn't defend policies I couldn't support. This came to a head when Michael Bassett proposed his policy on amalgamation of local authorities. Nothing was more set to inflame the passions of small local councils which were threatened with extinction. Once again, it could all have been done differently — telling authorities they could state their case to the Local Government Select Committee was not the way. People felt it was too late then.

In Pencarrow electorate, the proposal was that the Eastbourne Borough Council serving around 4500 people and the Wainuiomata

District Council serving approximately 19,000 people would be amalgamated into the Lower Hutt City Council. This was tiger country and both councils reacted accordingly. My three terms on the Nelson City Council had given me experience of the varied work of local government. I had been given the task of amalgamating the electricity authorities in the Nelson district. That had been fraught enough — though when I visited Nelson some years later, and talked to people about those days, it was obvious that all their dire predictions had faded.

But this was quite different — arbitrary and lacking in proper consultation. Michael Bassett had appointed a Local Government Commissioner, Brian Elwood. Brian had been mayor of Palmerston North, so he was experienced in local body affairs and also knowledgable about Local Body Association affairs. One of his tasks was to deal with problems which arose due to amalgamation. To him I took the unhappiness of both Eastbourne and Wainuiomata. He listened carefully to what I had to say, was almost dismissive of Eastbourne's claims, but said he would think carefully about Wainuiomata, talk to the people there and then make a recommendation to the minister.

The people of the Bays held a meeting in the Wellesley College Hall to discuss their future. It was a very tough meeting, at the end of which I joked that the only thing they hadn't brought with them was the tumbril to take me to the scaffold! I told them that I had talked to the commissioner and that, in his opinion, they didn't have a case. Because of this, I said, we should explore possible benefits; but they didn't want a bar of that. The area covered by their local borough council was and is, of course, special, with its backdrop of native bush and views across Wellington Harbour, but its small population of about 4500 people meant that, in the foreseeable future, there wouldn't be the financial ability from rates to meet their needs.

They asked me scornfully what possible benefits could result from amalgamation. I outlined several; and I also said we needed a council-assisted childcare centre, an after-school centre and a women's refuge. A woman stood up and said in a cultured voice, 'Ms Davies, there are no battered women in the Bays.' I told her she was wrong and said that the methods were slightly more sophisticated there. I then talked about the wife of a professional man who had had her face ironed with a hot iron, and the woman who had arrived at my front door on a Sunday morning whose husband had lost most of his money in the stockmarket crash and who had tried to run her over with his Mercedes. There were others, I knew, because they came to see me at my clinics — mostly in Wainuiomata so local people wouldn't see them.

The Australian Foreign Affairs and Defence Select Committee came to New Zealand and we had a very useful exchange of views. They also had meetings with the Labour Foreign Affairs Caucus Committee and with Russell Marshall, our Minister of Foreign Affairs, and said they were looking forward to welcoming us across the Tasman in their new Parliament in Canberra.

A major issue exercising us was the New Zealand Government's proposal to buy four new frigates from Australia. Like many people, I was philosophically opposed to this. I knew that the navy needed new vessels, but it seemed obvious to me that the last thing we needed was high-tech state-of-the-art frigates. New Zealanders, post Second World War, have increasingly shown themselves to be excellent peacekeepers and skilled at rebuilding bridges, houses and hospitals in the Pacific following tornadoes and other disasters. We needed vessels designed to do that work; and also to police our 200-mile economic zone, to perform mine-sweeping operations, and to go south into the ice of Antarctica to carry out rescue work and research. Opponents of these very expensive frigates also believed that New Zealand shipbuilders were capable of producing such vessels.

Through an engineering friend in New Plymouth, Harry Duynhoven made contact with a Danish shipbuilding company, with whom he had highly technical discussions on the telephone. Ultimately, representatives of the company came to New Zealand to visit him and to try to talk with our current Defence Minister, Bob Tizard.

That Harry was not successful in persuading the Government that the Danish prototype was much more appropriate than the Australian proposal was not due to his lack of informed persuasion but more to the political climate between Australia and New Zealand. Closer economic relations (CER) with Australia were developing at this time. We argued in caucus and with individual members and after that with ministers about the frigate decision but they were adamant and not prepared to make any concessions, which made us suspicious. Out in the real world, a large section of the population was outraged, and letters flooded in from all over the country; buildings and walls were covered with anti-frigate slogans. Taxi drivers reported that their passengers were substantially against the frigates. Treasury ministers had told people that, because of the parlous state of the economy and the size of the nation's indebtedness, they had to restructure, slash jobs, cut back state spending — and yet here they were planning to spend billions on four expensive and inappropriate toys.

The fact that David Lange, who had been so splendid about the nuclear-free policy and acted with such courage against the pressures from powerful nations, was not opposing the frigate purchase was very strange to us. It became very evident that there was more to this deal with

Australia than met the eye. The peace movement, which had been delighted with the nuclear-free legislation, was appalled about the frigates and turned against Labour, with some going to New Labour.

In May 1988, the Select Committee travelled to Canberra to study the work of the Australian Foreign Affairs and Defence Select Committee. We were shown their spectacular new Parliament which had been set into a hill, some distance from the city. On its roof was a huge lawn, where people could picnic. They showed us all the amenities, the bank, the shops, the self-filling swimming pool, the gymnasium. But when I asked where their childcare centre was, there was a pause of puzzlement. 'A childcare centre?' they said. 'Well,' I told them, 'I can't imagine why, with a modern Parliament some way out of town with 1700 or so workers, you don't see a need for a childcare centre for those workers.' At the official lunch that day I was asked to speak, and I traversed a number of areas which I felt were in our combined interest. Then I mentioned the child-care centre. At question time, I was asked whether the New Zealand Parliament had one. I explained that my cousin Whetu Tirikatene-Sullivan had had three babies while she was in Parliament, and had it not been for her whanau who brought them in for her to breastfeed and cuddle, she could not have continued her work as an MP. I told them about Ruth Richardson, who had had her two babies as a parliamentarian and had nowhere allocated where she could breastfeed them; and about my colleague Liz Tennet, for whom the Whips had allocated a small room where she could care for her son Matthew. She and the Labour Women's Caucus had started campaigning for a childcare centre. They had estab-lished that there were more than enough parents — MPs, journalists, executive secretaries and other staff — with small children who would use such a facility to justify a centre in Parliament. I told them that when we moved across to Bowen House, which was where all the parliamentary officials and staff except for ministers and their staff would be housed while the old Parliament House was being refurbished, the prefab build-ing that had housed some of us would be relocated behind Parliament House and developed into a childcare centre.

At a meeting of World Women Parliamentarians for Peace held after the Joint Select Committee meetings, I met Bob Hawke, who had come to speak to us. I knew him from my trade union days when he was presi-dent of the Australian Council of Trade Unions and I was vice-president of the New Zealand Federation of Labour. He looked at me and said, 'Good God, you're surely not an MP?', to which I replied, 'Good God, you're surely not the Prime Minister!' He said, 'I hear you've been stirring about a childcare centre here. If we had one, manufacturers and other employers would feel that we wanted them to establish one too.' 'Well, what's wrong with that?' I said, and he retorted, 'You always were a damn difficult woman!' and stamped off.

When the joint committees met, several MPs and senators were present. This was a real eye-opener. One of the senators was Jo Vallentine from Western Australia, a woman totally committed to peace. I couldn't believe the way she was treated by the more macho men on the Australian Foreign Affairs and Defence Select Committee. At a function later that day, I said to one of the Australian MPs that if our men were to behave like that to the women on a select committee, they would be very firmly dealt with. What I actually said was that they would get a belt up the bracket. That was quite at variance with my views on peace, of course, but I was angry. He said, 'Well, that's one of the differences between Aussies and Kiwis.'

Apart from these hiccups, it was a good visit. I talked to the Australian MPs about aid and development and they told me how their first visit to the Pacific Islands had changed their perception of aid. They were due to go again later in the year. They arranged for me to visit their separate aid and development department, the Australian Development Assistance Bureau (ADAB). It was a useful and worthwhile meeting. Not that it did much good when I got back to Wellington — our bureaucrats were strongly opposed to a separate body.

The meeting of the World Women Parliamentarians for Peace was stimulating and inspirational. West Australian Senator Pat Giles, whom I had last met in 1977 at the Australian Working Women's Conference, chaired this meeting. She had come to New Zealand for our Working Women's Conference in 1977. Among the international delegates was the controversial German Green MP, Petra Kelly. She was quite uncompromising but extremely brave and I was very shocked when some time later she was murdered by her partner. Europe was still very pro-nuclear, and she suffered because of that.

In 1986, I became the chair of the New Zealand Women's Refuge Trust, an organisation established to raise money for New Zealand refuges to address the shortfall between government funding and the growing needs of the refugees. Although funding had been increased by Labour, the needs always outpaced the means. We were continually trying to find innovative ways to raise money. We had concerts at Government House, dinners with well-known speakers, and were always exploring ways of fund-raising. When I became an MP, I asked for permission to hold our meetings in Parliament itself and was allocated a committee room on the ground floor of the House. It had a telephone, so if I was needed in the House or elsewhere, the Whips could ring me.

We learned that the successful businessman Bob Jones was interested in our work and might agree to donate some money. So, I was asked to arrange lunch with him to discuss our needs. At the Yangtse Restaurant, Bob said he knew why I was there, but he had a number of other issues he wanted to discuss with me. Bob is a great conversationalist and it was a challenging and very pleasant lunch. All too soon, it was close to my next appointment. The Trust had told me I should try for $45,000, but when Bob stood up and said, 'Well, how much do you want?', I said, '$100,000,' and prepared to negotiate. But he said, 'Okay,' and brushed aside my astonishment and delight. In addition, he decided to get some celebrities together and fly them around the country in his executive jet to perform celebrity debates, as long as the local refuge staff would arrange venues for him. Bob later provided an office for the Trust on The Terrace.

As I travelled round the country to speaking engagements, I tried always to set aside some time to visit refuges and to learn first-hand their needs and problems. I met some outstanding women who worked long hours for very little or no financial reward. Working with women and children who have been physically and/or mentally abused requires great skill. In overseas countries I also visited refuges where possible. In Kuala Lumpur I was taken to one in a very affluent suburb. When I asked whether local people had objected to having a refuge in their midst, I was told that indeed they had, and pointed to the very high walls around the property. These had been provided by a sultan's wife. As I arrived, a chauffeur-driven car drove off. The refuge workers told me that a battered woman from Penang and her children had arrived four days previously. She was married to a very wealthy man, who hired detectives to find out where she was. On this day he had arrived and persuaded her to go back to him. Refuge workers everywhere will recognise this situation. Women sometimes come back again and again before gaining the confidence to leave their abusers permanently. This Malaysian refuge relied on donations to provide a service to battered women and children. People had donated furniture and whiteware, and they were beginning to use counsellors.

In August 1988, I was contacted by Government House and advised that a ceremony would be held to present medals to the people who were to be awarded the Order of New Zealand. I had twice refused to accept the honour of 'Dame' because it simply wasn't me, but this was a far more New Zealand award, which I felt was more appropriate.

I was sent the details of the ceremony, to be presented by the then Governor-General Sir Paul Reeves, and told that I was welcome to bring three members of my family or close friends. I asked my brother David and his wife Lyn, and Mary. Mary came out to Eastbourne on the morning of the ceremony to collect me. I was really concerned about what I should wear for this occasion. I had been held up by telephone calls from constituents and had forgotten to have any breakfast, and eventually felt so dizzy that Mary made me sit down and have some sweet tea and toast to raise my blood sugar levels. While I was still dithering, Mary asked me what time the ceremony was due to begin and I handed her the invitation. We realised with horror that we had just enough time to get to Government House if we moved very swiftly. I had told David that I would meet him and Lyn at Parliament and I insisted on calling there, only to find that they had gone ahead, thinking I'd forgotten them. The traffic that morning was very heavy and the taxi driver we called to Parliament decided to travel via The Terrace. This was a disaster as many others were doing the same and we became firmly stuck in a traffic jam.

Finally, in a state of great agitation, we arrived at Government House. I was whisked in one direction and Mary in another. As I entered the ballroom where the ceremony was to take place, it was obvious that I had been holding things up. David Lange raised his eyes heavenward in mock exasperation as I shrank into my allotted seat. Then the Governor-General Sir Paul Reeves entered the ballroom and the ceremony began.

When the Order of New Zealand had been created, it was decided that there would be a limit of 20 recipients at any one time. In the original group announced on Waitangi Day 1988, along with myself there were Sir Edmund Hillary, then High Commissioner to India, the Maori Queen Dame Te Ariki nui Te Atairangikaahu, Dr Clarence Beeby, and Sir Arnold Nordmeyer. Subsequently another five recipients had been announced: Lady June Blundell, Jim Knox, Professor Douglas Lilburn, Frederick Turnovsky and Professor Richard Matthew. This was the first investiture ceremony for the Order.

The medal itself is very beautiful and quite heavy. The men had theirs hung on a red, white and black ribbon round their necks and the women had theirs attached to a bow of the same ribbon and pinned to the front of their dress. At the luncheon following the ceremony, Phillip O'Shea, who is the herald at Parliament in charge of all ceremonial orders and medals and their presentations, talked about the difficulties he had had contacting the recipients to tell them about the establishment of the Order some months previously. Sir Edmund Hillary had been in a remote area of Nepal and I had been tracked through Delhi, Moscow, Helsinki and Portugal; the Maori Queen had been at a remote marae which had no telephone and the information was conveyed to her by a person on a bicycle. We were told that the medal must be returned when we died. Since that time, a number of others have joined, some have died, but we have never yet reached 20!

*The Governor-General Paul Reeves confers
on me the Order of New Zealand at
Government House*

From the beginning, I was not happy about having my medal attached to a bow. I thought it looked much better on a ribbon, worn around the neck. When I approached Phillip O'Shea about this, he told me that no other woman had ever raised this issue. Over the next month I gently kept up the pressure. Some time after the award ceremony, the Queen was due to visit and would meet the existing ONZ members and officiate at the investiture of the new recipients. A few days before she arrived, Phillip rang me and said that the ribbon had arrived for my medal. He asked me not to change from the bow until after Queen Elizabeth's visit as she might not approve of what I was doing.

Getting the Gong, 1990

Following the ceremony, I found myself alone with the Queen. We sat together on a settee in the large drawing room. It was not long after Prince Edward had decided that a naval career was not for him, despite the opposition from his father Prince Philip. I told Her Majesty that many New Zealanders liked Prince Edward; that he had been very popular during his time at Wanganui Collegiate and that I thought he was a very principled young man. All mothers are pleased to hear their children praised and she was no exception. Then I told her about my problem with the medal and asked her if this proposal would offend her. She touched my hand and said, 'My dear, wear it any way you feel comfortable with.' When I got back to Parliament, I rang Phillip and told him, 'The Queen says it's okay, so you don't need to worry about her being offended!'

A medal, however attractive, is too grand and valuable to be worn other than on official occasions, so a small brooch of the same design was produced, and I wear it with pleasure on my jacket lapel.

Siberia

In the middle of 1988, David Lange entered hospital for an angioplasty. He had not been well for some time. The angioplasty cleared a blocked artery and marked the beginning of a series of coronary difficulties. None of this was helped by the fact that Roger Douglas was increasingly going public with his dissatisfaction about David's political activities. Roger was to say later that Labour should have stayed in for ten or twelve years — not admitting that his actions, the way he had forged ahead without regard for the social implications of his policies, the destablisation of Labour Party members and supporters, had sealed Labour's demise. There were too many angry, untrusting people around within the Party and outside it.

By 1989, along with a number of my colleagues, I was living in a state of tension and despair. I dreaded caucus on Thursdays because I knew that either Roger Douglas or Richard Prebble or both would be charging on with their policy of rapid change. Many of their decisions cut through everything I'd ever believed in, and we didn't have the numbers to oppose them successfully.

With the now frequent 'urgent' sessions of Parliament, and an indigestible legislative programme, I was delighted to receive a fax from Ray Stewart in Helsinki asking me to come to a World Peace Council (WPC) meeting in Amsterdam. It happened to fall in the next parliamentary recess, and as I said to Mary, it would give me the opportunity to view what was happening from a distance, in a new environment. She said that she had been thinking about travelling on the Trans-Siberian railway, about which I had told her so much. She suggested we take the Trans-Siberian to Moscow, which she had never been to, then go to Leningrad and by train to Finland, where she would leave me and go to Scotland while I went on to Amsterdam with Ray and the rest of the WPC secretariat. We would meet up in London, where I would stay with Wendy and Ian Dear and she would stay with her friend Jean. We planned to see the garden at Sissinghurst, and also a few plays. On the way home we would visit Helen and Chris Laidlaw in Harare, Zimbabwe, where Chris was the New Zealand High Commissioner. Mary loves Africa and really wanted to get back.

Then I was approached by the First Secretary at the Chinese Embassy, who said that his ambassador had heard that I was going on the Trans-Siberian railway. He had been suggesting for some time that I should visit his country, and he now asked whether I had time to include China on my itinerary: I might consider starting the train journey on the Trans-Mongolian at Beijing Station (something I'd always wanted to do), after seeing something of China. They asked me to specify where I'd like to go, and said that, from Hong Kong on, I would be their guest within China. I told the First Secretary that I would have Mary with me, and he said he was sure that would be fine. Because of the time constraint I knew I would have to restrict my Chinese itinerary. I mentioned I'd like to see something of rural China and Shanghai — I've had a strong wish to visit that city ever since I was a little girl at Woodville School, where we had sung the song about old Shanghai.

I contacted two women friends at Beijing Hospital, one the chief paediatrician and the other the chief gynaecologist. They had both been at the two meetings of the Asian Population and Development Association I had attended and we had established a good rapport. I told them we would be in Beijing.

It was all very exciting. We had our visas, our tickets and other travel documents and the itinerary all planned. And then, one week before we were to leave New Zealand, the Tienanmen Square incident burst upon our television screens in all its horrifying detail. Officials from the Ministry of External Relations and Trade (MERT) came to see me and advised me that it would be very unwise for me to go and that it could be quite dangerous. In the House, David Lange asked me what I was going to do. I told him that the Chinese officials so far felt I should still go but that the MERT officials had advised against the trip. He said, 'Oh well, I expect the Chinese know best what is happening in their country.'

During this period of indecision, we alerted our travel agent that he should perhaps begin to explore an alternative route as we were only days away from our departure date. Then the Ambassador himself rang me and said that they now felt it would be unwise for me to go to China at this time and, much as he regretted it, I should postpone the visit till a later date. In the end, the travel agent arranged for us to fly to Hong Kong, spend a day and a night there, then on to Tokyo, up to Niigata by bullet train and fly from there to Kharbarovsk to pick up the Trans-Siberian train.

In the weeks prior to our departure, our group of dissident MPs began to hear murmurs about replacing David Lange with someone more compatible with the views espoused by the Douglas/Prebble clique. I knew that there would be two caucus meetings while I was away, and at

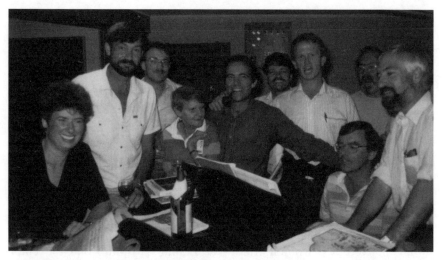

Evening sing-song around the piano at a three-day Labour Party caucus in Wanganui: (from left) Fran Wilde (now Mayor of Wellington), Ken Shirley (now ACT list MP), Phil Goff, myself, John Terris (now Mayor of Lower Hutt), Ross Robertson, Jack Elder (now a New Zealand First Minister), Russell Marshall, Harry Duynhoven and Trevor Young

the last caucus before I left New Zealand, I said loudly as I left the room that if anyone was contemplating any sort of coup during the time I was away, I would hear about it and come home. The Douglas supporters told me not to be ridiculous. A number of us would be away during the recess: Jonathan Hunt to Dublin; Graham Kelly on a Speaker's tour of South America with Jim Sutton; Fran Wilde to Rome; Peter Simpson to the US; and Margaret Shields to Spain.

As I lay in bed in a motel near Auckland Airport on the eve of our departure for Hong Kong, thoughts of what could happen raced through my head. I told myself that so far, all I had heard was conjecture, too ephemeral to cause me to cancel this journey. The next morning Mary and I were riveted by the news on Morning Report that part of the Trans-Siberian Railway had been blown up by a gas explosion. Mary said the trip was doomed, and I was inclined to agree. And then I remembered that there was more than one line on the Trans-Siberian and I said to Mary, 'Let's take a chance'. And off we went.

We flew to Hong Kong and arrived during the day. We were booked into the YWCA opposite the famous Peninsula Hotel, which of course we couldn't afford, though we did go to dinner there on our first night. We went to the shops and bought gifts and one or two items of clothing, which was just as well, because the next morning Hong Kong was shut: in an unprecedented action, the shops and restaurants closed in sympathy with the Tienanmen Square student protesters. We ventured out and saw thousands of students demonstrating outside the Chinese Embassy about what had happened to their counterparts in Tienanmen Square. They all wore white with black armbands. We knew that we were witnessing a historic moment.

We explored Hong Kong, went out on a harbour ferry and then flew to Tokyo. There we were met by a member of the Japanese Peace Movement who had been alerted about our arrival by Ray, Stewart and at dinner that night we met some very interesting people involved in the struggle for peace. The next morning, we set out for the railway station to board the bullet train. Unfortunately, that station had very steep, high stairs. Our slight young interpreter felt it his duty to take our heavy luggage to the top. With my bung lungs, I would have found that task impossible. When I finally and breathlessly reached the top, our interpreter looked fragile and bade us farewell with considerable relief.

The bullet train was not geared to people on a round-the-world tour — we had difficulty finding somewhere to put our two large suitcases. I had been on the bullet train before, but I was still amazed at its speed and the brief amount of time that passengers had to board or leave it at stations. In Japan, efficiency is a paramount aim. When I saw how people were crammed into local trains by guards wearing white gloves and how difficult it would be for the elderly and mothers with young children to operate at this speed, I felt that efficiency was more important than people.

We travelled so fast that we didn't see much of the country we passed, though when we reached the outskirts of Niigata, the train slowed down and we saw a number of houses sporting windowboxes filled with pink oxalis. We couldn't believe our eyes — in New Zealand it is a dreaded weed in the same league as couchgrass.

At Niigata Airport, as we stood in the queue to present our tickets and passports, I remarked to Mary with some relief that it was great to be where no one knew me and I could really relax. She said 'I wouldn't bank on it. Look over there.' To one side stood a man in shorts and a T-shirt that read 'Tim Round's Tours'. In his hand were about 40 New Zealand passports. My heart sank. Then, in the background, I saw what could only be New Zealanders: people with red, weather-beaten faces and conservative country clothes. It turned out that they were Waikato and Southland farmers and their wives. When they saw me, they came over and asked what I was doing there. I told them I was going to Kharbarovsk to board the Trans-Siberian train and they said, 'So are we!' I doubted if there was even one Labour supporter among them.

When we reached Kharbarovsk Airport, I lined up at the end of the queue to go through Customs. The New Zealanders wanted to know why

I was standing in line — shouldn't I be at the head of the queue? I told them that, on this journey, I was an ordinary traveller and wanted no privileges. They obviously found that very strange.

At Kharbarovsk, we stayed in an Intourist hotel. After a rather spirited discussion with the Intourist guide at the hotel when she realised that we had only a photocopy of our Trans-Siberian rail tickets, due to the last-minute alterations to our travel plans, we settled into our room. We weren't due to board the train until the following afternoon, so after a good night's sleep we set out to explore the city, which is situated beside the mighty river Amur.

The last time I had been in Kharbarovsk, it had been mid winter with snow up to my knees. Now it was spring and the parks were full of wild-flowers. Just before we left New Zealand, there had been a photo on the front page of *Time* magazine of David Lange lying in some long grass, so we decided that Mary would take a photo of me lying among the wild-flowers to take back to him. I tried to discover the hotel where I spent my traumatic visit in 1971, when I was stranded there in the middle of winter with no other English speakers, little money and an expiring visa, but it was difficult, eighteen years later. I could see that in the summer, it was really a very attractive city.

When we reached the railway station, we found our compartment and settled in. We met Ludmilla the provodnik (or conductor) who was in charge of our carriage and who spoke no English. Drawing on my previous experience on the Trans-Siberian, I had asked the travel agent to book us a two-berth airconditioned compartment and it was as well that I did because it was quite hot. I remembered the variability of the conditions in the dining car, and while it might well have improved in the intervening years, Mary and I each took a large plastic box full of basic provisions, just to be on the safe side. We had cheese, crackers, a tin of butter, salt and pepper, Vegemite, small sharp knives and a spoon each. We also took packets of instant noodle soups, which were invaluable.

Along the 8000 kilometres to Moscow, the train stopped many times. When we left the carriage, Ludmilla intimated that we should lock our compartment door, and she stood guard at the main door of the carriage. At the first station I saw a number of Hyde Park prams beside the food stalls. I said there must have been a population explosion, but when we approached the stalls, we saw that the prams had been used to transport the villagers' food for sale. In the stalls we found all sorts of goodies — sausages of many types, hot cooked potatoes, radishes, spring onions and local cheeses. We had to keep a weather eye on the train as it was inclined to take off at a moment's notice.

The New Zealanders came to visit us in groups. They asked how come

(Left) in David Lange pose among the wildflowers; (right) stitching Mira Szaszy's cushion

we had an airconditioned two-berth compartment when they had four-berth ones without airconditioning. They obviously thought I'd pulled influential strings.

We made friends with an English couple, Tom and Jennifer Lord, who were train enthusiasts and gave us a lot of useful information. Our travel agent was also a train buff and had asked us to take photos of any steam trains we saw, so Mary was busy with her camera whenever we passed station yards where steam trains were parked. Mary and I had brought our respective bits of tapestry embroidery with us. Mary was embroidering a cushion cover, and I was doing one on behalf of the Labour Women's Council for Mira Szaszy, for whom I have a great regard. Ludmilla was fascinated by this activity and came often to inspect progress and admire.

One of the real bonuses of this journey was the magnificent wildflowers all along the route. There were also banks of lilac, the delightful scent of which assailed us at each stop. In eastern Siberia, there were masses of purple Siberian irises as far as the eye could see. As we travelled, these were replaced by the glowing colours of Russell lupins, then masses of dianthus and, closer to Moscow, double gold ranunculi. It wasn't until much later, in South Africa, that I saw anything comparable. Most of the houses in the rural villages were wooden, unpainted except for the fretwork around the windows, which were bright green or blue.

At one station we saw through an open door a huge ceramic floor-to-ceiling stove, which we were told was never allowed to go out in winter. Each household had a stove like this to see them through the freezing cold temperatures. The last time I had been in Russia and got off the train at

Irkutsk, halfway across the Trans-Siberian line, at midnight, it was 30 degrees below zero, so I could appreciate the value of these stoves.

Spring and summer are a very busy time for the Siberians. The fine weather lasts only a couple of months, and during that time the villagers gather wood and chop it into the right lengths for their stoves. These logs are stacked high along the fencelines around each house. The people gather mushrooms that grow under the forest trees and preserve them in large ceramic jars. They grow potatoes to store, pumpkins for food and vodka, red cabbage, onions and radishes. Theirs is a very harsh environment, so these few weeks are crucial.

Shortly after we left Kharbarovsk, Ludmilla came to our compartment and, using sign language, indicated that we should look out the window. Soon we saw a large head of Lenin, complete with cap, carved on a chalk hillside, which reminded us both of England's white horse.

At Irkutsk, the Tim's Tour people got off the train. The lucky things were going to visit Samarkand and Tashkent. At a number of stations, various couples and groups from the tour had asked to have photographs taken with me. Mary, who was determined that I was on holiday and not public property, stood guard most of the time, and they had to wait until her attention was elsewhere before they brought their cameras out. We wished them a splendid journey and the train went on its way. As we travelled on, someone threw a stone at the train and it shattered the outer part of our double-glazed window, which made seeing out very difficult. Ludmilla was very put out. Tom Lord got up a ladder at the next station and tapped out the shattered glass and we were in business again.

And then we were approaching Moscow. At the beginning we felt it was going to be a long journey, but time had gone very fast. We had become quite attached to Ludmilla and when we said goodbye (dosvedania), which was one of the few Russian words we knew, we gave her some gifts that we had gathered together. Looking back, we waved to this sturdy indomitable woman who had been our protector and provider on the journey.

At Moscow Station we were to be met by a representative of the Soviet Peace Committee (SPC), but when we got off the train and searched along the platform, it was obvious that no one had turned up. Fortunately I had their telephone number and once I had worked out the intricacies of the station's public telephone, I reached the person who was supposed to come. He told me that they had been advised that we would arrive the day before, and several of them had come to the station bearing a New Zealand flag and had decided we had changed our plans. He asked us to go across the road to one of the other stations, where he would meet us.

We had been booked into the Hotel Ukraine, which is very large and looks out across Moscow. The architectural effect of the hotel's exterior was of a giant pink wedding cake and its reception rooms had vast high ceilings. We surrendered our passports as is required in Russia, and were shown to our room. I had told the SPC that I was going to be a tourist in Moscow for the first time, and wanted to visit places I had never before had the time to visit. They told me that they had allocated a university lecturer named Eugene to interpret for us while we were in Moscow and Leningrad, and they had asked a WPC woman who was an expert on art and ceramics to accompany us in Leningrad when we visited the Hermitage Museum. They were always very thoughtful towards foreign peace people.

After dinner, we joined the many people who were dancing in the dining room to the strains of a very good band. The next morning, we set out to explore. We joined the huge crowd that streamed up to Red Square and the Kremlin and soon reached the huge courtyard. I was rather blasé about being in Red Square as I had always been brought here when I had been attending peace conferences or passing through Moscow, but Mary was quite moved by the experience of actually standing in this famous place and seeing St Basil's Cathedral and its wonderful spires, the gates to the Kremlin, the long wall seen so often on newsreels with the Soviet leaders reviewing the military parades on May Day, and Lenin's tomb. We went on to look in the cathedrals and museums in the Kremlin itself, some of which housed incredible jewels, art treasures and icons.

By this stage of the journey, the arthritic vertebra in my neck was giving me a lot of pain. I had brought my Wellington chiropractor's notes about it, but decided to wait to find a chiropractor in London. It meant that climbing stairs was difficult for me, so if the stairs were steep, I sat outside and watched the constantly changing stream of people around me.

We went across to the huge GUM department store, which is a series of little boutiques and shops on several floors of an amazing building that runs right along one side of Red Square. We plunged into the maelstrom of people and shops and thoroughly enjoyed the sights and sounds of this extraordinary store. The only other shops we found in Russia were the Berioska shops, which were large shops set up for tourists and not available to Russian citizens. They were found in major hotels and tourist centres, and sold all the wonderful colourful Russian china, artefacts and other mementoes so attractive to tourists.

I had rung my friends Boris and Maya, and Boris had arranged to meet us after work and take us by Metro to have dinner with them. At this time, the stations of the Metro were still very beautiful, and we travelled a long way to the huge, grey, rather dreary block of flats where they lived. But if the outside environs were bleak, inside the flat, all was colour and gaiety. It was wonderful to see Maya again. By this time she was upwardly mobile in the film-producing world; she had been working in the United States with poet Rod McKuen, and was about to go with a crew to make a film at Loch Lomond in Scotland. She was always great fun to be with, and I regretted all over again that we lived so far apart and that communication with Russia was then so difficult. Boris was off to Mexico to teach at the university in Mexico City for a year. I was not surprised to learn later that they had split up. Maya now has her own film studios, is married again and has another child.

While Mary explored, I went to visit various people at the SPC head-quarters, and I spent a whole afternoon at the Soviet Women's Committee. It became obvious that change was in the air. We saw a number of wedding parties in and around the Kremlin, all of them very young couples, most of whom I was told would have to live with their in-laws. In accordance with tradition, many laid their bouquets on the tomb of the Unknown Soldier with its central eternal flame, and had their photos taken there.

And then it was time to go to the railway station to catch the overnight train to Leningrad. Eugene arrived at the front desk of the hotel. He was a very pleasant young man whose wife held a senior position in the SPC. He told us that, since it was the university vacation, he was free to inter-pret for us. We arrived at Leningrad at six-thirty a.m. It was the time of the 'White Nights' when for three weeks the sun never sets. We had been booked into a very pleasant hotel right on the edge of the Baltic ocean. We learned from Eugene that the next night, the opera *Eugene Onegin* was to be presented at a large old theatre in the city. When we said we would like to see it, he told us that he didn't like opera but would come with us and interpret if necessary. We went down and bought the tickets and then went off to explore Leningrad, which has been referred to as the Venice of the north because of the waterways throughout the city. Mary said she preferred Moscow, but I have a very soft spot for this historic old city with its gracious buildings. It was once called Petrograd or St Petersburg, then Leningrad with the Revolution, and then St Petersburg again after the changes instigated by Gorbachev. Certainly the large statue of Peter the Great on his horse dominated the landscape.

I had told Mary that in Moscow at the Bolshoi ballet and at operas, Russian people could only see one act per night as the seats were at such a premium. The first time I ever went to the ballet at the Bolshoi, I couldn't understand why the people around me changed after every act, until Maya explained what was happening. It would take people three nights to see a three-act ballet or opera. The same thing happened in this Leningrad theatre. The first act of *Eugene Onegin* was not too riveting and our Eugene looked totally bored, but not far into the second act, which

moves ahead and has some wonderful music, I noticed a change in his attitude and nudged Mary to tell her about it. By the end of the evening he
was most enthusiastic and said how much he had enjoyed it.

We came out of the theatre about eleven-thirty p.m. into a twilight
which was neither night nor day. Back at the hotel we looked out of the
bedroom window across the metallic grey of the Baltic Sea and saw an
amazing sight: a huge bright orange sun skimmed across the horizon to
the edge as far as we could see and then very slowly began to rise. It was
quite stunning.

The next morning Eugene took us to the Hermitage, the main part of
which is a large gracious green and white building which had been the
Winter Palace of the Czars. It was crowded with tourists. We met Vera,
the art expert from the Leningrad office of the SPC, and she told us that
there were four cruise ships in port. The air was full of a babble of different languages, and there were groups of tourists, each with their own
slightly distraught guide trying to tell them what they were looking at, or
waving umbrellas or furled newpapers to indicate where the groups
should go next, and interpreters all scurrying about. Vera was a charming
woman, very efficient and knowledgable. She suggested we give her some
idea of what we wanted to see and she would take us there, rather than
push our way through all the tourists. We opted for the Impressionist
paintings and said we were fascinated by china and ceramics.

The Hermitage is a treasure trove of very beautiful articles, including
many rare and quite breathtaking works of art, wonderful wallhangings,
precious stones set in filigree gold and silver jewellery, all displayed in
rooms walled and pillared with semi-precious stone such as lapis lazuli,
malachite and marble. We had only one day to see at least some of these
delights. In the end it all became an indigestible blur. Eugene made his
farewells and Vera called at the hotel the next morning while we were
having breakfast before we caught a very comfortable train to Helsinki.
We were sad to see the last of these two special people.

Helsinki was bathed in spring sunshine and looking its best. Once
again I had only seen it in mid-winter. We met Ray Stewart and his then
partner Helen Gilbertson from Hawkes Bay, who took us off to explore
this very attractive city and its environs. It has delightful small villages,
which we walked around. We saw the stunning Sibelius memorial, went to
dinner on Mary's birthday with Martti Gronfors, a Finn who had lived in
New Zealand and now lived in a marvellous historic artisan's house in the
centre of Helsinki. At one stage during the evening, I went into the
kitchen to use the telephone and saw on a shelf above me a black and
white pottery hen with a bright red comb. I knew straight away that it was
a Happy Hen from the Otago Peninsula in New Zealand. I had often

taken these attractive gifts overseas, and asked Martti where he had bought it. He said he got it in a shop in Hamburg.

Yvonne Sutherland had started making these little hens during the first years of the Douglas 1984/87 restructuring, in the hope that the business would flourish and she could employ some of the people around her who had lost their jobs and careers during that restructuring. By the time I visited her to order some hens to take overseas, she was employing a number of staff in the upstairs of her house which was right across the road from the Otago Harbour. It had been built for a sea captain at the turn of the century and I remember wondering if my great-grandfather Richard Driver, who was the pilot of the port, had known this man and perhaps visited this little house. Since then Yvonne has exported Happy Hens all over the world, so I was most excited to see one in Helsinki.

The next day Mary boarded the ferry *Finlandia* on the first leg of her journey to Scotland via Oslo and Bergen. I viewed the ferry with some astonishment because of its pristine state and enormous size. There was a similar Russian ferry preparing for departure as well, and we were told that there was great rivalry between the two crews. On the wharf there was a really good market which I gathered was set up by different groups of people at different times of day. I had to be firm with myself to stop going mad and buying up large. As Mary left, I said, 'See you in London.'

Later in the day I flew off to Amsterdam. The WPC meeting was being held at a hotel somewhere between the airport and the city. I had never been to Amsterdam before, and because of where the conference was, I felt I was unlikely to see the city and would probably just go straight to the airport and fly to London at the end of our three-day meeting. As always with WPC meetings, the actual content of the agenda was not as useful as the discussions behind the scenes with peace people from many countries. Many peace initiatives are of no interest to the international press, so we certainly don't hear of them here. But they are happening and I was to learn about inter-country peace marches, huge petitions against nuclear weapons, peace rallies and peace work in schools. Away from the rhetoric, we heard what was actually happening around the world. We met local Dutch peace activists and from what they told me, I was sorry all over again that I didn't have more time to explore and was so isolated. I had always felt that Holland must be an extremely interesting and stimulating country. I rang New Zealander Sylvia Borren, who is of Dutch ancestry but grew up in New Zealand, and was now living and working in Amsterdam. Today she heads one of Holland's major aid agencies. She is part of a talented family, some of whom I had met through her brother Tur and his wife Pip, who had been instrumental in establishing the Orangi Kaupapa Trust, about which I have written later in this book.

Sylvia said I just couldn't leave without seeing something of Amsterdam, so she arranged to collect me on my last evening there. She lives near the red-light district of the city, and as we drove through that, my mouth was almost permanently agape with astonishment. Karangahape Road in Auckland paled into insignificance in the face of this colour and open soliciting by scantily clad prostitutes from their open windows and doors. Sylvia lives in one of those very narrow houses on the banks of a canal. It was only one room wide, with steep stairs going to the top. We had dinner and she then took us on a magical journey on a barge on the canal, which is one of my life's treasured memories. We stopped off a number of times at lovely old pubs and had drinks or coffee.

When I got back to the hotel, the behind-the-scenes discussions were still continuing. I stayed with the activists for a while and then went up to do some last-minute packing as I was leaving for London early the next morning.

In London, Wendy and Ian were waiting as I came through Customs and were obviously pleased to see me. But when I heard what they had to tell me, my heart plummeted to my boots. Wendy said, 'A fellow called Trevor Mallard rang. He said he was a Government Whip and that you were not to leave Heathrow Airport without ringing him.' I didn't have to ask what all that was about. It was then Tuesday night in New Zealand so Trevor would be in his constituency in Hamilton until the morning. In case I didn't have the number with me, he had passed on his home number.

We searched the airport and found a telephone (one of two) at which I could place an overseas call. No matter how I tried, I couldn't reach Trevor. Then I remembered that I had Russell Marshall's home telephone number with me. I forgot that it would be 1.00 in the morning. Just as I started talking to a sleepy Russell, the man on the phone next to me started shouting, 'But darling, I do love you, I love you. I'm sorry if you're feeding the baby but I can't ring later. I'm just off to Paris but I do love you.' In the next pause I could hear Russell shouting, 'Who on earth is this?' I said, 'It's me, Sonja, ringing from Heathrow where I've just arrived. What's up?' He told me that Lange's opponents were planning to depose him at Thursday's caucus and confidently expected to succeed because of the number of MPs overseas. He said I had to get back to New Zealand by Wednesday night at the latest: I should go now and book a seat on whatever airline would take me.

So we took my bags on a luggage trolley and went round the airlines. Air New Zealand was fully booked, Air Singapore as well. Qantas said they could take me on a flight at eight o'clock that night, which would go via Sydney but would get me to Auckland at seven p.m. on Wednesday. I cashed in my round-the-world ticket, paid the extra with my credit card, took a change of clothes and put my huge suitcase in a security locker. I then went back to Wimbledon with Wendy and Ian. On the way there, Wendy said, 'It's too bad, we have tickets for a wonderful show tonight and had a champagne dinner planned. Well, we'll just have to have a good lunch, drink the champagne, then you can have a shower and change and we'll take you back to Heathrow.' I had to book in at 6.00pm, and as they said goodbye, Ian asked me to try to stay the night next time I came.

On the plane, I wondered whether my colleagues who supported David and were overseas would be able to get home in time. As I sat there, I became very angry and anxious to get back. About a couple of hours out, the captain spoke to us and said he was terribly sorry but there was something wrong with one of the engines and he was having to return to Heathrow. I was horrified. This journey was going to be very fine-tuned as it was, and I couldn't imagine what this delay would mean. I thought to myself that I'd aborted our visit to London and Zimbabwe, and for what, if David lost out by one vote because I wasn't there? The next time the purser came through, I relayed my reasons for wanting to get back and my fears about being there in time. He said he'd talk to the captain, and when he came back, he said they thought I'd still be all right. I had to change planes at Sydney, and he said I might have to accept that my luggage might not arrive until the next day, and I would have to run between the arrival area and the Air New Zealand terminal. As it happened, there was a later flight that Heathrow didn't know about from Auckland to Wellington. Of course, I could have gone on the first flight in the morning to Wellington, but I didn't want Douglas and his supporters to know that I was back and they could well have been on that plane. In the event, several hours out of Heathrow again, the captain talked to us and said they had made up a lot of time, had a tail wind and were now reasonably confident that people with onward bookings from Sydney would be able to meet them. I sincerely hoped so.

At Sydney Airport I was put off first and raced along endless corridors to where my flight was due to depart. In the departure lounge I saw two officials from the Ministry of External Relations and Trade and asked, wearing my hat as Chair of the Foreign Affairs and Defence Select Committee, what they had been doing in Australia. They said they had been in Canberra having talks with the Australian Government officials. My intuition prompted me to say, 'You've been talking about those damned frigates, haven't you?' and they admitted they had. In my current state of mind it was as well that they were in business class and I in economy.

At Auckland, it was nine p.m. when I got through Customs, amazingly with my luggage, and I hurried over to the domestic terminal, booked in for Wellington and went up to the Koru Lounge. There I rang my old friends Hutt Taxis, told them I had been away for three weeks and why I had come back, and asked if a driver could meet me at Wellington Airport and take me home. All through my time in Parliament, these drivers gave me splendid support. We went through the trauma of deregulation together. When I came into the airport at Wellington, there was my driver waiting. He said, 'The cab's out the front. Give me your luggage chit and tell me what to look for. You sit down.' I sank into the back seat of the cab, hardly believing that I was really there. On the seat beside me was fresh bread, butter, milk and orange juice. I wanted to burst into tears. When I thanked him, he said, 'I reckon you've got enough ahead of you tomorrow and that you won't have much in the house.'

Arriving at Eastbourne, I settled up with the driver, who insisted on carrying my bags up the three flights to my apartment, opened my door for me and switched on the light. He said that a driver would pick me up at 8.30 in the morning to take me to Parliament. Inside, I filled the electric jug, plugged it in and then sank into the settee while I waited for it to boil. The phone rang. It was Mary from London. She had arrived after I had left. 'What's happening?' she asked and when I told her, she asked if I wanted her to come home too. I told her that the next day was the crucial one. There was no need for her to spoil her holiday and she should continue as we'd planned, finishing up with the visit to Zimbabwe.

She had no sooner rung off than the phone rang again. It was Graham Kelly from Brazil. He said he'd been trying to reach me so I told him the whole saga. He asked whether I thought he should come home on the first available flight, which was on Friday, but I told him too that he should continue on for the rest of his tour. I asked him where Jim Sutton was and said that, while I was fond of Jim, I wasn't sure how he would vote in a leadership challenge. I suggested that Graham should not let him out of his sight. Graham was quite distraught about not being here for the vote, but I said I hoped that others who were in places with more frequent flights might make it. I hung up, had a cuppa, chose something from my wardrobe to wear the next day, had a shower and fell into bed to get what sleep my jetlag would permit.

I knew that Hutt Taxis would ring me at seven a.m. to make sure I was awake and so they did. As it happened the traffic on the Hutt Road was particularly congested that morning and we didn't get into town until about twenty to ten. I asked the driver to go up Bowen Street and round the back of Parliament so that I wouldn't need to go past the press offices, which were next to the Government Caucus Room in the old Parliament Buildings. As I'd dressed and prepared for the day, I'd heard on Morning Report that the MPs who hoped to depose the Prime Minister were confident of success. They listed all the MPs who were out of the country and said that I had been unable to be contacted. So I didn't want to see the press until I had to. Besides, I was very jetlagged and not in any shape for repartee with them. They did catch sight of me as I went through the door into caucus but I closed it behind me. I saw that Jonathan Hunt was back, but could see none of the others. Just before ten o'clock, a tired Fran Wilde arrived all the way from Rome, then Margaret Shields from Spain, and about 10.15 a red-eyed Peter Simpson arrived from New York.

I just hoped we had the numbers — and we did. It justified all the hassle. Then, six weeks later, David resigned as Prime Minister. But that is another story.

Fighting Back

While I was at the meeting of the World Peace Council in Amsterdam, I received a copy of an article about me by journalist David Cohen in the *Evening Post*, in which he criticised me as a socialist who came in from the cold to find a warm, well-lit Parliament with cheap food and perks galore, and thereupon became a quiet, docile Government member.

When I arrived home, Rosemary Vincent, a very competent journalist with a social conscience, rang me and said she'd read this article and wanted to interview me for the *Woman's Weekly* about my reactions to his opinion. In the interview, I told her that I was still the person I always had been, but that when you go into Parliament, nothing is as simple as you first thought. For me, the years between 1987 and 1990 had been incredibly hard, especially with a Minister of Finance like Roger Douglas, who, I said, '. . . has a brilliant brain but he's like a kamikaze pilot in the way he goes for things without necessarily thinking of all the consequences, and without going downstream to see what's likely to happen.' I knew changes needed to be made in order to deal with the incredible debt we had inherited from the Muldoon era; but I questioned whether we needed to move so fast and not take the country with us. I already had serious reservations about free-market policies that enrich those at the top of the heap and, despite ministerial assurance, do not trickle down to those at the bottom. I said that, of necessity, I had become pragmatic.

It was becoming increasingly hard to know what to do, feeling so isolated within the Government, as well as facing such suspicion from outside. All I could do was try to serve my electorate. The electorate party machine, consisting of the Labour Electorate Committee (LEC) and the various Party branches, was always a barometer of what Labour Party members felt about Government policies. The electorate of Pencarrow had several quite different communities and I needed to be sensitive to these. From the very beginning, I had a wonderful support group in Eastbourne. The Labour women there were largely responsible for my election. They offered me sustenance at the end of my working week and on Saturdays after the Wainuiomata clinic, and bought my groceries and even clothes on approval, because time for personal shopping had become a rarity. They set up stalls in the main street of Eastbourne to raise party funds, and offered their homes for meetings.

There were also special individuals in my electorate whose hard work and generous support were welcome relief from the divisions inside Government. Warwick Flaws was representative of these unique saviours. He had a strong social conscience and I had worked with him before my election to Parliament. Not long after I was elected, he had been diagnosed as having a brain tumour which was then treated by specialists, successfully, it appeared. One night, because of my work schedule and because I wanted the LEC to become familiar with Parliament, we had arranged to have our monthly meeting in one of the huge old select committee rooms in Parliament. Years ago, it had been Bill Rowling's office. During the course of our meeting, Warwick became extremely unwell. I went to find Peter Tapsell, who was one of the two qualified medical men in the Parliamentary Labour Party. After he had examined Warwick, Peter said Warwick should rest at home and consult his specialist.

1989 began sadly when Warwick died. We were very much saddened and would miss him very much. Our hearts went out to his family. His funeral was held in St Ronans Presbyterian Church in Eastbourne and there were no spare seats. I had been asked to speak of his life and work. I agonised over this and finally just spoke from the heart. He was such a special man and would be sorely missed.

When I first drove over the hill to Wainuiomata after my election, because of all the trauma associated with my selection and the campaign, I had to force myself to go. Slowly, however, my constituents there came to accept the fact that they had an MP who was a woman with a liberal social conscience. Invitations began streaming in to meetings of a wide variety of organisations, and to meet the tangata whenua, who were then very involved in the finishing stages of their urban marae, Pukeatea.

When my brother David and his wife Lyn came to visit me, I took them to see the almost completed marae. As a man, David was invited to go inside and see what they were doing. Maori culture decreed that, even as an MP, because I was a woman I couldn't enter the building until it was opened. On the way home, David said to me, 'How do you cope with that situation, mate?' and I told him, 'Not very well, but I have to accept it in the meantime,' adding that one day Maori women would resolve these problems.

All through my time in Parliament, I felt close to both the Maori and Pacific Island communities. The Pukeatea Marae, when finished, was very handsome and was used for a wide variety of functions. There is something about a well-run marae that is very healing. When staying overnight, I am always impressed at the efficiency of the tangata whenua, who are excellent hosts and do everything possible to make their guests comfortable. Waking up on a marae in the early morning is one of life's joys.

The Wainuiomata Pacific Island community had supported the building of a new church. It is very beautiful and has a vivid Pacific atmosphere. The building is much more than bricks and mortar, being central to the lives of the Pacific Island constituents, and I was privileged to be involved in fund-raising and included in the opening ceremony.

I was, of course, also meeting teachers and parents at all the schools, and a warm and enriching experience it was. An organisation I was very interested in was one called Friends Who Care. This group of volunteers cared for physically and mentally disabled people from the Wainuiomata community. People who were suffering from Alzheimer's or Parkinson's would spend one day a week with the group, and this gave their spouses and caregivers a rare break. A retired cabinet-maker inspired people to make things with their hands, and other talented people helped to extend their interests. The core group who ran the place had become very knowledgable and skilful: they could estimate when a schizophrenic was not taking medication; and they became adept at dealing with epileptic fits. Each Wednesday there was a well-attended lunch for participants in Friends Who Care activities in the Louise Bilderbeck Hall, and usually there was a speaker. I felt we needed organisations similar to this right around the country and that they should have adequate financial support, and I argued for this in Government.

At this time, people with psychiatric disorders were being discharged into the community from psychiatric hospitals. I believed that, apart from those who were clinically insane and who had a violent history, many people would be better off out in the community; but — and there was a real but — there had to be the necessary supports in place to make rehabilitation possible. I knew that the United States had adopted this same policy of discharge of psychiatric patients, but what I had seen in New York alarmed me.

In 1989, I was walking down Fifth Avenue one evening after the conclusion of a meeting at the United Nations, when suddenly a man darted out into the heavy late afternoon traffic and was run over by a bus and killed. I was horrified, but the New Yorker beside me said, 'Don't worry, it's one of those nuts out of a mental home. Often happens. They sleep in subways, driveways and under bridges and steal food.'

Then in 1991, I was scheduled to have dinner at a New York restaurant with Margaret and Pat Shields, who were visiting from their base in Santo Domingo. I had almost reached our meeting place when a man leapt at me, seemingly from nowhere, put his hands round my throat and tried to strangle me. Fortunately, Pat was looking out for me, ran to my rescue and disengaged the man's hands. He went off muttering incoherently.

I was therefore delighted to learn that the Housing Corporation house opposite my Wainuiomata electorate office was to be the home of five people newly discharged from psychiatric hospitals, and that they were to have support. All had varying disabilities; and one was a man of 50 who had been in Lake Alice Hospital since he was a teenager. I wondered how Wainuiomata would cope with this new development. We all know of suburbs where people object to kindergartens, women's refuges or child-care centres in their area, stating that they 'believe in those facilities but not in our street'. But Wainuiomata rose to the challenge magnificently. The day the five people arrived, local residents brought hot scones, cakes and flowers and welcomed them to the community. They were so delighted to be in a caring environment and out of hospital. They went as a group to the supermarket, and once a week to Friends Who Care.

At this time, the Labour Government believed that every child born in this country regardless of any handicap was entitled to be educated to the limit of their ability and to be integrated into school classrooms. The theory was called mainstreaming, and to be successful needed a system of support teachers or teacher aides, because mainstreamed children required extra help with such matters as toileting and behavioural prob-lems as they entered a strange new environment. There were mixed feel-ings about this development, particularly among teachers with large classes, who couldn't see how they could cope with such children without adequate help. What constituted adequate help was and still is a matter for debate.

For some time I had been talking to women's groups and individual women in the electorate about the possibility of holding a meeting for the women of Pencarrow. After much discussion, it was decided to have the meeting on a Sunday at one o'clock. It would start with lunch, and I would ask a number of senior Labour women in Parliament such as Margaret Shields and Annette King to speak. We wrote to all the women, inviting them to come to Vogel House, which was not occupied at the time. We were amazed at the response and soon realised that we couldn't accom-modate all who wanted to attend, which was disappointing. Nevertheless, it was an excellent event. Women from Wainuiomata and Eastbourne very competently dealt with the food as it arrived (it was pot luck) and it all seemed like a family affair. All the usual issues of interest to women — health, education, housing, family violence, social welfare and unemploy-ment — were explored.

Concern about Government's intention to purchase four new frigates from Australia still raged on. It was decided to hold a seminar on the frigate issue and I was asked to chair it. It was proposed that Government officials, senior staff from the then Ministry of External Relations and Trade (MERT) and the Ministry of Defence would debate with anti-frigate activists — the first time the two groups actually confronted each other in debate. Malcolm McNamara, who was the liaison officer with the Foreign Affairs and Defence Select Committee that I chaired, was with the Defence group but their deputy director of international affairs, Commander David Wood, was to present the case for the frigates, and Terence O'Brien of MERT was to explain the wider needs associated with the purchase.

The seminar was organised by the Pacific Institute of Resource Management and Peace Movement Aotearoa. I predicted that it would not be an easy one to chair and it wasn't. The protagonists all held very strong views about the need for and desirability of the frigates; whereas the opposition felt that frigates were not needed in the South Pacific and that different types of vessels would be better suited to carry out the work that New Zealand was moving toward.

At best, I felt that the seminar would clear the air. That the ministers spearheading the frigate purchase floated, with the anti brigade, the proposition that Government might only purchase two frigates rather than four, demonstrated clearly that they had no understanding of the deep philosophical reasons which were the basis of the opposition. It was not a happy time. Caucus was divided and the Labour Party was bitter and demoralised. It was not a subject which would simply fade, and the resentment lingered long.

At this time, Australia's Channel 9 TV, headed by presenter Peter Couchman, came to New Zealand to arrange a programme for Australian and New Zealand viewers. It had two aims: to gather together pro- and anti-frigate people; and to discuss the possibility of this country becoming the eighth state of Australia. Russell Marshall, then Minister of Foreign Affairs, and I represented the Government, and Doug Graham and other pro-speakers the Opposition. I looked at the audience and saw peace activists and pro-frigate people. I really liked Russell and was saddened by his support for the frigates purchase, but realised that with a pro-frigate department and a pro-frigate Minister of Defence in Bob Tizard, he was between a rock and a hard place. On this question we presented opposing views.

Then we came to the question of New Zealand becoming a state of Australia. The discussion became very vigorous, but Tipene O'Regan summed up in a few pithy words what most of us felt. He said: 'It's like this, Mr Couchman, we don't mind living with you but we don't want to marry you!'

Back in the House, the divisions between David Lange and Roger Douglas festered on, not helped by Roger's public criticism of what he saw as David's intransigence. It was becoming increasingly clear that the philosophical differences between them were making it impossible for there to be a common meeting ground. They couldn't even discuss the situation they were in and resorted to writing letters to each other. David believed that we needed to raise taxes so that we could deliver the improvements in social conditions that he had campaigned for in 1987; Roger was still supportive of a flat tax, the withdrawal of state involvement from as many areas as possible, and continued economic reform.

It was a potent cocktail. The public reacted to this disunity; and Party members started resigning in worrying numbers. This didn't concern Roger, who I suspected saw the Party as irrelevant in the society he was hoping to create, whereas many of us felt that the Party was pivotal to our well-being. One of the most worrying experiences for us was that David couldn't accept our offer to help him, nor that of pro-Lange supporters in Cabinet. Together we would have been quite a force to reckon with, but somehow it seemed impossible for him to unite.

At this particular time, Cabinet ministers whom my group trusted were busy doing the best they could with their portfolios, and apart from visiting them on behalf of constituents or in caucus, we didn't see them. It is hard now to explain the climate we operated in. Helen Clark became Minister of Health and wanted to make sure Area Health Boards delivered state-funded, quality health care for everyone who needed it. Her decision to sack the Auckland Area Health Board, which included her husband Peter, because they were not delivering what she felt was badly needed, was a tough one. She fought for funding for health against a Minister of Finance who believed in private health insurance and a privatised health service.

I had been involved in the establishment of Area Health Boards as the FOL representative on the Area Health Working Party when Aussie Malcolm was Minister of Health. As a former Nelson Hospital Board member, I could see the real need for change. For one thing, there was far too much waste. I had gone to Australia and seen how the Australian unions and the hospital authorities had worked together to minimise waste. And I felt at that time that there was insufficient financial expertise on the then Hospital Boards. The proposed Area Health Boards would provide that.

In late winter 1989 I developed a sharp cough. It was not a cold, but was persistent. One morning I woke at five-thirty a.m. and coughed, and when I looked at the tissue I'd used, it was stained with bright red blood. I was horrified. Had my tuberculosis returned? I looked at the clock and decided it was far too early to ring my doctor, Rosie Fenwick — she had young children and a busy practice. I lay there wondering what my chances were. At seven-thirty a.m. I rang Rosie, and then Mary, who was most alarmed.

Rosie came and shortly afterwards an ambulance arrived to take me to Hutt Hospital. After doing x-rays and tests, the senior medical officer was at a loss to say what was wrong with me and, after a few days, told me I could go home. My friends and constituents had come in large numbers with flowers, fruit and other goodies. On the day I was to leave, I had another haemorrhage. No one could say what the cause was. Finally, I was discharged and sent to see a chest specialist at Wellington Hospital. After further x-rays and tests, he told me that because my lungs had suffered so much during my years of tuberculosis, my arteries had been damaged and one of them had ruptured — hence the haemorrhages. Sputum tests revealed no TB.

Once I was fit and well again and back in the House, Fran Wilde talked to me about a Human Rights Conference in New Zealand that the Government wanted me to chair and help organise. The subject of human rights is always tricky and I knew that this conference, just like the Frigates Seminar, would not be easy: Maori would want their rights considered; and supporters of Israel and Arab rights and the PLO would want to be represented. We have become a multicultural society and all these strands needed to be joined together. The passions which exist in Israel and the Arab States and in the Far East are represented in this country. Government officials and activists spoke at the conference, and workshops were held by the different interest groups. In all, the conference offered a fascinating view of where we were in terms of race relations in the broadest sense. We were beginning to realise that we were not an outpost of the British Empire, but part of the Pacific and South-East Asia, that immigration had brought to our country people from many parts of the world, bringing different cultures and values and that we couldn't just ignore these, but accept that these new citizens added an important dimension to the fabric of our society. Then, too, the aspirations of Maori, their deep-seated resentment and their desire for justice were causing thoughtful people to understand that positive action was needed.

On the night the conference ended, Fran Wilde invited those of us who had been responsible for organising it to have dinner with her at Zino's Restaurant in Island Bay. Zino's was then owned by Alick Shaw, who later became the unsuccessful Labour candidate for Wellington Central in the first MMP election. All through the meal, Fran was called away from the table to answer the telephone. At the end of the evening, as I went back to my car, she followed me and said, 'David is leaving.' I said, 'For where?' and she told me that in the morning he was going to resign as prime minister.

I was devastated. In spite of all the difficulties we had had trying to support him, he was a fabulous man. When he became convinced that his country wanted a nuclear-free New Zealand, he not only supported but also strongly promoted the idea, against considerable odds. His speech in the Oxford Union Debate in Britain was spectacular. He withstood the pressure from Britain and the United States with reason and panache.

Like many of us, I mourned his departure. I drove home in floods of tears. I wondered how I could cope with him out of office; and I thought how devastated and demoralised he must be feeling.

Geoffrey Palmer was David's successor and Helen Clark his deputy. I really respected Geoffrey as a Nelsonian and as a principled person. On the night of his election to this high office, he appeared in my office in the bleak prefab building. I looked up with astonishment. Here was the Prime Minister visiting me. I asked him what he could possibly want to talk to me about, and he said that he had come to talk about the frigates, about why it was absolutely essential that we purchase them. I told him not to bother, that we were philosophically opposed on this issue and that he was wasting his time: he should go away. And he did.

But both Roger Douglas (now elected by caucus back into Cabinet) and Richard Prebble took to coming to our weekly caucus and telling us that they needed to sell XYZ government department, and that further-more it must be decided by midday or business confidence would suffer. This was patently nonsense, but they always had the numbers in caucus to carry the day.

That year, in and around everything else, in my capacity as a marriage celebrant I married Michael Cullen and Anne Collins at Anne's brother's house in Havelock North. Jonathan Hunt was best man, so it was quite a parliamentary happening. I also married Karen Fisher (a respected parlia-mentary radio reporter) and Steve Jones at the Port Nicholson Yacht Club. Then Susan Kedgley and Denis Foot decided to marry and asked me, along with Jim Kebbell, a former Catholic priest who had left the priesthood to marry Marion Wood, to officiate. It was a very stylish wedding held in Sue and Denis's home in Oriental Bay. Brett Lineham and Clare Robinson, with whom I stayed in Kiribati when Brett was high commissioner, had returned to Wellington and rang and asked me to marry them at Clare's mother, Marijke's home. I had not long arrived home from hospital and was still quite fragile, but apart from leaving my glasses at home and having to borrow a pair from a wedding guest, I managed to officiate at what was a very happy event.

Marrying people was such a positive act of union, it was a wonderful antidote to the divisions in caucus. One of the overwhelming feelings I had, apart from anger, during those first three years from 1987 to 1990, was that of loneliness. When I said that I was going to write this book, a number of people assumed that I would be revealing steamy accounts of affairs between MPs or MPs and staff. Well, I have no intention of doing that. But I do have to say that particularly for MPs from out of Wellington, separation from wives, husbands or partners and children is not an ideal situation. My only observation is that I don't know where they found the time (and energy) to indulge.

I often had reason to be thankful that I wasn't in Parliament when my husband Charlie was alive and my children were young. Going home to an empty apartment late at night wasn't exactly fun, but at least I hadn't had to miss important family occasions or school functions because of the work of the House. Now that we have electorate secretaries, MPs' families, particularly wives, don't have to be unpaid workers, except of course during election campaigns. This means that they can live their own lives, develop their own interests; but that too can cause conflict and times of loneliness. Most do the best they can in this situation.

Today, when list MPs are finding the debating chamber a hostile place, I have a sneaking sympathy for them. There are people who love being there and who enjoy the cut and thrust of Parliamentary debate, but most of the time it bored me. There was so much time-wasting and so many second-rate speakers; though I have to confess that good debaters — and there were a number of them — were a joy to listen to: people who could think on their feet, and didn't have to shout to get their message across.

I knew that the 1990 election campaign would not be easy. Apart from bitterness about asset sales and the closure of post offices, there was rage about the enforced amalgamation of Pencarrow local authorities. I hadn't singlehandedly stopped any of this, so I was part of the problem. And my constituents let me know it.

Before the House rose for the campaign, our four retiring MPs, Colin Moyle, Michael Bassett, Russell Marshall and Anne Collins made their valedictory speeches and we all geared up for a stormy campaign.

Many times I wished that I had had three years in the House before I was flung into that 1987 conflict. I would have been more confident and assured. I might have dealt more positively with the fact that several of the free-market ministers didn't speak to me for the first months I was there. Presumably they were very angry that several trade unionists had come to

A cottage meeting at Ora Eddy's home during the 1990 Election Campaign

sully the ranks of the academics and entrepreneurs.

Although I had faced the election campaign with some trepidation, I knew that if I survived it, I would go back to Parliament a very different person: tougher, more streetwise, but still, as ever, a convinced socialist and determined to continue the fight.

Out there in the electorate, the diminished but very valued group of people who would work for me in the campaign discussed with me the type of campaign that we would wage. At that time, meetings in halls were not well attended and street-corner meetings in the evenings had been overtaken by television. We decided that we had to find ways and means of meeting and talking to as many people as possible. We planned dozens of cottage meetings in people's homes, and Noeline Colman was a tower of strength in working to set these up. In Eastbourne and the Bays, my faithful women did the same and a variety of people arranged cottage meetings in Epuni and Waiwhetu.

During the campaign, Mike and Yvonne Moore came to Wainuiomata. We went to Wainuiomata College first, where they were greeted with great enthusiasm, and then went on to walk through the local mall and visit work sites. Ann Hercus, newly retired as our ambassador to the United Nations, came and visited the college too and then spoke at a well-attended cottage meeting at Noeline and Fraser Colman's home. Geoffrey Palmer's wife Margaret came to speak at Ora Eddy's home, Michael Cullen came and visited work sites with me. They were great occasions but otherwise I flung myself into the campaign, the pamphlets, the billboards, newspaper articles and interviews.

Visiting the Wainuiomata Mall during the Election Campaign; left to right: Shona Robb, myself, Noeline Colman, Mike and Yvonne Moore

And then we had the three-yearly combined churches pre-election meeting at Epuni. In 1987 this was a warm supportive meeting but this time around, the anger and lack of trust showed. All I could say (despite Roger's lack of commitment in his latest Budget) was that I would fight very hard for social issues to be top priority in the next Labour Government and that there were a number of other Labour MPs who agreed with me, that I would work with them to make this possible.

In Eastbourne, the Lions always have a candidates' meeting in the Muritai School Hall. This one was very lively, and I enjoyed it. There were a large number of candidates so it was a long meeting, lightened by the contributions of the young person representing the McGillicuddy Serious Party.

In the second week of October, I presented the Pencarrow residents with the 1990 Commemoration medals at Premier House. This was a really special occasion. I had consulted widely in the electorate and chose people who had served the community well over a period of time. Premier House is a charming example of the architecture of its time and has been lovingly restored and maintained.

And then it was Election Day. We had again been offered the Wainuiomata Kokiri and when the results started coming in, I knew that we were in big trouble. Hamilton West and Hastings are often the litmus for the final result, and when both Trevor Mallard and David Butcher lost their seats, it was obvious that we might not be the Government. As the evening developed, we knew that we had lost 27 seats, 23 sitting members and the four candidates who had stood in the four seats where members had retired — Otara, Te Atatu, Wanganui and East Cape — were not successful. I held Pencarrow by a slim majority. I knew I would be in Parliament for the next three years, but it would be a very different place.

The next afternoon, I kicked off a soccer ball at a fundraiser for Arakura School in Wainuiomata, so it was business as usual — well, maybe not quite.

In Opposition

Going back to Parliament as part of the Opposition was very strange, particularly as there were 27 fewer members in our caucus. It took some time to adjust to that. The loss of seats made the Rogernomes aware that their policies were unpopular and caused a reassessment of the direction in which the Labour Party was to go. While Roger and his cohorts started planning their eventual defection to ACT, the new Government took on Rogernomics and made it their own. While the Labour Party reassessed itself internally, there were also plenty of things to be getting on with.

We were in the throes of moving from the about-to-be-refurbished Parliament House to Bowen House across the road. Jonathan Hunt was Chief Opposition Whip and had the task of allocating offices for MPs and staff in the new building, not an easy job as everyone concerned had strong feelings about where they wanted to work. He told Mary that he had sorted out a very nice office for me on the fifteenth floor and said we should go over and look at it. It certainly was a most attractive office with spectacular views across the city to the harbour. What particularly pleased me was that I could see my electorate of Pencarrow and, at night, the magical sight of the lights on the hill road over to Wainuiomata. Our neighbours were Koro Wetere and Fran Wilde, and Graham Kelly and David Lange were just down the hall.

Once Governor-General Cath Tizard had opened Parliament and the new members were sworn in, work was underway. To our horror, the new Government's first act was to rescind the Pay Equity Act and, even worse, the minister who led the debate in her capacity as Minister of Women's Affairs was Jenny Shipley. When I thought of the struggle that women had been engaged in since the inception of the National Council of Women at the turn of the century, and how strenuously Helen Clark had battled in Cabinet and in the House to have the legislation introduced and to steer it through, I was sickened. I didn't accept Jenny Shipley's contention that there were other and more effective ways of achieving pay equity. We'd tried all those and they hadn't worked.

Women's pay is still 17 per cent below men's. This was highlighted recently at a Council of Trade Unions meeting, where women debated ways and means of getting pay equity back onto the public agenda. Men, it seems, still have the view that they work to provide for their families and women for pin money and their golf subscriptions. This theory is part of a timewarp and bears no relation to the realities of family life today. The number of homes where Dad earns the pay and Mum stays home and cares for the children is greatly diminished. Many solo parents, mostly women, are supporting families on unequal pay. It seems the well-worn battleground will have to be traversed again right back to Parliament.

This session, I was allocated to both the Foreign Affairs and Defence Select Committee and the Maori Affairs Committee. Both of these weekly committees, I found, met at the same time on the same day of each week, which meant that I was constantly called away to one or the other.

At the first meeting of the Foreign Affairs and Defence Select Committee, we discussed what we would choose as our major study, on which we would produce a report to Parliament. I said that it would be useful for us to investigate what had happened to the lives of people in countries such as East Timor, Tibet and Cyprus since external forces had altered their culture, religion and existence. There was no support at all for this proposition, not even from my own colleagues on the committee: 'We can't do that, Sonja, we have to think of our trade links with Indonesia, China and Turkey.' Instead we studied the cost of the frigates.

At the Maori Affairs Select Committee, Ian Peters, MP for Tongariro and brother of Winston, was elected chair. The committee decided to do an in-depth study on Maori education, and we embarked on a revealing and quite outstanding series of meetings with Maori around the country. We had endless discussions with Maori artists and within the committee about the proposed artwork for Bowen House's new Maori Affairs Select Committee room.

At this time, there was growing concern about what the new Government would do with the health system; meetings were held in all parts of my electorate and elsewhere. I attended as many of these as possible. I also visited health officials, including Karen Poutasi (who later became Director of Health), to find out what was likely to happen. The mayor of Lower Hutt, Glen Evans, who was always very good about liaising with MPs in his area, held meetings with me and the other two Hutt Valley MPs, Joy McLauchlan and Paul Swain, to discuss future health services and what effect the changes might have on services at Hutt Hospital.

Simon Upton was Minister of Health and wanted to press on with health reforms. Later he was to produce his Green and White Papers, outlining what the Government intended, which he believed would produce a quality health system and reduce waiting lists. I liked Simon, despite the fact that our political philosophies didn't mesh. I knew he was a passionate gardener; we discussed gardens from time to time, and he invited me to come to the Waikato to see the garden that he was developing. Because the Opposition was so unhappy about his health reforms, I was sure that Jonathan Hunt at least would not be pleased to see me consorting with the enemy, so to speak.

One night, when Simon was steering his health reforms through the House in urgency and we, the Opposition, were practising delaying tactics with a myriad of amendments, each of which had to be voted on, I met Simon at ten minutes to midnight in the middle of the House floor as we were going to our separate lobbies to vote yet again. He told me that slugs were really decimating his delphiniums and he was depressed about that, especially as his mother's ones were untouched and flourishing. We discussed several possible slug destruction programmes, and then both raced off to our respective lobbies to record our votes. When my turn came to vote, Jonathan asked me what I had been discussing with the Minister of Health, and I told him that we had been talking about the decimation of his delphiniums by slugs. Jonathan looked at me scornfully and said that he didn't believe me. I was very cross: was he assuming that I was doing some unilateral deal with the Minister? I said as calmly as I could that Simon and I were both keen gardeners, and politics didn't come into that.

I didn't get to see Simon's garden until after I retired. Although he was a busy Cabinet minister, he had found time to set out the bones of his garden in a very inspirational way, and had planted many trees, shrubs and perennials. He, his wife Bhardy and their two small children live in a splendid old two-storeyed house, and the garden blends in well with it. He has also planned and planted an arboretum around what will ultimately be a man-made lake. Because of the type of trees he has planted, when it is fully grown and the lake is well established, it will be quite spectacular. Just how much so I realised when visiting gardens in Scotland with Mary and her cousins and we saw a well-established arboretum that was magnificent. As Simon said to me, 'I've got plenty of years ahead, I can afford to wait for the trees to grow.'

In January, I had gone to Christchurch one weekend to participate in a panel discussion on the implications of the Gulf War, which was exercising our minds at that time. When I returned, I found a fax from Ray Stewart asking me to go to Cyprus for a World Peace Council meeting at which the Gulf War would be on the agenda. I talked about this with Jonathan, who finally said that if I could fulfil my electorate responsibilities, I could have leave. He knew I would want to report back when I returned.

On Saturday 2 February, I held my usual clinic in Wainuiomata, attended the opening of the Waterloo Kindergarten's new playground, took a late afternoon plane to Auckland, had dinner with my friend Charles Chauvel, and flew out to Larnaca at midnight, via Hong Kong and Zurich. Because of the Gulf War, planes were flying into Larnaca only in the early hours of the morning, so I was hardly scintillating on the first morning of the meeting.

We had a long, detailed and sometimes heated debate about what was happening in the Gulf War and what, if anything, the WPC could usefully do, together with various peace movements in countries surrounding Iraq, to help resolve what was becoming a very serious conflict. Ray had already met with a number of these groups and reported his findings.

Another agenda item was that of reconciliation with past enemies, which the Russians were promoting. I was quite startled that, in a peace organisation, there was considerable opposition to this idea. One Brazilian delegate, who I later discovered was a multi-millionaire, said he believed that the only way to achieve peace was through violent means! Quite mind-boggling. He had never been to any WPC meeting before, and why he came I shall never know. I was told by a Brazilian friend much later that he lives in what is virtually a castle, is ultra-rightwing and quite ruthless.

At this session I was sitting on my own, for once, behind the Japanese delegation. They were adamantly opposed to reconciliation with their past enemies and said the times were not right now. I was incensed. After the Brazilian's outburst, this was too much. I poked my finger into the back of the Japanese delegation leader in front of me and said, 'My daughter's father was killed in the Battle of Tarawa. If I didn't believe passionately in reconciliation and forgiveness, I would have shot you in the back before this.' I had always been on friendly terms with the Japanese, and to say that they were taken aback was an understatement. Nevertheless, the matter was not resolved at that meeting.

I flew home via Geneva and stayed a day and a night with my friends Tord Kjelstrom and Adrienne Taylor, who now live in Moens across the border in France, with its stunning views of the Alps. Adrienne works nearby, as the Industrial Health and Safety Officer for the Public Service International. Tord, as a director of the World Health Organisation, works in Geneva: he travels across the border each day, and has to carry his passport and both French and Swiss currency. Both of them travel extensively for their work. I then flew home through Los Angeles and arrived back in time for a function in Eastbourne and a Monday clinic in Wainuiomata. Shona and Mary briefed me about events while I was away, and I went back to Parliament the next day.

I was now spending a lot of time in Wainuiomata, meeting people in their homes, organisations, Lions, Rotary, the firefighters, women's groups — I now felt quite at home there. Ora and Keith Eddy, founding residents of Wainuiomata and much loved by the community, were towers of strength from the beginning. I grew to know and appreciate their lovely home in Isobel Grove. It backed onto native bush and whenever I went to visit, there were tui and fantails, and now and then native pigeons. They were cat-lovers and keen gardeners too. They were great friends of Fraser and Noeline Colman, who had moved to Wainuiomata when it was developing and had been pivotal in its progress. Betty van Gaalen represented Wainuiomata on the Hutt City Council and was a mine of information. Through these and other local people, I learned to know, understand and love Wainuiomata.

On 25 March I attended the ceremony to close the old Maori Affairs Select Committee room in Parliament Buildings. At four a.m. the next day, tangata whenua from around the country were to come for the opening of the new room in Bowen House. Leaving home at three-thirty a.m. was not a very attractive proposition, so I arranged to sleep at Parliament and be awakened at three forty-five a.m. in time for a shower. When I stepped out of the lift at the new room, I found a large crowd present. Winston Peters was Minister of Maori Affairs at the time and he and Koro were there. The ceremony was very moving. Afterwards we all had breakfast in the banquet hall in the Beehive.

At this time, Oxfam was being established in New Zealand, and because I believed in what it stood for, I became involved in that. I was also involved with the Lower Hutt Women's Centre, opened in 1987, and helped the women who, virtually on a shoestring, provided services for Hutt Valley women. This year, they celebrate their tenth anniversary. They tell me that the ability to provide services is still limited by resources, but demand for help has risen.

During one recess at Parliament, Graham Kelly and I went down to Sydenham to show the Labour flag, which had been obscured from view there, in Jim Anderton's electorate, since the rise of New Labour and the Alliance. We had a splendid day, met dozens of people and local Labour members, visited shopping malls and two homes for the elderly. The first home was a recently built one run by the Catholic Church — and one of the best I've seen, with small sitting and dining rooms, and bedrooms looking out onto beautifully landscaped gardens. The little sister who took us round told us that most people who came to live in a home were in their late seventies or early eighties: they were survivors and tended to be very independent. She took us to see a wonderful old lady who was having her hundredth birthday in a couple of days. She was sitting knitting booties for

Speaking with members of the Indian community in Wainuiomata

a great-great-grandchild in two-ply wool on steel needles. She had a glass of sherry beside her and was watching a Spencer Tracy/Katherine Hepburn movie. As we left, I remarked that she seemed to be doing very well, but the sister said that they were rather worried about her. She had persuaded her doctor that she should have a sherry before lunch, one before dinner and one before she went to bed. I asked whether they were worried on account of the expense, but she said no, her family provided the sherry. What they were concerned about was that she might become an alcoholic!

At the next home, we met a couple who had just come in, leaving their family home. It was a poignant discussion. We met another 100-year-old — quite a different character. She had a word processor and a telephone and was obviously in touch with the outside world. She directed Graham into the only easy chair and told me to sit on the bed. She knew who we were and made her political affiliation to National quite clear. I said we hadn't come to be political but to meet her and see how she was at this great age. When it was time for us to leave, she patted me on the arm and said that she wanted me to do something for her when I got back to Wellington. I assumed that she wanted me to contact a grandchild or another family member — but no. She said that she wanted me to drown Ruth Richardson and Jenny Shipley. I thought she was joking, but she said that, in her opinion, they were not good for the Party. Still thinking it was a joke, I said maybe I could manage Ruth but Jenny was another matter, and she said strongly, 'Take a pole and hold her down!' I realised she was in earnest but made no promises. We went away in gales of laughter.

In October, the Labour Caucus chose me to go to Chile to attend an

Inter-Parliamentary Union (IPU) conference in Santiago. The Government was sending Tony Ryall, the MP for East Cape. For me, this was a historic first visit, as I vigorously opposed the Pinochet regime during my FOL years: when the women of Chile had asked me to go and speak to them, the Pinochet Government had refused to allow me into the country. So, here I was, going as an official delegate. Pinochet's regime had been overcome, though I was told that Pinochet himself was still in charge of the military. Tony and I met with our Foreign Affairs officials and with the Chilean Ambassador, and were given our conference papers. He left before me, flying via Easter Island, but I had an electorate engagement that I didn't want to miss, so went the next day on Aerolineas Argentinas to Buenos Aires.

It was not the most comfortable flight I've ever had. I don't know whether the staff were more friendly and attentive to their business or first-class passengers, because we certainly saw little of them. We arrived at the Buenos Aires Airport in the late afternoon, and by the time we aliens had gone through Customs, it was after six p.m. Those of us who were going on to Chile were told that we would be collected at 5.00 the next morning, and that we would have to walk clear across the huge tarmac to another airport. Then the officials said goodnight, locked us in and went home. To say that we were put out was an understatement. We had been able to buy a cup of coffee when we arrived, but there was no food and the prospect of spending eleven hours upright in a stiff plastic chair was more than a little daunting. There was absolutely nothing we could do as there wasn't a soul in sight.

Then I remembered that I had my business-class lounge card in my wallet. Even though I had travelled economy, I was entitled to use the lounge and I cursed myself for not telling the officials that before they left. I asked my fellow passengers if anyone could open a locked door and was quite astonished when several said they could. In no time at all, we were ensconced in the lounge. I felt no guilt about this because we all felt that we had been very badly treated. So, we had tea and coffee-making facilities, milk and sugar, liquor for those who wanted it, and some food. When a lone official arrived in the morning, we had at least had a rest in comfort.

It was still dark and quite chilly, but, at the other airport, officials were loading passengers for the Lan Chile plane to Santiago. The officials were not, of course, Chilean, and when we asked if we could have breakfast either before we left or on the plane, they said no to both requests. As it turned out, Lan Chile put us into first class and gave us an excellent breakfast.

Tony and I had been booked into a hotel opposite the presidential palace where Salvador Allende had been shot. When I had unpacked, I

rang Tony, and found he was out but would be back soon. I went down to
the lounge to wait for him. A bus drew up at the hotel's front door, out of
which streamed a crowd of tourists. I soon realised that they were Kiwis.
They were delighted to see me. Several of the older ones told me that they
had decided to spend their money on this journey as they were angry
about the New Zealand Government's plans for the financial resources of
the elderly. They wanted to enjoy their savings rather than hand them
over if they or their spouses ended up in hospital or homes.

When Tony arrived, we decided that we would travel by Metro to the
conference session that afternoon, as the hotel was some distance from
the conference venue. At lunch times, we took the Metro further, to
explore downtown. We ate local food in open-air cafés and found the
shops amazing. For one thing, there was the astonishing number of staff.
Roger Douglas would have had a fit! The locals realised that we were
foreigners and pointed to our gold Kiwi badges. I had brought a good
supply of these and gave half to Tony, and every day we handed them out
to the many people who wanted them.

One of the things that disturbed me in Santiago was the smog: I never
saw the famed Andes, even from the top floor of a university building.
When we first reached the conference venue, I was looking up at the
pollution when I saw that on top of the opposite building were armed
soldiers. I was stunned, and thought, 'Shades of Pinochet.'

International conferences of politicians would make an interesting
study. There are delegates who, like Tony and me, are chosen in a caucus
ballot and are unlikely to be at the next one; and then there are the peren-
nial delegates who come year after year, who know each other and tolerate those who are passing through. They greet each other with glad cries
and then settle down to see what other flotsam and jetsam they have been
landed with. Tony and I decided that we should concentrate on the issues
we had highlighted in our conference papers.

On the second night, there was a reception in the presidential palace.
It was a magical occasion, overlaid for me with sorrow at how a socialist
president — Salvador Allende — who wanted justice, health and education for all had died under suspicious circumstances before he could
implement his policies.

One day during the conference, Tony and I decided that we would talk
to the French delegation about the upcoming French nuclear tests on
Moruroa Atoll in the Pacific. When they saw who we were, they made it
clear that none of them spoke English. We found an interpreter and told
them how strongly opposed we and the countries of the Pacific were to
nuclear testing in our area. All through the discussion, the leader of the
French delegation looked at us scornfully and then, as we left, said in

perfect English: 'What are you worrying about? Moruroa is a long way from your country.'

I went to a meeting of women delegates, but there was the same problem of the transients and the perennials. I never felt any of the sense of sisterhood at this IPU meeting that I felt at the Commonwealth Parliamentary meetings. There were, however, some very special women there, and we debated a number of agenda items, won some and lost some.

One night I went to a socialist meeting in a very historic building. I had limited time because Tony and I had been asked to dinner with our ambassador to Chile. When I got to the meeting, I found that the writer Isabel Allende, Salvador's daughter, and her mother were present. The speeches from the top table were sometimes in English but mostly not. When the time came for me to leave, I tried to extricate myself quietly from my seat. I finally reached the aisle, but then tripped on a rucked section of the carpet. It was the ultimate international disgrace — I fell flat on my face, picked myself up and limped back to the hotel.

We had a wonderful evening with the ambassador. Also present was Hamish MacIntyre, the son of former minister Duncan MacIntyre, who was later to travel with me as a diplomatic escort for my friend Ram Subramaniam, the Indian peace advocate, when he came to New Zealand.

While in Santiago, I also met Helene Todd, a New Zealander who ran a clinic for brain-damaged children. When I visited her, she told me that, during the Pinochet regime, she was teaching at the university. As a strong supporter of Salvador Allende and his policies, she came under the scrutiny of the Government. As time went by, she realised she was in danger, and one afternoon towards the end of her lecture, she was told that a plot had been uncovered to shoot her as she left the university. However, friends had arranged for her to be taken secretly to a remote area in Southern Chile. Knowing that these friends would never have told her this had she not been in serious danger, Helene asked if she could go home and get some clothes, but they said no, as assassins were likely to be there, too. She lived in the south for several years, and, when she returned, the only way she could contact her friends was at mass in one of the cathedrals, where they exchanged notes.

Helene gave me a lot of information about Chile that I could never have discovered at the IPU conference. I also met a number of key women, including some of those who had tried to get me there some years previously.

After the conference, I went briefly to Washington and New York to see friends and colleagues in the peace movement, then on to Boston to visit my sister Beverley's eldest son Tony and his wife Liz. I hadn't seen

With Helene Todd at the school in Santiago

Tony for years, and it was great to get to know him again. It was autumn, or rather fall, and they took me out to see large plantations of trees in spectacular shades of crimson, orange and yellow. I had read many books about Boston, which is a city full of character — I felt it was quite familiar. Tony was studying for his PhD at the Massachusetts Institute of Technology, and he took me to visit Harvard, where he had also studied; both are impressive institutions. He and Liz are Episcopalians, and they took me to their church on Sunday. Accustomed to a more formal Anglican service, I found their one very relaxed and the congregation very friendly. The vicar had been a Harvard Dean, and the quality of his sermon was very much appreciated. At the morning tea later, Tony and Liz introduced me to their friends. It was a short visit, but I felt glad I had met those two impressive young people.

I flew to Santo Domingo via San Juan in Puerto Rico and was met by Margaret and Pat Shields. Margaret was director of the United Nations Institute for Training and Research for Women (INSTRAW) and travelled extensively. Pat told me that he was struggling with Spanish and was doing some work in one of the local theatres. They lived in a large, delightful apartment with a balcony, in a complex that was surrounded by a high fence with an armed guard at the gate. I had realised as we drove from the airport that the level of poverty was very high. Rubbish disposal seemed to be non-existent and I felt sure that the shacks so many lived in had none of the amenities we take for granted. But the people seemed unfailingly cheerful. Like most Caribbean islands, the countryside was very beautiful.

I met and talked with Margaret's staff at INSTRAW, and was introduced to artists and sculptors, people producing a very high quality of artwork. One night we went to dinner at a local restaurant, and on display were some attractive sculptures made of local mahogany. One in particular appealed to me — it was of a Taino Indian woman who was said to be very beautiful, with long flowing hair. Her name was Anacoana, and she had resisted the invasion of the Spanish who were going to burn her at the stake. In the end, one of her captors garrotted her, which was considered to be more humane. I counted up my money and found I could afford the statue. It was very heavy, as I found when I carried it in my hand luggage, but it now stands on my dresser as a memento of a Third World country that deserves help of all kinds.

One day I was sitting on the balcony when I saw a very strange sight. A procession was approaching, with a number of motorcycle outriders in front, then a truck with soldiers displaying guns facing all sides, then a large black stretch limo with tinted windows. Behind the limo was the same number of guards. Pat told me it was the president, and that this was his normal form of transportation: he was then 90 and blind, but continued in office.

All too soon, I had to leave for home, and flew back into crisp sunshine. The recess was over and I had a packed itinerary for the rest of the year. Looking through my diaries recently, I remarked to Mary that, from this distance, I couldn't imagine how I managed so many diverse activities. She reminded me that as the diary filled up, she kept saying that I couldn't do all that, but somehow I did.

Early in December Jim Knox died and I was asked if I would organise his funeral. Old St Paul's Cathedral was overflowing for the occasion, which marked the end of an era. Jim had lived through incredible times and a number of people talked about these during the service.

Taking Sides

1992 began with a busy schedule — being in Opposition certainly didn't mean there was no work to do. Housing was becoming a serious issue, and seldom did a Saturday clinic go by without a variety of housing problems being brought to me by constituents. The proposition of charging market rents for state housing was also surfacing and this terrified state tenants, particularly those on benefits that had been slashed, and those whose Government Retirement Income was static. While doorknocking in Epuni, I came across several very elderly widows who had been notified that they must leave the family home and find a one-bedroom state unit. The path to the Housing Corporation became well worn by Shona and me.

Sexual abuse of various kinds was by now being openly discussed. I spent time with police in Wainuiomata and Lower Hutt, talking about ways and means of dealing with this. I received a great deal of mail on this subject from all over the country. I perceived that police attitudes were changing. The old 'She must have asked for it' and 'Look what she was wearing' attitudes about rape, and the attitude that domestic abuse was none of their business, were obviously no longer viable. There were some older police who found these changes hard to accept; when I spoke to police in groups, I could tell them by their body language. I went out to the Police College at Porirua to talk to tutors about the curriculum and learn what they were teaching trainees about rape and other sexual abuse. I found to my dismay that this topic had been dropped from the curriculum for a year because of other priorities.

For me, the nastiest debate in the House centred on the Employment Contracts Act (ECA). From the beginning, it was obvious that National Government MPs did not know or understand the basic philosophy of the trade union movement; and furthermore, they had no wish to. It soon became clear that if, by the stroke of a pen, they could have made unions disappear, they would. They made reference in their speeches to 'cloth cap mentality', 'restrictive and destructive influences' — which simply reinforced their ignorance. My explanations that since the 1980s, unions had changed dramatically and in fact were still changing, that the union activities of the past reflected those times; and that unions were now changing to meet new challenges, were greeted with derision. If ever there was a need for proper consultation between workers and government, this was it, but there was no desire on the Government's part for that. The debate went relentlessly on, and people making submissions at the Labour Select Committee told me that they had the distinct impression that Government MPs were just going through the motions and had no intention of making any relevant changes to the legislation.

The Government's contention that workers would prefer to negotiate with their own employers and that this would create better industrial relations, I knew to be fatally flawed. Today, sixteen-year-olds who ask if they can take their employment contract home to show their parents before signing it are being told to sign now, that there are plenty of others wanting this job . . . and they are not confident enough to talk the issue through. In the years since the passing of the ECA, we have seen real attitudinal changes, many stemming from the fact that job security no longer exists for many people. Employment contracts that may be terminated at the end of the period, or at best renegotiated (seldom to the workers' benefit); the large number of redundancies; the fact that people are working longer hours for the same or less money: all these are a direct result of the philosophy underpinning the ECA.

Experienced state servants were made redundant and replaced by seventeen and eighteen-year-olds. I experienced an example of this in Lower Hutt ACC when I took a constituent along to discuss what could be done for her. She had been flung out of the rear door of a work van and seriously injured her back; she was unable to do housework or gardening, and work outside the home was impossible. All this had caused tension in the home because her husband had a very demanding job and her teenagers were trying to make their way in an uncertain world. I had personally rung and made the appointment and had explained that my constituent was very disabled and found sitting for anything but a short period very painful. When we reported at the front desk, no one had heard of my appointment and I was asked to wait until the receptionist had a chance to make some enquiries. Half an hour later, when I could see that my constituent was flagging, a young woman who looked every day of eighteen, wearing harem pants and a T-shirt, arrived, took us into a cubicle and said to my companion, 'Well, what seems to be the trouble?' I pointed out that I had asked to see the manager but was told that that person was out. I then pointed out that there was a file in the department which contained details of the accident and the actions that had been taken so far and suggested that it would be helpful if she went and got it. She said that searching for files wasn't in her job description.

Fortunately, at this point, the manager arrived. The message about my appointment with her hadn't filtered through, but I think she sensed that my temper was reaching danger point and took us into her office and called for the appropriate file. We discussed how my constituent could be helped. As I left, the manager told me that she had been summoned to her head office and told that, from here on, she would be responsible for an expanded district, as one of the managers was being made redundant. It was all par for the course.

Health groups from around the country started asking me to speak to them. Everywhere there was unease about the fact that there were to be no elected people administering hospitals. Everyone realised that health was expensive and there was a need for people with business acumen to be involved, but no one was happy that hospitals were more and more being run as businesses. There was the first hint of private wards in public hospitals for wealthy overseas patients. Day surgery, whereby the patient came in for the day only and returned home after the operation, began to operate in hospitals. For many people, there was little objection, but the concern was that when the patient got home, there would not be proper or adequate support services for the post-operative period. Anyone with nursing experience will tell you that if good, efficient post-operative care does not follow surgery, it negates the skills of surgeons during the operation, and not only causes pain and distress to the patient, but also undoes a degree of the good that the surgery was supposed to provide. This is also a time when the patient is particularly prone to infection.

We had a huge outdoor meeting outside Hutt Hospital. Thousands came, and there were many speakers, including Mayor Glen Evans, health professionals and the Hutt MPs. Around the same time, there was a similar meeting in Masterton, which was very well attended. People were beginning to wonder whether their hospitals would survive. The next to approach the Hutt MPs were the hospital cleaners, who had been told that cleaning services were to be contracted out. We had always been proud of the standard of hospital cleanliness in this country, and knew that reliable workers, proper supervision and high standards kept cleanliness at a very satisfactory level. Workers knew that it wasn't poor standards that were behind contracting out, but cost-cutting, and that they would be asked to clean more wards in less time and that a lower standard would result.

Paul Swain and I went to discuss the proposal with an official in an office in what had been the nurses' home when nurses were trained under the old system. It soon became obvious to us that the authorities were determined on contracting out, and our arguments against this were to no avail.

Planting Mark's replacement totara at Rangipo with Lyn and David and Ian Peters

In 1992, invitations for me to speak at Labour Party meetings, to health workers, to women's groups, teachers, students, poured in. Mary, who is good at jigsaw puzzles, somehow juggled all these with House and electorate obligations

One day, as I arrived at the committee room for a meeting of the Maori Affairs Select Committee, the chair, Ian Peters, told me that the previous weekend he and his family had gone to Rangipo. There they had seen that the totara tree that had been planted by Mark's plaque after he was killed in the tunnel had been snapped off by a turning vehicle. He said that he had found a good strong replacement in a nursery in Tokoroa and suggested that we all go and plant it very soon. Around this time, I had three more reminders of Mark in the space of two days. First of all, arriving home at a very late hour, I found a narrow oblong parcel sitting outside my front door. Was it a bomb? I kicked it, realising with hindsight that had it been a bomb, I could have blown up the whole apartment block! I picked up the parcel and took it inside. It was the box containing Mark's ashes, which had disappeared when I moved from the rear apartment to the front. The next afternoon, I had a speaking engagement in Blenheim. In the taxi on the way to the airport, the driver told me that he had been beside Mark in the Rangipo tunnel when the machine that killed him went out of control. We talked of Mark and he told me he had been at his funeral. The following day, I had been asked to open a small smoke-free restaurant in Eastbourne. When I arrived, the proprietor told me that his name was Frank Macskasy, and that he was a friend of Mark's. I realised that this was indeed the schoolfriend with whom Mark had argued politics during his Wellington High School days. Frank said that Mark had changed his right-wing ways. He said he'd been out of Wellington and lost touch, and asked how he was. I had to break the news of Mark's death and he was very affected by it.

I arranged with David and Lyn to visit them in Taupo during recess and liaised with Ian Peters for us all to plant the totara at Rangipo. I decided that as Mark had so dearly loved the bush and river there, I should bury his ashes under the new tree. And that's what we did.

Later in July, caucus chose me to go to Delhi to a meeting of Asian parliamentarians. I stayed with Priscilla Williams, who was at that time the New Zealand High Commissioner. She was there when the High Commission moved into the new mission designed so exquisitely by Sir Miles Warren. Priscilla's living quarters had a small dining room and bedrooms around an attractive central courtyard. I first met Priscilla in Mexico in 1975 when she was the Foreign Affairs official with the all-women delegation to the International Women's Year Conference. She is a very efficient diplomat and a splendid hostess with an endearing sense of humour. She told me that just days before Don McKinnon, Minister of Foreign Affairs, was due to arrive to formally open the new mission, electricity had not been installed. The contractors said that it would take a year to install, and when Priscilla was firm with them, they demanded a large amount of money without guarantee. They obviously didn't know about the steel underlying the pleasant exterior. Priscilla went over their heads and the electricity was on by opening day.

The Asian Parliamentarians Conference was fascinating, all the more so as I met so many politicians that I knew from other Asian conferences. We were able to catch up with events in each country, discuss the problems and some solutions. It was while staying with Priscilla after the conference was over that I read the book, *May You Be the Mother of A Hundred Sons* by Elizabeth Bumiler. It is an excellent and intelligent study of the lives of Indian women. I was told that paperback copies of this were available in the markets, so went to these exciting places and bought a number of copies for friends back home.

Ram Subramaniam came to see me and told me that he and his wife were now living in the countryside. He asked if I would like to go with them to see their house. I realised when we arrived that Ram's idea of country and mine were rather different. It seemed more like a house in a suburb to me, very pleasant and of course a real contrast for them to the huge crowded city where they worked.

From Delhi, I flew to Nepal for a brief World Peace Council meeting. I had met a Nepalese woman MP in Delhi and she wanted me to stay with her, but the WPC was working day and night so it wasn't practical. We stayed in a modest but very pleasant hotel with delightful gardens.

The first thing that struck me about Nepal was the level of pollution — I never saw the Himalayas, but had the strong feeling that they were there, somewhere high above. The second thing was the unrelenting poverty of the people. One day, after our meeting was over, I went with Ray Stewart and an interpreter to the nearby market, arriving just as it was closing. We saw a very young woman with a tiny baby gathering up her goods and weeping. I asked the interpreter to find out what was wrong. She told me that the woman had not sold anything that day and had no

(Top) in Kathmandu with Ray Stewart, who has just witnessed a Nepalese funeral where the corpse is consigned to the river; (above) speaking at the WPC meeting in Kathmandu

food at home. I asked Ray and the interpreter to stand in front of her and scrabbled in my bag to find the stack of Nepalese money that I had. I reckoned that in our terms it would be around $50. I gave it to her and asked her to stuff it into the front of her dress. She was overwhelmed and told me that that amount of money was more than she would earn in six months. I felt very overprivileged.

We met politicians of all persuasions and realised that their problems were unlike anything we had to face. Life expectancy was low, health services marginal or non-existent, and thousands of children went to work at a very young age in the carpet industry. Despite all this, the people were invariably cheerful.

Back home, I found Mary embarked on an election campaign for a seat on the Wellington City Council. Because of my wall-to-wall commitments, I wasn't much use to her. I felt that, with her organisational skills and her sense of justice, she would be an excellent councillor. But it was not to be.

Fran Wilde had resigned from Parliament to become mayor of Wellington, and we went to her swearing-in ceremony in the Town Hall. Her replacement in Wellington Central was Chris Laidlaw, who was now my next-door neighbour in Bowen House.

Early in October, I received a fax from Japan, from Takeshi Asami, the secretary of the Campaign for a Nuclear-Free Kanagawa. David Lange and I had been invited to attend a Nuclear-Free Municipalities conference in Yokohama in November. Takeshi asked me to come a few days earlier and to go on the Shinkansen super express from Tokyo to Hiroshima to meet unionists, peace activists and members of the Co-operative Movement, to see the museum, and talk there with survivors of the atomic bomb (called Hibakushas). The conference was to be held in Yokohama, beginning on 5 November, so he planned for me to be in Hiroshima for two days, have a free day and then go to Yokohama to speak for an hour at a pre-conference one-day International Symposium on Denuclearisation of the Globe. There were to be four other speakers. As I was to have one free day, I faxed my friend Ritsko Kondo at the Japan Free Press in Osaka and asked if she could spend some time with me. She faxed back that she was just about to fly to Korea to continue her research on Korean comfort women, who as very young girls had been abducted by the Japanese military during the war and forced into prostitution. She said she would be back when I was there and we could spend as much time together as I could spare.

So, in and around my schedule in October, I prepared two major speeches and boned up from peace worker Kate Dewes on the latest developments of the World Court Project. Rob Green, chair of the British campaign to have the legal status of nuclear weapons tested at the World

*Ritsko Kondo with her husband and their three children
in Osaka*

Court in The Hague, was going to share a workshop on that subject with
me in Yokohama. Rob is a former British Navy Commander who left the
service to campaign against nuclear weapons. He is also a thatcher and a
lovely man, now happily married to Kate. She arranged for Rob to bring
me a variety of information about the World Court Project and also her
long colourful rainbow banner to use at the conference.

I set off for Tokyo at the very end of October and arrived at Narita
Airport to be met by one of Takeshi's people and taken to the railway
station. I travelled to Hiroshima with a Scottish ex-naval officer from
Edinburgh. I found Hiroshima to be very beautiful, memorable and
disturbing. The city of course has been rebuilt, but specific buildings have
been left as they were after the holocaust. The Red Cross Hospital is one
of these, and there I met the staff, who are still working there, and also
survivors of the bomb, and heard their accounts of terror, pain and
despair. I went to the museum, which is full of pictures and accounts of
what happened to people when the bomb was dropped. Many of the
Hibakushas seemed to me to be completely trapped in their ghastly experiences. For them, there was no better tomorrow, only the memory of a
tragic past.

I went on to Osaka and met Ritsko at my hotel. She brought her
delightful, intelligent four-year-old daughter with her and they stayed for
dinner as we caught up on our respective news. The next day, Ritsko took

me to see her boss, Koji Komori, whom I had met on a previous visit. We went to a traditional Japanese restaurant and had a splendid early lunch, because they had arranged for me to meet unionists and co-operative people.

At Yokohama, I met Takeshi at last, a dedicated, work-driven man, and very charming. He told me that the symposium the next day would be held in an auditorium within the headquarters of the Kanagawa Prefectural Government. He explained that this prefecture was an umbrella local authority that included 37 cities and towns, 27 of which had been declared nuclear-free. Takeshi said that the local authorities' nuclear-free status was a nominal one, that mayors, councillors and bureaucrats were under the strong influence of central government, that Japan's representation system through local councils did not work adequately, and that local people had no input into council affairs. In his experience, strong and conservative bureaucracy prevailed.

The symposium itself was invaluable. The other speakers were Rear-Admiral Eugene Carroll from the Centre for Defence Information in Washington; Professor Roland Simbula, national chairperson of the Nuclear-Free Philippines Coalition; Roman Bedor from Belau; and Chuck Johnston, executive director of Nuclear-Free America. Diverse though our subjects were, it soon became obvious that we shared a great deal of common ground. After question time, which was lively, Professor Bato of Hosei University summarised our presentations from the point of view of how Japan could contribute to the cause of nuclear-free international relations. It was very useful to understand the positions from other countries' perspectives, and the symposium gave us invaluable information on the new military developments in the Asia Pacific region and of the nuclear-free organisations of that area.

The next day, when the actual conference began and delegates filed in, I saw that there a large number of delegates from all round the world. One of the first who came to my notice was an amazing-looking Australian, complete with Aussie hat with corks bobbing round the edge. He told me he was shortly to stand for Parliament in the upcoming Australian election. David Lange and his secretary Lorna Best were there. Lorna had been his unstoppable secretary for years, in the Beehive and out of it. The Japanese love and admire David so much because of New Zealand's nuclear-free legislation. When he spoke, another delegate and I stretched Katie's rainbow banner across the front of the stage and it looked fantastic.

Early in the conference, we started hearing about a ship called the *Akatsuki Mara*, which was about to leave France with a tonne of reprocessed plutonium on board, en route to Japan. The Japanese Government was refusing to say which route the ship would take, but because of strong objections from many countries and statements from the governments of Argentina, Brazil, Chile, Uruguay, South Africa, Malaysia, Singapore, Indonesia and the Philippines, which barred access to their ports, it seemed likely that the ship would sail between Australia and New Zealand. Japan has a high incidence of shipping accidents: the Japanese Ministry of Transport reported that in 1990 there were over 5000. The amount of plutonium on board the *Akatsuki Mara* was said to be enough to make 150 nuclear bombs. I sent a faxed press release to Mary outlining all this and asking whether our Government had been consulted by the Japanese. This apparently sank like a stone in the press gallery, and it wasn't until later, when the ship neared our area, that the press started taking an interest.

On that first evening, the Australian delegate asked several of us to go over to his hotel across the city. It was where David Lange was staying. He said he had brought a picture from Australia which he wanted to present to the Mayor of Yokohama at a function to be held the next evening. When we got to the hotel room, we saw a large crated flat object about 3 metres long and 1.5 metres wide. I asked him how on earth he had managed to get it into the Qantas hold. We insisted on opening the crate and seeing it. When it was uncovered, we were all stunned into silence and then asked what it was. He told us that it had been painted by an artist friend of his and depicted the Australian outback. It was a picture of brown and ochre desert with some black tracks across which he said were Aboriginal. I wondered if the mayor would appreciate its subtleties. I was asked to help take it up on stage the next evening for the presentation, and I said I would.

It was very clear that the conference organisers didn't want delegates to discuss the plutonium ship in the plenary sessions, but of course in the workshops it was a top priority. Because of pressure from delegates, a committee had been established to draw up an acceptable resolution on the transportation of plutonium by ship. The Australian was on this committee, which was a good thing because he was quite passionate on the subject.

The next evening, delegates attended a very swept-up function and were to be addressed by the Mayor. When the Australian came to me with the picture and asked me to take my end, David Lange said as I passed, 'What on earth have you got yourself into now?' The Australian made a very spirited speech, emphasising the goodwill of his local authority, handed out gifts from it and then damned the plutonium ship. When he presented the picture, the mayor looked quite dazed. The last I saw of it was when two staff members carried it out.

The next day, Rob Green and I presented our World Court Project workshop. It was not well attended as delegates were not aware of what it was about. However, several young Japanese lawyers came, and Takeshi and a few delegates, and it was the beginning of what was to become strong Japanese support for the project. In workshops, we talked about every aspect of local government, and I realised just how very complicated the Japanese local government system was and how little input the people had. They were astonished to hear that in New Zealand's central government MPs had electorate offices and held clinics around their electorates and that a number of us sent out newsletters every month to party members and interested constituents.

At the final plenary session, I was handed a copy of the resolution on the transportation of plutonium across the oceans by ship. David Lange and Rob Green had left by then, as had the Australian, who was said to have been unhappy about the resolution and had kept the committee up until the early hours of the morning before being outvoted. That didn't bode well. I sat in the huge hall where the plenary session was being held, among delegates that I knew and trusted. When I read the resolution, I was horrified, particularly about a paragraph which read that 'some delegates, no matter how misguidedly, had been strongly opposed to ships carrying plutonium' and then went on to virtually sanction it! I said to my companions that I couldn't agree with that. They said that I couldn't alter anything. It was the democratic decision of the majority of the committee; and the British and Americans, for strategic reasons, would never support any change. They also said that no delegates could speak at this session. An Italian delegate was in the chair with an interpreter. As soon as he opened the session, I stood up, went to the microphone and said that I wished to speak on the resolution concerning ships carrying plutonium. The chair shook his head, so I went down through the crowded auditorium to the stage and stood in front of a microphone. In as measured tones as my rage would allow, I told the conference that if they voted for the resolution as it stood, I would refuse to be associated with it. I said that I came from a nuclear-free country and that the people that I represented would be appalled if I associated myself with such sentiments. I wanted those words deleted and a new sentence to replace them, stating simply that at workshops many delegates expressed strong reservations about the transportation of plutonium by ships. There was a roar of approval from the audience, which grew as I resumed my seat. When the noise abated, the chair said that he assured the New Zealand delegate that what she asked for was agreed to and the resolution would be amended accordingly.

After the conference, I had a day and a night to spare, so Takeshi took some of us to visit small villages, exquisite temples, magical gardens and also the city of Yokosuka where the US naval base was. We spent time at an outdoor celebration of the co-op women, saw lots of markets, watched children dancing and singing — a lovely ending to a memorable visit.

At home I was into the maelstrom of political life, end of year functions for the Fire Service, organisations, school graduation ceremonies and parliament rhetoric.

From the first day that I entered the debating chamber, John Banks called me 'Granny'. What pleasure it gave him I'm not sure. At first I was outraged and retaliated by telling him that he hadn't even made it to first base and that I was proud to be a grandmother. After that, I ignored him. It wasn't until Paul East, then attorney-general, came into the House one afternoon before the Speaker arrived and called me 'Auntie' that I snapped. After the prayer that starts each day, I rose to my feet on a point of order. I told the Speaker that I was sick of ageist name-calling from his colleagues who had called me 'Granny' and 'Auntie' and asked him to discipline them. It was a Thursday afternoon. Rob Muldoon was in the House and called out, 'If you can't stand the heat in the kitchen, girlie, you'd better get out of it.' As he left the House, he stumped over to me and poked his tongue out. I said, 'It's dirty, Sir Robert. You need syrup of figs.' He gave one of his famous derogatory grunts and stomped out. Several Goverment women MPs came across to tell me that they were glad I had spoken out.

Some time later, I was having dinner with grandsons Tim and Ben in Bellamy's. They looked across during the meal and said, 'That's John Banks over there, isn't it?' I looked over and indeed it was. I told them not to get any ideas about talking to him. While I was signing my chit to pay for dinner, I looked over and saw the two large young men (both well over six feet) standing at John Banks' table. I signalled to them to come away, and in the lift, asked them what they had said. They told me that they had been perfectly polite and had told Banks that they didn't call me 'Granny' and they didn't give him permission to either, and that the next time he did this, he would be dealing with them and not me! I think Banks must have been quite impressed because he never called me 'Granny' again in public.

Suffrage Year

In 1993, the House didn't resume until 23 February. Because this was to be my last year in Parliament, it was tinged with sadness, which was increased by my own and family illnesses. However, with it being Suffrage Year as well as my having normal parliamentary duties and, by now, customary conferences overseas, I had little time to indulge in sorrow or self-pity.

Before I left for Japan in late 1992, Jenny Shipley had established a Women's Suffrage Committee on which were to be women representative of all parties. We had started planning for the centenary of the year when New Zealand women were the first to win, by Act of Parliament, the right to vote. When the House resumed in late February, a Joint Women's Suffrage Committee meeting was scheduled in Jenny Shipley's office.

One of our first discussions the previous year had been about the fact that the photographs around Parliament were mostly of men. There was little evidence that any women MPs had existed. So we had decided to collect photographs of all women MPs past and present and hang them on either side of a lobby through which MPs would pass on their way to the debating chamber. This exhibition engendered an amazing reaction from some of the male MPs. Whether the sight of so many women — not in reality a very large group — threatened them, or whether they hadn't realised that there had been as many women in the House and didn't like it, I don't know, but there were mutterings as some of them passed through.

One night I came down from my office as the bells were ringing for a vote. I was walking behind two tall Government MPs. They looked at the photos and one said to the other that it was like going past your grandmother, aunts and sisters each time he passed. I poked them in the back and said, 'Don't you like yours?' and they both had the grace to look ashamed.

Another issue that the committee was considering was the fact that although there were plaques in the debating chamber celebrating the battles that men had fought in two world wars, we felt there was absolutely no recognition of the contribution that New Zealand women had made in both: those who had stayed behind; the mothers who raised families alone on reduced incomes; the women who knitted khaki sweaters, socks and balaclavas, rolled bandages, baked cakes and sent them in sealed tins to their men in the trenches. There were the women who went into engineering shops, drove trains and acted as conductors; and those who went out into the country as land girls when more and more men were sent overseas. There were few workplaces that women didn't enter and work hard in, learning skills they had never experienced before. This contribution was simply taken for granted. True, women weren't sent into the trenches, or bayoneted or blown up, but they were at the other end of all that, mourning the deaths of husbands, sons, friends and lovers, their lives changed forever. There is no doubt that women played a major role through all those dark days.

We considered having a plaque to celebrate those efforts and decided to ask women artists to submit designs to the committee. The problem was, where could this plaque be placed? We started talking to our male colleagues about this, and soon understood that there was incredible resistance to any one of the existing plaques being replaced by one of ours. I asked, 'What about Vietnam? We should never have been there.' There were howls of protest: 'My RSA would never stand for it!' Well, it seemed like an impasse, and then someone noted that there were two empty panels on either side of the Speaker's chair and we began negotiations about that and won.

Suffrage celebrations all round the country meant that women MPs were much in demand. In Murchison, the women decided to celebrate by holding a 'Grannies Galore' weekend for older women and asked me to go down and be their guest speaker on the Saturday night. They sent me their programme and it looked amazing.

The Grannies were going to go abseiling, white-water rafting, target and rabbit shooting, tramping, canoeing and other quite bracing activities. In addition, there were workshops on pottery, watercolour painting, quilting and weaving and microwave cooking. I was told that there were women enrolled for the weekend who had been recently widowed, had never used a chequebook, driven a car or made major decisions, other, of course, than those made during the raising of three, four, five or six children. This was to be an empowering weekend and during the journey from Nelson to Murchison, I was told that there had been a splendid response from older women, far more that had been expected.

The organisation of the weekend was superb. I gave away physical outdoor activities and attended a number of workshops. I had been accommodated at the wonderful old hotel, at which it was said that the

With Helen Clark and Hawkes Bay women after a suffrage meeting in Hastings,
1993. Hawkes Bay Herald Tribune

legendary Captain Moonlight had stayed early in the century. There
aren't very many of these hotels left now and it was a nostalgic experience.

When I arrived at the Saturday night dinner, I could see that the
Grannies had had a great day, and I felt very privileged to be able to speak
to them. I finally tottered across the road to the hotel, fell into bed and
slept soundly. Early next morning, there was a champagne breakfast on
the banks of the river, a church service with a woman minister, and then
lots of discussion, before the local Lions and Rotarians arrived with a delicious lunch. It was an outstanding success. If only these sorts of events
were run on a regular basis throughout the country as a matter of course.

In March, there was a two-day meeting of the World Peace Council in
Hanoi. I particularly wanted to go to this meeting because, as someone
living in the Pacific and on the edge of Asia, I tended to find the WPC
rather Eurocentric. I knew that it was essential for peace on our planet
that Asian countries be part of the peace process. Japan certainly was, but
there were reasons for that. I also have to admit that I longed to see
Vietnam and what had happened to it since that unspeakable war. I found
it was possible to fit it all in, and set off for Hanoi via Bangkok. I find
Asian cities absolutely fascinating and Hanoi was no exception. We stayed
in a Vietnamese hotel which was within walking distance of our meeting
place. Walking along that crowded street, dodging bicycles and motor-

bikes, each with as many people on board as could be managed and some-times with a Buddhist monk on the rear, the word which sprang to mind was 'vibrant'.

It was obvious that Vietnam was pulling itself out of disaster to recovery. Our hotel had a dining room open to the public, and there we met some very interesting people. A number of expatriate New Zealanders came as well, who were working in various agencies, and I learned from them about the free market political and social policies being developed by the Vietnamese Government.

The two-day meeting itself taught us much about Asian aspirations. Given cultural differences, theirs were not so far removed from ours. They want peace, education for their children and adult education for themselves, quality health care for all and full employment. To my horror, I found that former Cabinet ministers from New Zealand had been there, promoting a market-driven economy as the way to go for them. I raised my concerns at the meeting and ultimately was interviewed on television with a Vietnamese Cabinet minister who had been sold the great economic vision. I told him what had happened in New Zealand, warned him about what happens when the free-market theory becomes more important than people, and suggested he should visit New Zealand and meet not only the people who have done well out of Rogernomics but also the people who have not; only then, I told him, could he make an informed decision.

I took time to visit with the Vietnam Women's Union and to talk to them about our Suffrage Year and also about a project initiated and funded by the Labour Women's Council in New Zealand. The project, spearheaded by Cath Kelly, aims to help nomadic women in the highland region of Vietnam to be self-sufficient, by means of a health and education programme including animal husbandry and money management. This project is run by indigenous women. Cath Kelly and Jo Fitzpatrick, a Labour Women's Officer, visit Vietnam each year to check on progress, and they say it is going very well, in spite of a limited budget.

Vietnam is an incredibly beautiful country and my short time there didn't allow me to see much of it, apart from the lushness of vegetation, the beauty of the people, their seeming fragility and innate strength. I had demonstrated with thousands of others against the Vietnam War, and have never regretted it.

Back home, I was into my crowded schedule. No sooner had I unpacked than I was off to New Plymouth to speak at an International Secretaries Day breakfast early the next morning. Secretaries, who for years have been regarded as necessary but not important, are at last being given the status that the quality of their work deserves. MPs, on days when their secretary is absent, are like rudderless ships and go round distractedly asking where their select committee papers are.

Liane Dalziel had invited me to Christchurch to speak at a women's dinner, and I was then going on to Gore and then to Nightcaps, in the uttermost south of the island, to speak at a Women's Suffrage dinner on the Sunday night. As I went to the airport, I became aware that I was developing a cold, which was hardly surprising.

The Christchurch dinner was splendid, and we all talked about what Suffrage Year meant to us. Christchurch women had been very active in the fight for women's suffrage and Kate Sheppard belonged to them, so there was particular pride expressed at the dinner. I stayed with Liane in her idyllic home with its old and very special garden. My grandson Ben, then studying law at Canterbury University, came to visit, which was great.

On I went to Gore, invited by my friend Alison Broad who works at Southland Polytechnic with the Rural Education Action Programme. She runs self-defence courses for young women and wanted me to speak at the graduation of her latest group. By the time of the graduation ceremony, I was feeling rather grotty, to say the least, but pulled myself together. To meet those wonderful women who had been empowered by their self-defence course in what was becoming a more and more violent society was a great privilege. I was cared for very well, had a warm bed and good food.

The next morning, feeling progressively tatty, I met a mother and daughter who, hearing that I was there, came to talk to me about incest and what had happened in their family. I was convinced all over again that we had to come to grips with the causes of incest and rape and cope with the results. We had a lunch with the women of Gore who wanted to be part of Suffrage Year. One of the wonderful things for me about Suffrage Year was that, wherever I went, I met amazing women.

In mid-afternoon, Alison and I set out for Nightcaps. We were expected there at six o'clock. By the time we arrived at the hall, I felt decidedly unwell and knew that I had a fever and was aching all over. I was just about to tell Alison that there was no way I could speak, when she opened the door and I saw a packed hall of women. Nightcaps had been a mining town, now greatly diminished in population, but it was estimated that there were at least ninety women there that night. How could I not talk to them? By that time I knew that I couldn't stand to talk, so I arranged with the organisers that I would sit out front on a chair. Alison disappeared, and I later found that she had gone to ring her parents in Invercargill to ask them to go across to her house and turn on the electric blankets on our beds.

Despite my failing health, it was a memorable night and I met so many women that I regret not being able to see them again. We set off around midnight and, back in Invercargill, had a hot milk drink and I fell into bed. I found that, despite the electric blanket, I couldn't get warm. I realised that all was not well with me. In the morning, Alison delivered me to the airport.

At the airport, the plane on which I would travel north had just landed. Among its passengers was Tim Shadbolt, then mayor of Invercargill, and his current partner. The media was in full cry. Before leaving for Japan on a twin-sister city visit, Tim had sold the story of his new relationship to a women's magazine. The press thought they had a chance to discredit him, but they underestimated this entrepreneurial man. Hidden behind a pillar, I heard Tim say, 'I'm a celebrity mayor. I make no apologies for that. You'll just have to get used to me.' There was no way I could cope with all that, so I stayed hidden.

Back in Wellington I was able to fit in a visit to my daughter Penny before realising I was really in trouble and rang my doctor, Rosie Fenwick. When she arrived and examined me, she told me that I had pneumonia and should go immediately into hospital. I didn't want to go and foolishly persuaded her that, with her help, I could cope at home. My dear friends Rona Ensor and Brian Small heard about this and set up a roster of people who would stay with me at all times. Mary at this time was in Paris attending a UNIFEM meeting.

Peter Franks was rostered on for the first night. He told me later that he hardly slept, he was so concerned that I might have a crisis during the night. In the morning, his anxious face appeared round my door asking what I wanted for breakfast. I realised that I hadn't eaten for over a day, so asked Peter if he could make me some porridge. Peter is a sensational cook and I had often enjoyed delicious meals at his house, but porridge was something else. Before we could come to grips with the making of porridge, Rosie arrived. It was very early in the morning and I knew that she was serious when she said that I couldn't be treated at home and that she had called an ambulance to take me to Hutt Hospital. It was obvious that I had no alternative, and Peter and Rona gathered together what I would need for my stay in hospital.

One of the parliamentary secretaries phoned Mary in Paris, waking her at six a.m. in her hotel room, and told her about my situation. She rang Rosie, who said that she was sure I would survive and counselled against her coming home. When I got to hospital, there was a beautiful bouquet of flowers in the feminist colours, purple, green and white, from her. She told me later that she had rushed out to a Parisian florist near the meeting place and had discovered that flowers sent Interflora would cost her $150, so she had rung Shona in the electorate office and asked her to have our faithful Wainuiomata florist produce the wonderful bouquet for me.

The next few days were very stressful because I was so ill, but the staff were everything anyone could wish for. Many people wanted to visit me, but it was decided that I should have no visitors for a few days while I recovered. I felt so sorry for constituents and friends who came and were turned away. My room filled with flowers.

The changes in the health system were obvious: I was told that wards no longer existed; they were now business management units: there was no longer a ward sister but a business manager, who sometimes wore uniform and, on the occasions when she had to go to meetings, wore mufti. The 'business manager' on my 'business management unit' was a very special person, and I knew that all this was difficult for her as well as me. In spite of what was happening around them, the staff were efficient, caring and very hard-working.

There is an old saying that one knows when one is getting older when policemen look like boys. Apart from the senior medical staff, all the rest looked like teenagers to me. Early one morning when one of them came to change my intravenous drip, I had to stop myself asking was she really qualified, she looked so young. One evening as I was dozing with the oxygen which helped my poor old battered lungs, I opened my eyes and there, sitting at the end of my bed, dressed in what looked like baseball outfits complete with caps, were my friends Charles Chauvel and Greg Cleave. I decided that I was hallucinating, but they were real, and Charles, who was working in the health sector at the time, told me he had persuaded the staff to let them in for five minutes. They were a real tonic. When I was well enough to have visitors, I was astonished when Penny appeared wheeled in by her partner Mick with Tim and his girlfriend in tow. It was all quite bizarre, with me hooked up with tubes, Mick recovering from chemotherapy and looking frail, my poor ill daughter and Tim and Shelley looking appalled, but I was able to reassure them I was getting better.

Nevertheless, it was a long haul back to health, and when I finally made it back into the House, my colleagues, who had been very supportive, did all they could to ease my path.

During all this, there was a Cabinet discussion in which Geoffrey Palmer decided he didn't have majority support. He said that under those circumstances, he was not prepared to stay on. By then a number of MPs were feeling very uneasy about their chances of being re-elected. Mistakenly, in my opinion, they decided that maybe a new leader might be the answer to the Party's future. Geoffrey resigned and returned to his legal profession and, six weeks before the 1990 election, Mike Moore took over as leader.

I soon realised that Mike was gearing up for a presidential-style campaign and that colleagues were divided about this. When I looked back to the Mike I had known, this new version seemed to be someone quite different. As I travelled around the country, people started saying to me that, apart from clerical staff, Mike didn't seem to have any women in his campaign team in Parliament; and that when they saw him in parliamentary TV interviews, he was always surrounded by male staff. Women, in particular, felt that this was a retrograde step. This viewpoint was reflected in my electorate and I finally decided to discuss the matter with Mike.

I never learn. I should have remembered my attempts to help Norm Kirk and the disaster that ensued. Rather than seeing that I was trying to help him become prime minister with a supportive attitude towards women, Mike took it as a personal attack and was very angry indeed. I had the feeling that he wasn't really listening to me. He accused me of trying to undermine him, saying bitterly that if everyone worked as hard as he did, a Labour victory would be easily attained. As I said to Mary when I got back to the office, it had all been a great mistake and Mike had totally misunderstood my motives. I added that his assertion that we were not working hard enough showed how out of touch he was, because most of my colleagues were working their butts off. Mike's office poured out an incredible amount of correspondence to various interest groups, but from comments I heard, these were not particularly appreciated, especially when people received two or three letters on the one issue. But there was no way that I was going to raise this with Mike. It seemed to me that, sadly, the years of friendship and co-operation that Mike and I had shared had not held up in his quest for power.

Out in the electorate, there was much conjecture about who would succeed me as MP when I retired at the 1993 election. I was anxious that I should be replaced by another woman — but it was not to be.

In the meantime, Suffrage Year was proceeding with hundreds of meetings and functions all around the country. We planted a 'Kate Sheppard' camellia in a dell on Wainuiomata Hill with a group of women, and the Parliamentary Women's Joint Suffrage Committee planned to plant one on either side of the steps leading to the Parliamentary Library, when that building was refurbished.

One day, a woman rang Mary from Auckland and told her that she had been commissioned to paint my portrait and that she wanted to arrange a series of sittings. Mary told her that my diary was so tight that I was hardly going to sit down for the rest of the year, and suggested that the best we could do was have her sit in on a select committee meeting and sketch me there. Shortly after, the artist rang again and said not to worry, she had found a photo of me and was working from that. I was so busy that I forgot all about it. When I went to Auckland for their Suffrage Afternoon Tea, I saw at the entrance to the Aotea Centre a very large portrait of me displayed on an easel. It was just not me and I was quite shattered. Portraits are tricky things and I felt sorry for the artist, knowing that if she had actually seen me, the result would probably have been different. I was hurried past the painting by the organisers who were anxious to get me seated before the function began. After the function, I looked around for the artist but never met her, which I regret.

Some weeks later, a large crated parcel arrived in my Wellington office, which turned out to be the portrait. I leaned it against my office wall and colleagues came to see it. No one thought it was a good likeness and several went off into peals of laughter. Mary finally put it in the storeroom nearby and in the pace of the year, I forgot about it. When I retired, it was left behind. Mary's new boss Chris Carter, MP for Te Atatu, saw it, asked why it was there and was told the story. He said he would like to take it to his new apartment, and that's what happened. When he lost his seat, he and his partner Peter Kaiser kept the apartment and rented it to two new Labour list MPs, Mark Gosche and Marion Hobbs. At a meeting recently, Marion told me laughing that when she comes home very late, my eyes seem to follow her.

Around then, the Correspondence School children gathered together from remote areas on their annual visit to the capital. One of their experiences was to visit Parliament, and Ruth Richardson, Joy McLauchlan, Liz Tennet and I were asked to speak to them. One of the children asked Ruth what her children thought about her being a Cabinet minister. She said that her small son was becoming adept at cartoons, and when she went home the previous weekend, he had presented her with one which showed her with a balloon coming out of her mouth which said 'Blah, blah, blah.' She told them that, like all MPs, she spends a lot of time in the weekends talking to constituents on the phone. Sometimes her daughter becomes exasperated and puts a list in front of her mother, asking her to tick the appropriate spot. It asked whether she would be another five, ten or fifteen minutes. The children asked her about the Budget and she told them that because she was a woman Finance Minister, the media was more interested in what clothes she would wear to present the Budget than its contents. We all had a lively and enjoyable discussion. For years, I had admired the work of the Correspondence School, and had seen how much it was appreciated by families in rural areas.

All during these last years, I was a member of the New Zealand Council of the Labour Party and attended two-day meetings at weekends several times a year. It was good to work with key Labour Party people from the North and South Islands. I had come full circle, having been on the Council in the 1970s. Council members were more accountable to their constituencies than they had been in the past. When I first served on the Council this time round, Ruth Dyson was president and was then succeeded by Maryan Street.

It was great to work again with people I had known for years, like Tony Timms, Murdo McMillan and Jo Fitzpatrick, and to have Maori representatives on the council. Eddie Dickson was a strong advocate on the council for the trade unions. For years the Labour Women's Council, which was the successor of the Women's Advisory Committee that Margaret Shields and I had founded in the 1970s, was a force to be reckoned with. They were all part of the rich warp and weft of my last years in Parliament.

We were at a very interesting time for the Party. We knew that we would have a referendum on Mixed Member Proportional Representation (MMP) at the next election, and were gearing up to deal with it if, as we suspected, the majority of electors wanted it. Like most parties, we had people who were passionately in favour of MMP and others just as strongly against. I was not convinced that MMP would give us the sort of Parliament I felt would be better for all people; but the Westminster, first-past-the-post system was too adversarial and restrictive, and I wanted it replaced by one that allowed real consultation and consensus and a lot less time-wasting in debate.

MPs who were standing again in 1993 were honing up their election campaigns. In August, we were notified that the Commonwealth Parliamentary Association (CPA) Conference was to be held in Larnaca, Cyprus. The Government was sending Geoff Whittaker, MP for Hastings, and Jeff Grant, MP for Awarua. The Labour Caucus decided that I should go to represent the Opposition. My previous visits to Cyprus had been shoestring affairs, modest hotels, self-paid transport, but this was different. I found that, within the bounds of my travel budget, I could go via London and Geneva, which would give me a chance to see Wendy and Ian Dear in London and Tord Kjelstrom and Adrienne Taylor in Geneva. It was on this visit that Wendy took me straight from Gatwick Airport to see the wonderful garden at Sissinghurst in Kent. Tord and Adrienne were just back from Italy. We had a dinner party to which they invited Con's youngest daughter, who has lived in Geneva for many years. They saw me off to Larnaca where I arrived in bright sunlight.

The hotel where I stayed in Larnaca was alongside a wide sandy beach, and it was here also that the conference was to be held. One of the issues to be debated was the upcoming United Nations Year of the Family, and

(Left) Wendy and Ian Dear at Hazeldene in Wimbledon; (right) at Sissinghurst in the rain, admiring Vita's garden

what CPA countries could do to strengthen and support families. I had discussed this with the Labour Women's Caucus before I left, and had prepared a contribution which talked about ways of combatting violence, telling delegates about the work of the Hamilton Abuse Intervention Programme and what we were doing in our country to deal with rape and incest. The two Government MPs had brought the issues the National Government believed the Year of the Family should promote, and we were a good team. Both of them were retiring at the election as well, and we were determined to represent our country well.

Cyprus is a historic country and, out of conference hours, we were taken to visit ancient buildings and had dinner one night in the grounds of a huge old castle. Of course, we were taken to see the artificial barrier between Greek- and Turkish-occupied Cyprus. In this day and age, it seems tragic that mediation cannot resolve the impasse and that families remain lost to each other. We talked with local politicians about this issue, but they weren't too hopeful of a solution.

When I presented my paper, it soon became obvious from the body language of the predominantly male audience that they didn't want to debate the issues I was concentrating on. Several delegates spoke opposing the proposition that much violence begins in the home, and that the causes of violence need to be tackled, not just the symptoms. They implied that such issues had no part in the Year of the Family. My parliamentary colleagues spoke out in firm support of what I had said. It was finally decided that a resolution spelling out the causes of violence and what could

New Zealand's parliamentary delegation to the CPA Conference in Cyprus, from left: Jeff Whittaker MP, Jeff Grant MP, myself, and Kerry Scott from the Committee Clerk's Office

be done about it should be included in the report of the conference.

When this session ended, a delegate from the Channel Islands came to me and said, 'Mrs Davies, how do you spell that word incest? We don't seem to have heard of it in my constituency.' I wanted to say, 'In your dreams, buddy,' but controlled myself and said he should speak to social workers at home.

When the final report appeared, I discovered that my section, which had been agreed upon, was not included. I went to see the secretariat, where there was some embarrassment. I said I would raise it in the final plenary session, so they realised that I was in earnest and told me it had been accidentally omitted and would be reinstated. It is this sort of refusal to face and discuss the issues that is part of the problem; at least New Zealand can claim to be past that initial barrier.

When I returned to New Zealand, I found that my diary was even more tightly packed. With all the myriad strands of my life, getting through it all was going to need a super balancing act. Early in the morning on 16 September, I went to Naenae College for a Suffrage Breakfast with young women senior students. Joy McLauchlan, MP for Western Hutt, was there with me, and we enjoyed a great breakfast provided by senior male students — something that would not have happened when I was at secondary school. Joy and I talked to the female students about the long hard struggle for women's suffrage and the importance for them to be aware that they were the people of the future, and they needed to keep faith with Kate Sheppard and all the other women who had made it possible for them to vote.

In the next weeks, I was all over the country: a pensioners' meeting to support Phil Goff in Mt Roskill, followed by a suffrage speech at a packed meeting at the Auckland Museum; a speech at the launch of the book *Women in the House* by Janet McCallum in the banquet hall in the Beehive.

On 23 September, I made my valedictory speech in the House and was quite frank about my feelings on free market policies and asset sales. The previous night, the caucus had given me a splendid farewell. Koro Wetere came up trumps with smoked trout, Jonathan Hunt gave me a much-appreciated engraved silver tray, and I received other farewell gifts from caucus.

Back in Wellington, I opened the Frances Hodgkins Collection at the National Museum and raced around the electorate to various functions, feeling sad that it was for the last time.

On 28 September my favourite brother-in-law Larry died. A gentle loving man, a builder by trade, Larry was mourned by his large family and in particular by his wife Merle. They had married when they were very young and had a very good marriage. He is still greatly missed.

I was then asked to take part in a television programme to be used during the election campaign. It was filmed on the top floor of the now mammoth Majestic Building and one had the feeling that we were floating in the sky. Helen Clark was also in the programme, which was shown some weeks later.

The end of the year was so busy that finding time to sleep became problematical. We launched the Women's Policy early one morning in the function room at the Wellington Botanic Gardens and I went off to be interviewed by Kim Hill and later by Gordon McLauchlan. Early that evening, I flew to Auckland to speak at a fund-raising dinner in Te Atatu, and the evening of the day after I arrived back in Wellington, I married Kay Miller and Dennis Middleton.

When they first came to see me, I had asked them where the marriage would take place and they said they would like to be married in my parliamentary office. So that is what happened. A tiny baby was the youngest participant and behaved impeccably, lying in a carrycot on my desk. Kay is a speech therapist and had been very good to Penny when she came down from Kohukohu.

Two days later, I flew to Wairoa to open the Community Childcare

(Left) with Cath Tizard at my seventieth birthday party on the ferry on Wellington Harbour; (right) guests Franya Johnstone, Mary O'Regan and Gaylene Preston

Centre. This was a splendid centre. Wairoa is an amazing place. Years ago, playwright and author Renee had got me up there to open a women's centre. There is still one operating, though in a different place. It seemed to me that whatever the women of Wairoa did they did well, and the child-care centre was no exception.

The following weekend, Pencarrow Labour Party members gave me a farewell barbecue at the home of Trevor Mallard and his wife Stephanie in Wainuiomata. Trevor had been selected to succeed me, and he and Stephanie had bought a house not far from his old school. Many people I had worked with came to the barbecue, and I realised how much I would miss them all. I didn't have time to dwell on that, though, because I was still travelling — to New Plymouth to speak at Spotswood College, then to Wanganui to speak at a dinner.

November 6 was Election Day, and I was at the Kokiri in Wainuiomata when Trevor won handsomely. Hutt Taxis gave me a special afternoon tea and a huge bouquet of silk flowers. The Hutt City Council farewelled me at an evening function.

The next day was my birthday and I woke to posies of flowers. Birthdays are perhaps a time to take stock of one's life, but I barely had time to squeeze mine in! I had to fly to Christchurch to speak at a packed meeting, and flew back to be met by Mary, got changed and went off to my seventieth birthday party which was held on the Trustbank ferry on

Wellington Harbour. The days before the event were cold, wet and windy and we were worried this might continue over my birthday, but it was a perfect evening with a calm, flat ocean and, later on, a full moon. The ferry was packed with 84 of my dearest friends, and it was certainly a night to remember.

My brother David was about to embark on a tour of the South Island with his over-fifties motorcycle club. He stayed with me, and before I got back from Christchurch had gone with Charlie and Nancy Baldwin to Mary's to have a pre-party drink — or two. There were friends from all around the country and it was definitely my best-ever birthday party, with wonderful food and champagne and lots of music and fun. David and I got back to my apartment quite late, and in the morning he wheeled his huge bike out and was immediately surrounded by little boys.

I then had to get to the airport to go to Nelson to speak at the nurses' graduation ceremony at the Polytechnic. I had watched the development of this facility over the years and had opened their childcare centre a few years earlier. It had grown into a very important part of Nelson's education scene. I spent the whole day there and fell in love all over again with Nelson. Just so that I wouldn't be bereft of things to do at the weekend, there was a meeting of the New Zealand Council of the Labour Party.

The rest of the year was full of prizegiving ceremonies at schools in the Hutt Valley, and, everywhere I went, the students sang 'Bread and Roses' for me.

And then it was time to move on, to get on with the rest of my life. I had a phonecall from women in Wainuiomata, who said that they wanted me to meet them at the Wainuiomata Rugby League Clubrooms for a farewell function. When I arrived, I found many women I had worked with during my time in office. They showed me their farewell gift. It was a glowing patchwork quilt made up of individual patches donated by women, each containing a personal message, some of them embroidered. It was colourful and truly special and is one of my treasures. When I was ill with flu in 1996, I lay in bed covered with this quilt and kept finding new messages which gladdened my heart.

Part Three

Retirement

The Making of the Film Bread and Roses

When I was working for the Shop Employees Union, I first met Gaylene Preston, the film-maker whom Graham Kelly enlisted to do some illustrations for our union magazine. I was impressed by the quality of her work and her strong social conscience. When my son Mark died so tragically, it was Gaylene who produced exactly the right drawing of Mark in the New Zealand bush he loved so much, and we used it for the card that was sent to the hundreds of people who had given me support at that time.

Gaylene and another film-maker, Robin Laing, had teamed up to form the company Preston°Laing Productions. Over the years they have become respected and admired for the excellence of their work. In the early 1980s, they decided that the lives of women during and after World War II had not really been recorded and they started developing a fiction film along those lines.

In 1984, when my book *Bread and Roses* was published, Gaylene read it and Robin listened to me reading it on Radio New Zealand, and both decided that they could use it as the basis for a film. Over the next few years they both discussed this proposition with me. I must say that, at that time, I couldn't believe that investors would put money into filming what I'd written. I doubted that it would happen. In the event, I underestimated their tenacity and strength of purpose.

In 1991, Gaylene and Robin reported to me that they had obtained some developmental money and they intended to proceed. I was amazed, but shouldn't have been. By this time, with films such as *Mr Wrong* having successful runs, they were becoming well-known and respected in the film world.

Nevertheless, they knew that a television drama documentary costs a great deal of money and that would mean obtaining finance overseas. This would not be easy for such an obviously New Zealand film, so they employed an amazing woman, Dorothee Pinfold, as executive producer to negotiate investments. Dorothee later said that it was one of the hardest sells she had ever undertaken. But the film-makers' faith in her abilities was justified, and although the budget would never be quite enough for such a film, with super-careful handling, it could be done. In the end, funding came from the New Zealand Film Commission, from Australia, from a company called Beyond International Television, from Television New Zealand, New Zealand on Air, and from the New Zealand Women's Suffrage Trust.

In the meantime, Gaylene and Robin had enlisted an experienced scriptwriter, Graeme Tetley, to adapt the book for film. Graeme is a warm, intelligent man who undertook this task with confidence. We had a number of discussions about the script and, before long, copies of the episodes started arriving on my desk. By that time, my life in the House and outside it had become so frantic that I sometimes found myself going through the script at one o'clock in the morning.

When I came out of hospital after I broke my shoulder and was recovering from surgery, I went early each morning to Hutt Hospital to use the hydrotherapy pool and to have physiotherapy. Gaylene suggested that she come out to Eastbourne each morning, so that we could go through the script together when I got home. This we did and it turned out to be a most useful exercise. On fine days, we would take deckchairs onto the beach opposite my apartment and, in that peaceful environment, would go through the events of my life as they were to be portrayed.

Gaylene questioned me closely about the clothes we wore, the furnishings and the language we used. I realised that she was making up her mind about a great many things. An upstairs warehouse was leased in Adelaide Road, where the film crew and administration staff would be based.

The important issue of casting for the film began to be addressed. From the beginning, there was a lot of interest in who would portray me, and only weeks before shooting was to start, Gaylene told me that she and Robin really hadn't found the right person. And then Genevieve Picot appeared on the scene. From the minute I saw her on video, I knew quite positively that she was absolutely the right person. The fact that she was taller than they wanted and older, and Australian to boot, quickly became irrelevant.

Mick Rose was to play the part of Charlie, and Tina Regtien that of my dear friend Con. Tina worked closely with Con's granddaughters, who talked to her about Con as they knew her. Donna Akersten was given the part of my mother and Erik Thompson was chosen to play Red Brinsen. Erik was the only one I didn't meet or talk to, and I think that was a pity.

A great many extras were needed, and I kept meeting people who told me they had been co-opted. One of the requirements for the men was that they had to have their hair cut in the short-back-and-sides style. This was done by the makeup department, with mixed reactions. Graham Kelly told me that he was to play the piano with the band in the Majestic Cabaret scene, to be shot in the old Town Hall. I told him he would have to have his hair cut, so he went off and had it done by his own hairdresser. It was certainly shorter but definitely not what I knew makeup would want. I told him so, but he was confident that it would be all right.

On the Sunday when this scene was shot, Mary and I went to watch. I looked at the musicians on the stage and could see no sign of Graham. I commented on his absence to Mary, and she suggested I look harder at the man in the middle of the stage. Eventually, I recognised him. A very shorn Graham conveyed his feelings strongly to me. He had also been told to play the piano without his glasses on as they were too modern in design; it is rather unfortunate that when the film finally emerged, the camera didn't really cover him.

The search for clothes for cast and extras was intense, but sometimes what was needed was impossible to find and the garments had to be made. The sets that were created in the warehouse were a real example of Kiwi ingenuity. All the crew did the maximum amount of work on a minimum budget. Sets were dismantled after use and recycled for another purpose.

Around that time, another Wellington Hospital Nurses' reunion was held one weekend, and Gaylene talked to us about the nursing scenes in the film. She met members of my Gang and had lots of useful details explained. When some of the nurses' home scenes were shot at the old deserted Erskine College in Island Bay, members of the Gang came with me to comment on any aspect they thought not quite right. At lunch on the playing field, they told me that they were very impressed.

When the property people contacted Wellington Hospital to see if they could borrow some ward utensils that would have been used in my days as a nurse, they found that they had all gone to the tip. In the end, Wanganui Hospital provided them from its display of past uniforms and tools of the trade. I didn't know about this until I was invited to speak to the staff at Wanganui Hospital, when I was given a photo of the items they had loaned.

For me, the most dramatic and exciting event was the filming of the Nelson Railway protest. This turned out to be a very expensive exercise. The exact steam train we needed was actually on rails and in working order at Silverstream, but that line wasn't linked to the Wairarapa line on which was Maymorn, the small station close to the Rimutaka tunnel that had been chosen because it was the nearest thing to Kiwi Station at Glenhope. So the film-makers had to go to Paekakariki to obtain a different train and have it brought to Maymorn via Wellington.

I had been away for the weekend and caught the six-forty a.m. train in order to attend meetings on the Monday. A lot of people travel on that train, and when we reached Maymorn, I saw that its sign had been replaced with one that read 'Kiwi'. People were milling around the station

167

In the cab of the steam train at Maymorn during the filming of the Nelson Railway protest

and the train had to stop to pick up a couple of passengers. Everyone in my carriage wanted to know what was happening. Usually Maymorn is quiet and deserted, but here were dozens of people, camera crew and directors. I told them what was happening and they were most interested.

On the day the steam train was being brought to Maymorn/Kiwi, driven by Margaret Shields' brother Steve, I wanted to be there. I was due to attend an ecumenical church service to celebrate the beginning of Women's Suffrage Year at St Paul's Cathedral that morning. I had just emerged from the shower when there was a knock on my door. I wondered who on earth it could be so early on a Sunday morning and opened the door to find a very battered woman, who asked me to help her.

When I had given her a hot drink, I said I would ring the Hutt Women's Refuge and take her there, but she became very upset and said she didn't want anyone local to know and would prefer to go elsewhere. This involved my finding the best place to take her, and by the time I had delivered her and explained the situation to the refuge workers, I was running out of time. I hadn't had time to have any breakfast and felt rather light-headed, but drove to St Paul's. I found all the carparks crowded and in the end had to park almost at the top of Hill Street and run down the hill before the church service began. I took my place next to Fran Wilde and settled back to listen to the service.

Halfway through, I realised that all was not well with me and told Fran I was going out through the side entrance. Fran insisted on coming with me and asked the bishop if he had a sofa in his office. He said, 'I'm not

Lunch with the Gang at Paekakariki on a later occasion

that sort of bishop', but she was not amused and (over my objections) rang the ambulance, which arrived at the Molesworth Street entrance. The media was present, and that evening I appeared on TV, being wheeled to the ambulance. Mary had arranged to meet me after the church service and arrived just after I had left in the ambulance for Wellington Hospital. She actually beat us to the hospital and was there when I was wheeled into casualty. A young intern was determined to investigate me thoroughly until one of the nurses said, 'What she actually needs is a hot sweet drink and something to eat.' Mary was appalled to find I still wanted to go to Maymorn/Kiwi, but I wasn't going to miss that train for anyone. So we bought some food and off we went.

There were so many extras whom I knew. The men portraying the police who arrested me at Kiwi were dressed in 1950s uniforms. They asked me exactly what the police had said to us when we were arrested. There was a difficulty with the steam train, because when the Wairarapa train was due, it had to be taken off the main line and put on a siding.

Genevieve told me she couldn't understand how we could have sat in front of that train, not knowing whether it would stop or not; she found it scary enough when she knew it would stop. During the afternoon, Steve, the engine driver, asked me if I would like to ride in the cab of the train, so I realised an old childhood dream.

On another occasion, when the crew was shooting other scenes without the train, I told them that we had a marvellous homemade pie shop in Kuripuni in Masterton and that I was going to bring enough for everyone on the ten o'clock train. The House was in recess at that time so I was able to spend most of the day with them. I picked up the hot pies and the guards took the large covered carton and put it in the guard's van.

Sometimes, when the House was in session, Mary would tell me that the crew had a series of questions for me and could I approach Jonathan Hunt to see if he would give me a couple of hours to go to Newtown. Jonathan was then Chief Opposition Whip and always tried to accommodate me by changing the order of the jigsaw of events that was part of our daily lives. On one occasion I was taken to see Kit Rollings, the sound editor, in what was once the National Film Unit, and was amazed at the complexity and precision of his work.

Paul Sutorius was the film editor and over the time of film-making, I would go and watch what he was doing. Finally, he rang and said he had almost finished the first episode of the four-part TV film series (later made into a two-part film) and they wanted me to see it. I had seen some scenes by then but not the whole finished episode. I went on my own on a Friday when the House was not in session. That was a mistake, as I was so affected when I saw the film that I burst into tears and wondered how I could ever thank all those marvellous people who had produced such a faithful and skilful result.

I was fascinated by the camera crew, headed by director of photography Alan Guilford and camera operators Alun Bollinger and Leon Narbey. I watched them at work on a number of occasions and knew that the people who had told me that these were highly qualified, innovative and skilled craftsmen had not exaggerated.

My one regret was that it was not possible to use any of the wonderfully evocative songs of the war years because of the cost of permission fees which was quite astronomical — something the film budget was not. But of course the song 'Bread and Roses' was sung, and it is rich and moving.

Once the film was finished, plans for the launch swung into action. On 18 July, it was premiered as a two-part film in the Wellington International Film Festival. On the night, the Embassy Theatre was packed. I had seen the film in episodes at the studio in Adelaide Road, but it was different in a theatre filled with so many good friends and acquaintances, and on a wide screen. Dame Cath Tizard was there and Jenny Shipley, who at that time was Minister of Women's Affairs, and many people who had been my friends and companions over the years. Suddenly, I was extremely nervous. The film had been made as a four-part television series so it was very long, and I wondered how people would cope with that. Cath Tizard was sitting behind me and sensed something of what I was feeling. She leaned over and said, 'Don't worry, it'll be great.'

*Me, Gaylene Preston and Genevieve Picot on location at
'Kiwi'.* Guy Robinson

It was an amazing night and there was no doubt that people liked the film very much. As we left the theatre, people were saying, 'Why did it stop there? Where's the rest?' — as they did everywhere the film was shown. Over at the Opera Restaurant in Courtenay Place where the after-film party was being held, Jenny Shipley stood on the stairs and made a very graceful speech.

After the Wellington run, the film went to Auckland, and my daughter and son-in-law came down from Kohukohu to see it. We knew that the big test would be in Nelson, and Gaylene asked me to go with her for the first night there. At the end of the film, there was absolute silence from the packed theatre. I whispered to Gaylene, 'They hate it,' and then someone said, 'Three cheers for Sonja!' and the place erupted. As we left the theatre, we met the next audience waiting outside. Several of the first audience said that they knew that the Nelson scenes had not been shot there because the sky was different and the shape of the beach was wrong.

Preston°Laing, the cast and crew all richly deserved the good things that were said about the film. By now it was 1992; but it wasn't until 1993 and Women's Suffrage Year that the four-part mini-series appeared on four successive Sundays on *Montana Sunday Theatre*. Some time later, Learning Media published a video on the making of the film for the Ministry of Education, to be used in secondary schools here and overseas.

In 1994, at the Annual Film and Television Awards in Auckland, I accepted on Genevieve Picot's behalf the award for Best Female Acting Performance. She received that award for both film and television. Mick Rose received the Best Supporting Actor Award for television, and *Bread and Roses* was also awarded the Best Design Award. At the Melbourne Film Festival, it was voted most popular film by the audience. Not surprisingly, it had my vote!

By the Waters of Babylon

By the waters of Babylon,
When we sat down
And wept when we remembered thee

In 1984, my daughter Penny and her partner Mick moved from Newtown to Titahi Bay. Both of them found teaching positions at Porirua College. They lived very close to the seafront and it was here that my middle grandson, Tim, began his attachment to surfing. At times on that coast the conditions are quite wild; for Tim, the wilder the better. By this time, my eldest grandson Tracy (who became Tony in the macho climate of Brisbane) had gone to Australia to live and work, and apart from brief visits had not come back.

The house they had bought was close to the street, behind a hedge, on a long section with a stream running through. Had they had the money, the house could have been moved further back and another storey built on top so that they could see the ocean. It certainly had possibilities. Penny had a real gift for making wherever she lived as comfortable a home as possible.

Both Penny and Mick became immersed in the work and politics of Porirua College, which was very much a multicultural establishment. By 1986, they were thinking of moving north. In 1988, Penny applied for a position at Panguru Area School in the Hokianga, and she began teaching there in late January the next year. She and Mick were allocated a two-bedroom unit that was one of two on the property, close to the school. Neither Tim or Ben, my youngest grandson, moved north. Ben spent a year in Australia while Tim worked through his builder's apprenticeship. They left their two dogs, Freckles and Frisky, with Penny and Mick.

Mick stayed on in Titahi Bay until the house sale was finalised some months later and then joined Penny. He did a lot of relief teaching in schools around Northland and tutored an access course teaching computer literacy and keyboard skills. In 1986 he had had plans to build a waka at Porirua College. Up at Panguru, he dusted these plans off and, with the help of young unemployed people, created the waka.

Penny in London in happier times

Penny taught English at Panguru, was in charge of the library and was the guidance counsellor for the female students. She was a good teacher and was delighted to work in a school where the students were predominantly Maori. In the Panguru village there are two marae, and Dame Whina Cooper lived in a house not far from the school. On my first visit, Penny took me to her school to meet the staff and students. The area has a strong Catholic background, and there were two priests on the staff who lived in a house near Penny and Mick.

The whole of the Hokianga area has a dream-like, subtropical aspect, with mangroves along the shore of the harbour. At that time, a large proportion of the population was on a state benefit of one kind or another, due to the high level of unemployment. Many people had gone to Auckland to look for work. Penny was particularly keen to see her young women students go out into the world as well qualified as possible, but a number of parents didn't see the further education of their daughters as a priority. 'We just want her to get married and give us mokopuna (grandchildren),' was often the response to Penny's request that they consider university or polytechnic education for a bright, intelligent young woman.

Through her work as a guidance counsellor, Penny realised that a number of the girls were victims of incest, and others were being beaten. Late one night, a badly beaten girl arrived at Penny and Mick's home with her sister, seeking help. They took the two girls to the doctor the next day, contacted the Department of Social Welfare and spoke with the social worker responsible for these girls. The social worker's opinion was that the whanau should handle the problem. Penny and Mick felt that the whanau would simply leave it up to the abuser to deal with the problem, so they took the frightened girls to the doctor, who had the power to officially report the nature of the abuse and demand Social Welfare support. As a consequence, the girls were taken into care in Kaitaia and later lived independent lives. The incident reinforced my awareness of the difficulty victims have in getting free from their situations, the serious need for sound training for social workers, and the difficulties of reconciling conflicting priorities of cultural and ethical values (was the social worker putting respect for the whanau before the welfare of the girls?)

In the middle of 1990, Penny started telling me in her letters that she wasn't well, and that her leg was feeling heavy. Her doctor was unable to find any cause for this and she began living through a frustrating time, telling herself to brace up and stop imagining things. Then her right hand became affected, making writing difficult. She taught herself to write with her left hand, and her students began calling for her in the morning to carry her books to school. This was a touching indication of the affection they must have had for her.

In 1991, she applied successfully for an annual study grant for teachers in area schools. She gained one of the two grants that were available: this would give her a year's study in Auckland, where she was planning to gain a diploma in Teaching English as a Second Language.

Wanting to be fit for her year's study and becoming more and more concerned about her health, Penny went back to her doctor, who was still unable to make a diagnosis and referred her to a neurologist at Auckland Hospital. After a series of tests, the neurologist told her quite bluntly that she had motor neurone disease, that there was no cure for it, and that she was going to die. We were all devastated and had to try to come to terms with all that this brief information implied. We tried to find out what we could about the disease. I recently saw the mother of the English scientist Stephen Hawking on television talking about how he was diagnosed as having MND when he was 21. She went to see the neurologist who had made the diagnosis. When she asked what she could do to make her son's life more comfortable, he said, 'Very little,' in a dismissive way.

I knew that Nedra Shand, who works in the Parliamentary Library, was active in the MND Association and went to talk to her. She was very helpful and a tower of strength for me all through Penny's illness. Through Nedra I learned that MND is a group of conditions that affect the cells in the nervous system that control voluntary movement (motor neurones) so that progressive weakness and paralysis occur. The disease affects people in different ways: some have difficulty swallowing and voice loss before they lose the use of their limbs; others, like Penny, lose the use of their limbs and later their voice and the ability to swallow.

For some time, Penny and Mick had been talking about buying a piece of land out in the country and becoming as self-sufficient as possible. This was obviously not practicable now. I questioned the wisdom of staying in such a remote place where professional support would be harder to come by, but Penny was adamant. She loved the Hokianga and its people and that was where she wanted to stay. There were two other MND sufferers in the Hokianga, one a relatively young man and the other a former *Northland Star* reporter in his late forties, who was in the hospital at Rawene.

In December 1991, Mick and Penny reported that they had bought the lovely old Anglican vicarage situated beside the Anglican church in Kohukohu, some distance from Panguru. There was no longer an Anglican vicar in Kohukohu, and clergy from a variety of churches came from time to time to conduct services. Kohukohu itself was typical of small towns that had been affected by the curtailment of the post office service. Once it had had a fully functional post office with banking facilities; there was a garage where cars could be repaired, a local butcher, a draper, a local store and a coffee shop. Today, the post office is open for a couple of hours Monday to Friday but banking deposits and withdrawals are not possible; the butcher, draper and coffee shop have gone as has the mechanic service.

Across the harbour is Rawene, where the controversial Dr Smith practised medicine. In the 1940s, Dr Smith went to work in Northland and established a model health service there offering free, quality health care. He had very definite ideas about how this should operate and these didn't always find favour with more conservative medical people. The hospital is still there, but struggling. There is a car ferry which travels between Kohukohu and Rawene, much used by travellers and locals alike.

When they moved to Kohukohu, Penny could still walk but needed assistance, and before long she had to resort to a wheelchair. MND does not usually affect the patient's intelligence. I realised then that, while nursing at Wellington Hospital in the 1940s, I had actually nursed two cases of MND, though it wasn't called that then, and I was ashamed when I remembered I had simply taken for granted that the patient's brain was impaired as well because they couldn't speak or move.

As soon as I saw it, I liked the old kauri vicarage very much. I used to fly to Auckland, change to a much smaller plane and fly to Kerikeri, which was just over one hour's drive from Kohukohu. For as long as she could, Penny came with Mick to meet me, and we would shop before going home. On the next Waitangi Day, we went to Waitangi for the ceremony. We had a bit of a crisis when Penny needed to use the toilet and Mick had to go into the women's toilets with her because I couldn't lift her in and

Penny and Mick's Kohukohu home

out of the wheelchair. But when people knew the reason, they were very kind and helped.

Penny wanted to go to Purakanui near Dunedin to visit the graves of her ancestors. It took some organisation, but ultimately she was taken to Auckland Airport by Mick, who saw her settled on the front seat of the aircraft which would stop at Wellington, where I would join her and go on to Dunedin. Once there, we were met by my friend Heinke Matheson who helped me get Penny into her car and drove us to the motel that she had chosen for us, which had good facilities for disabled people. Social Welfare, through my then colleague Clive Matthewson, the MP for Dunedin Central, had provided two absolutely splendid nurses who were skilful and caring. After we had eaten and Heinke had gone home to her family, the nurses showered Penny and settled her for the night. She had had a long day and was very tired. It was almost midnight when the nurses went home. The next morning when she was rested, we were going to Purakanui to find Great-grandmother Maria's cottage and the graves of our family.

After the nurses had gone, I had a shower and popped in to see Penny. To my horror, I found her with cramp in all parts of her body. I tried everything I could, drawing on my experience to alleviate the severe pain I knew she was in, but with little success. I hated to do it, but I needed the nurses' help, so I rang the number I had been given, apologised and explained the problem. The nurse had just been getting into bed, but didn't hesitate and was soon with us, coping and relieving the pain. Even with her expert help, it took some time to ensure that all the cramps were gone and we could all retire thankfully for the night.

*Penny being hauled back up from the grave of her ances-
tors at Purakanui*

My Hutt Taxi people had given me the name of a Dunedin taxi
company which could provide a taxi van with a hoist so that Penny could
be lifted into it with as little strain as possible. Heinke arrived with
wonderful food and we set off with one of the nurses accompanying us.
We went first to Murdering Beach, where our ancestor Richard Driver
had come in with a longboat to get water for his whaling ship. The story
of all that is documented in *Bread and Roses*.

My great-great-grandmother Motoitoi had died of tuberculosis (introduced by the immigrants) after she had borne three little girls to her
husband Richard Driver. She was the founder of our whakapapa and the
mother of my great-grandmother. We tried to find her grave, but were
certain it would not be in a formal cemetery. When I had planned this
visit, I had asked my cousin Whetu Tirikatene-Sullivan to come with us,
but in the end she was unable to. We finally figured that a very young
Maori woman, no matter how highly born, would not be of much consequence in the society of the day and she was probably in an unmarked
grave.

On the way to Purakanui to find Great-grandmother Maria's cottage, I
tried to envisage it as I remembered it during my childhood, but most of
the surroundings seemed to have changed. There was no road past the
cottages when I was little and we arrived by boat. We finally pinpointed a
couple which may just have been right and then went off to the cemetery.

There was just one snag about the cemetery. The graves were at the
bottom of quite a steep slope. However, our splendid taxi driver and the
nurse said not to worry. They would take Penny slowly down there. We

found Maria's grave and those of Richard Driver, his second wife Elizabeth Robertson, and many relatives. Getting Penny back up in the wheelchair was something else, but it was done and I have the photos to show it.

The next morning, we went to the old Otago Early Settlers Museum and saw Richard Driver's portrait, taken when he was the first pilot of the port. And then it was time to begin the return journey and to say goodbye to the people who had made it all possible. I left Penny at Wellington in the care of an air hostess, and rang Mick, who said he would be at the airport in Auckland to meet her. They were to stay overnight in Auckland with friends Kate and Mike Donoghue, whom Penny loved and who were so supportive through all her illness, and then go back to Kohukohu. Mick reported that, though tired, Penny had found it a very worthwhile experience.

When Tony, Tim and Ben learned about Penny's diagnosis, they were devastated. Tony came over from Sydney, and Penny was delighted to see him. He came down to Wellington afterwards, and he and I, Tim and Ben and Penny's ex-husband Syd, father of Tim and Ben, all talked about what we could do to help Penny. It was a fraught time for all of us.

Penny loved the outdoors so Mick and local friends would take her to the wonderful Northland beaches. When her boys visited, they would go on expeditions with her and she enjoyed those. The people of the area were very supportive from the very beginning of her illness. She loved to visit her school and I went with her a couple of times. Teachers and students alike were always pleased to see her. When it was no longer possible for her to travel, the students would get one or two of their teachers to bring them over from Panguru during the school lunch hour. They would bring their lunch and their musical instruments so that they could play and sing to her.

When Penny and Mick first moved into the vicarage, knowing that Penny would spend a lot of time in her bedroom, and while she was still able to go to shops and choose paint and curtains, the two of them created a very attractive room. It looked out over the Hokianga harbour. For some time, Penny was able to sit out on the front verandah on sunny days — and there are many of those in that region.

Like most old colonial homes in this country that have been left intact and not refurbished, the vicarage had a less than upmarket bathroom, with a semi-detached toilet off the washhouse. The bath was a very high one and above it was a shower. To shower Penny, Mick had to lift her in and out of the bath. At that time, her body had a fair amount of water retention and she was heavier than she was later as the MND progressed. It put a lot of strain on Mick's back.

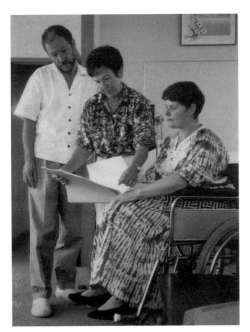

Penny and Mick visiting her old school, with principal Jill Parker

Penny and Mick had made enquiries and had found that, for terminally disabled people, it was possible to obtain a loan from Social Welfare (which would have to be repaid later), and that they could have an en suite bathroom custom-designed for Penny so that she could be wheeled in and under the shower in a special chair. This seemed to me to be eminently sensible, so I suggested that the time had surely arrived to apply for the loan. Not long afterwards, I was in the House at question time when a messenger came and told me that there was a tollcall for me in the lobby. It was Mick, very angry because their application for a loan had been turned down on the basis that Penny was not completely immobilised and they would need to wait until she was. I told him to hang in there and I would see what I could do.

By this time I was part of the Opposition; I had three years' experience of living in the belly of the beast under my belt, and was a much more assured person. Jonathan Hunt was Chief Opposition Whip. He was very understanding about the situation I was in. This was in pre-MMP times and it was not the done thing to ally oneself publicly with the politicians across the floor of the House. After question time, I crossed the floor of the House and sat beside the Chief Government Whip, John Carter, who at that time shared the electorate of the Far North with Northern Maori MP Bruce Gregory. I looked up and saw that Jonathan had questions on his face.

I told John what had happened and suggested that he go and see Penny and Mick at the weekend to satisfy himself that what I was saying was true. I said I was desperate enough to talk to *Fair Go*, as it was all so patently unfair. From time to time, John and I had arrived on the same plane in Kerikeri and I had introduced him to Penny waiting for me in her wheelchair. He knew that I had a genuine grievance. He asked me to leave the problem with him and he would see me later. Just before the House rose, he came across and sat beside me, causing his colleagues and mine to stare, and said I should ask Mick to get three quotes for the work and submit them to Social Welfare, who would get in touch with him as soon as they had a recommendation. And so that was done. The en suite bathroom made all the difference to the quality of what was left of Penny's life. I couldn't help but think about all those others terminally ill but not quite immobilised people who are out there unable to get a grant but don't have the same lobbying power as I had.

By this time, it was obvious that Mick couldn't manage alone, and three carers came to help on a part-time basis: Kay Walker, Angela Schnaderbeck and Penny Collyns. Each had a different approach, each brought something valuable and special, and each really cared for Penny. Then there was Jackie, who created and maintained the garden that Penny had designed and which brought her great joy. There was a South African District Nurse who covered a large area but came as often as she could. She was unflappable, practical and a great person. Also Leah came several times a week to wash and iron and keep the house ticking over. She was a solo parent, lived in a lilac-painted house across the road, and had two teenage daughters. She was bright, fun and a great amateur theatrical person. She was accompanied each day by her white woolly dog, Elvis, who got along well with Tim's dog Freckles and was tolerated by Penny's small, shy cat, Hecate, a real witch's cat. In the house in front of the vicarage lived Daphne, a violin teacher of much passion who inspired many young musicians in this remote area. She was a good neighbour and visited Penny often, helping her in many ways.

Caregivers were essential to Penny, and yet their profession is undervalued and underpaid. Recently, someone was widely quoted in the media as saying that caregivers deserved to be paid very little as they only sit and watch television most of the day; from watching the hard physical work, the patience and caring that Penny received, I know this is a gross injustice.

One of the terrible things about MND is the inexorable advance of the disease. The patient has to come to grips with a new disability and find ways to deal with it, and then wake up days or at most weeks later to find yet another ability lost. We were told that the life expectancy for MND sufferers was two to four years, and that, at any given time, there were around 250 cases throughout the country; so I suppose it was not surprising that GPs were not exactly au fait with the disease. I had contacted my friend Merle Hyland's son Brian, who is on the staff of the Otago Medical School, and talked to him about MND. He told me that research was in progress into the causes and possible cure, but that the research was long-term and certainly not likely to have results in time for Penny. Like many neurological diseases, MND still has more questions than answers.

Mick's very elderly parents came from Devon every year. In the beginning they would stay for a while and then go on down in a campervan to spend some time on the beach at Kaiteriteri near Nelson. When age started to catch up with them, they would stay at a delightful homestay in Kohukohu.

As time went on, Penny began having difficulty with breathing and was initially supplied with a nebuliser. Eating was becoming problematical as well. The last reasonably stress-free meal I remember having with her was when Mick and I took her to Mangonui. We had lunch out on the deck at the famous fish restaurant — their scrumptious fish and chips: fresh fish caught that morning and crisp chips. For me, it was the last truly happy day that we all spent together.

Early in 1993, Mick was diagnosed as having cancer and went into Kawakawa Hospital for surgery. The surgeon was very hopeful but suggested that he go to Wellington for follow-up chemotherapy, just to be sure. It was arranged that Penny would be cared for at Te Omanga Hospice in Lower Hutt. I knew some of the staff and, as a Hutt MP, had met the board administering the hospice, knew their work and so was comforted to know that Penny would be in good care. One way or another, it was a difficult time. In the middle of it, I was admitted to Hutt Hospital with pneumonia. Once I was deemed strong enough to have visitors, each of whom was told to make their visit brief, I was astonished when the door opened and Mick wheeled Penny in to see me. With them were Tim and his girlfriend Shelley. I knew what an effort it must have been to get Penny there and was very touched. It was all quite bizarre really. Here was I hooked up with tubes, Mick just recovering from chemotherapy and looking frail, my poor terminally ill daughter, and Tim and Shelley looking appalled. But given all that, it was great to see them.

By then, the vicarage had had its sitting room redecorated and Mick had installed a woodburner with a wetback in the hall. Penny still had the use of two fingers, and with these she wrote poetry on the computer and answered as many as possible of the letters that came to her from all over the country, particularly those from old friends. Music had always been very important to her and was even more so now. I borrowed compact discs for her and Mick got her a good stereo. Robin Laing, one of my film-makers, sent up some great videos. She had talking books, and National Radio was a great support.

The next time I went up, Mike and Kate Donoghue were there. I told them that I had a growing sense of unease at the lack of medical overview and direction of Penny's MND. It seemed to me that because she was going to die, local doctors (who were run off their feet anyway) didn't feel there was much that they could do, and basically left her treatment to the carers and the district nurse. I felt there had to be something better than that. Kate and Mike said that they had a friend in Whangarei who was a GP, and they would talk to her on their way back to Auckland. As a result, we had a call from Dr Jim McLeod, who was then working at the Whangarei Public Hospital and was also the senior medical officer at the hospice there. He asked if we would like him to see Penny, assess her case and suggest things he could do for her. We consulted Penny who agreed, and we settled on a time for him to come.

From the minute I set eyes on him, I knew we had done the right thing. He spent a long time talking to Penny on her own, gave her a full physical examination — the first for several years, and made a number of practical suggestions. It is quite a long distance from Whangarei to the Hokianga, especially for a busy doctor. He said he would talk to the local GPs in Rawene about his proposals and was sure he would have their co-operation. He proposed to provide Penny with a morphine pump, which she could activate when her pain became severe. He also arranged to come back and check on her whenever possible. This was all very reassuring.

It was not long before this that Penny, who had become quite desperate about her total lack of independence, her pain and the thought of carrying on for some months, if not years, without hope, had asked me if I would give her an overdose and end it all. I was quite shattered because I believed it was her right to choose, but I just couldn't do it. I found out later that she had asked each of the boys and Mick, but none could agree. We all felt terrible about this.

Grandson Tony came from Australia late in 1993 to see his mother, and I went up to Kohukohu to be with them both. It would be the last time Tony saw Penny alive, though he didn't know that at the time. He had a demanding job in the transport industry and getting away was very difficult for him. Penny just loved having her firstborn with her, and it was hard saying goodbye.

On 15 March 1994, Mick rang me at night at Parliament and said that it had been a funny old day: in the morning, Penny had been in such bad shape that he thought she was going to die. He was deciding whether to ring me and suggest that I come when the Archdeacon of the Far North, Tony Ross, arrived and asked to see Penny. Mick said that he thought she was dying. The archdeacon, who had visited Penny whenever he was in the district, said to Mick, 'I always said that there were two things I could do for you and Penny. One is to marry you and the other to administer extreme unction when Penny is dying.' He suggested that now was the time to do both these things and came back later to do so. Penny Collyns was the carer on duty that day, and she flung herself into wedding mode

By the Waters of Babylon

and did everything she could to help. After the archdeacon had left, Mick was trying to make Penny comfortable and found that the morphine pump had become dislodged, so she had been coping with pain without it.

By now she needed to be attached to an oxygen mask and cylinder almost continuously. Mick had made her a special padded reclining chair on wheels, so that she could lie out in her garden among the flowers and trees or watch television at night and not be shut away. I had bought her a soft light mohair shawl in a marketplace in Kathmandu, and unless it was very hot, she liked to use this as it didn't press on her.

I went up once more to be with her before she died. It was obvious that time was running out, and when I left to go to the airport, I wondered if I would see her alive again. It was a wretched time for us all. During the next weeks, I spoke to Penny on the telephone on a number of occasions. I think that not being able to speak, and worse than that, not being understood, was one of the worst aspects of MND for her. She became very frustrated because, of course, she knew what she was trying to say, and we all felt so stupid that we couldn't understand her. Mick and the carers who were with her all the time understood a lot of what she was saying.

Late on a Sunday evening in July, the phone rang. It was Mick. He said that Penny wanted me to speak to her so I did, for quite some time, and when I said goodbye, I told her that I loved her very much. Mick said, 'She's smiling'. When I hung up, I said to Mary that I felt sure I would never speak to Penny alive again. In the morning, quite early, Mick rang and said she had slipped away at seven-thirty a.m. I felt a mixture of gratitude and sorrow — gratitude that she was now released from that MND straitjacket, and sorrow because she was such a loss and had so much to give. This was the second of my children to die before me. It just wasn't right.

I had made arrangements to go to Kohukohu for the funeral because that was where Penny had said she wanted to be buried. But when I got there, I found a note on the door telling me to come to Panguru to the Ngati Manawa Marae as the Maori there had claimed her body first. It was 28 July. The Labour Caucus was meeting in Christchurch, but before I left home, I had a message to say that David Lange and Graham Kelly were coming to represent the caucus and would be at Kohukohu for the funeral the next day. I travelled from Masterton on the early train. When I got to Wellington Station, dear friends from Pencarrow, Lynne Bruce and a number of others that I couldn't see for tears, were there to comfort me. Ben was at the marae when I reached Panguru, but not Tony, who had rung me from Sydney to say that he would fly to Auckland and drive to Kohukohu. I found out later that his plane was delayed and he didn't

183

arrive there until late that night, to find Tim and his girlfriend Shelley at the vicarage. They came over to Panguru the next morning.

After we had been welcomed onto the marae by the tangata whenua, I went to see Penny. She looked incredibly beautiful with all signs of pain and struggle wiped away. She was dressed in a blue silk kaftan, one that I had given her because I thought she would look lovely in it and because her carers could easily slip it over her head. I had bought it years ago at Whetu Tirikatene-Sullivan's ethnic dress shop in Willis Street and had worn it on a number of occasions overseas. Penny had decided when she saw it that that was what she wanted to be buried in.

There were a lot of people on the marae, including many of Penny's students. Just before sunset, Mary arrived with Kate and Mike, and Syd with his mother, who is of course Tim and Ben's other grandmother. Heinke, who had flown from Dunedin, stayed in Whangarei and drove to Panguru following my instructions and arrived in time for the tangi.

It was an amazing night. After people had been fed and settled their mattresses around the walls of the marae, people started speaking about Penny and about what she had meant to them. All through the night, two students at a time sat at the foot of her coffin, and one after another stood and told us about what she had done to help them. One young man said he had been a wild child, and when he first entered Penny's class at school, she had told him that he had two options: one was to continue to refuse to learn and to end up on a benefit because he was unemployable, and the other was to use his undoubted intelligence which would take him on to tertiary training. He said he had resisted this but finally realised she was right. He told us that he was going to Auckland University next year to do a business administration course. It was a heartwarming experience.

When the students were finished, later in the evening, Penny's carers talked about what it had meant to them to look after Penny, to work with Mick to do their best for her; how she had always thought of their well-being and encouraged their own development. I looked at these young women who, for minimal wages, had done such a magnificent job and my heart went out to them. It was very late when we all settled down to fitful sleep, I on one side of Penny, Mick on the other. Ben had brought a beautiful piece of polished pounamu and placed it between Penny's hands.

In the morning I went with Ben, who is fluent in Maori, to talk to the kaumatua, who said that the service would begin at ten-thirty a.m. I told them about David Lange and Graham Kelly and said we must wait until they had reached Kohukohu, seen the notice about the changed venue and come on to Panguru. They knew David. Not only had he been prime minister, he had also had an office in Rawene as a young lawyer and had acted for them on a number of occasions. They agreed to wait until he

Ben, Tim and Tony the day after Penny's funeral, at Kohukohu

arrived. In the event, Christchurch Airport was closed due to fog, so Graham couldn't come, but David, who had been in Auckland, drove up with his wife Margaret and they were welcomed onto the marae. He came and looked at Penny and there were tears in his eyes. I really appreciated having those two representing my Labour family. Tony Ross conducted the service and the children from Panguru School sang beautifully.

At the graveside, I stood with my brother David and sister-in-law Lyn and was comforted. Earlier, the family had been asked to select a site for Penny's grave. She lies looking out over the land she loved.

Back at the marae, I talked to local people who had been Penny's friends, and to her friends and mine who had come long distances to be there. The boys found it all hard to take, and the months ahead would not be easy either. I thanked all who had done so much to help. Back at Kohukohu later that evening, a friend of Penny's, the principal of the local school, came to see me. She said she had a message from Penny for me. She said she had spent almost a day with her and despite the difficulties, had written down what Penny had to tell her. Penny had said, 'My mother won't understand why I suddenly decided it was time to go.' She told her friend that on the Monday evening, she saw her brother Mark, that he was standing beside a pohutukawa tree which had its roots in the water. He held out his hand to her and told her it was time to come. She and Mark were very close. The next morning, she had decided what she wanted to do before she died. On Tuesday, she asked her carer to call all her women friends together for the evening. I have a photo of her on that night and she looks radiant. On Wednesday she painstakingly dictated to Mick separate letters to her three boys and to me, to be given to us after her death with a photo of her. On Thursday night she went out to dinner at the home of friends with Mick, and on Friday Mick took her across to the church which had a new organ and they listened to a concert of Mozart and Bach.

On Sunday night, Kay decided to stay overnight as she sensed the end was near. Late at night, Penny let them know that she wanted a shower, she needed to be clean. And she died peacefully the next morning. She who had been so dependent had arranged her own death, as she wanted it. I found that absolutely mind-boggling and was, and am still, full of admiration.

I found these words and they seemed right for Penny, so I read them to her at her graveside:

> Do not stand at my grave and weep;
> I am not there. I do not sleep.
> I am a thousand winds that blow.
> I am the diamond glints on snow.
> I am the sunlight on ripened grain.
> I am the gentle autumn's rain.
> When you awaken in the morning's hush,
> I am the swift uplifting rush
> Of quiet birds in circled flight.
> I am the soft stars that shine at night.
> Do not stand at my grave and cry;
> I am not there. I did not die.
>
> — Anon

Rangiiti

The day following the funeral, Mary, Heinke and I went to Mangonui and explored the area around there. For me, it was so full of memories. Tony, Tim and Ben were coming to terms with the loss of their mother and it was good for them to spend some time with each other. Tony was to drive them to Wellington — a long haul — and I suggested they might stop off in Taupo to see David and Lyn, and, as well, to have a swim in the AC Baths, Taupo's mineral hot pools. Mary, who had Chris Carter's car, was to drive Mike and Kate back to Auckland, and we arranged to meet Tony in Wellington. He wanted to see my new home, Rangiiti, and spend some time with me.

When we arrived, it was a chill Wairarapa afternoon and my first thought was to get the Kent fire going. We walked into the kitchen, and I sensed something was different. For some time I'd been hassling Charlie, our almost resident carpenter, to put in one of those garden windows. He'd put it on his list of 'things to do'. And there it was — Charlie's way of making coming home not so sad. It was and is delightful.

Tony and I had a quality time together. The film *Bread and Roses* had not then reached Australia, so I gave him the video and he watched that. I regretted once again that he did not live closer — but that's life.

When I wrote the book *Bread and Roses*, I was still living in Brooklyn in Wellington in the cottage on the Sutch estate, tucked in below Mitchell Street. It had been either a gardener's or a farm labourer's cottage in earlier times and Bill Sutch had refurbished it for tenancy. From it, I had stunning glimpses of Wellington and its harbour, which I saw across a mass of rhododendrons, azaleas and tree ferns planted by Bill, an indefatigable gardener. It was a magic place and I lived there for just on fifteen years.

In late 1985, before I retired from the Shop Employees Union, I decided to find somewhere warmer, though still in Wellington. Thanks to my old PSA boss, Jane Galletly, who lived nearby, I found an apartment in a three-storey block on Marine Parade, Eastbourne, across the harbour. It was a rear apartment that looked out onto the bushclad slopes of the hills, which merged ultimately with my old friends the Orongorongo Mountains. From a slim south window in the lounge, I had a sea view out across Cook Strait to the seaward Kaikouras which, at sunset in the winter when they were coated with snow, looked like giant pink icecreams.

Across the hall, one of the two front apartments was owned by an older couple, Dee and John Smythe, who had lived there for 23 years, since the apartments were first built. Their apartment had two bedrooms, whereas mine had only one. Their windows looked out over Wellington Harbour north to the Rimutakas and south to Cook Strait. I was in Parliament by then, and so didn't have much time to socialise, but sometimes on a Sunday or during the recess, John and Dee would ask me to come over for a cup of coffee or a drink. One day when I was settled in their cosy sitting room, they told me that they had decided to move to the Gold Coast of Australia to be closer to their daughter and her family; and they asked if I would like to buy their apartment.

Would I what! And so it happened; and for most of the six years that I was in Parliament, this was my home. In the crazy days between 1987 and 1990, when Roger Douglas forged ahead with his drastic economic reforms which turned the whole country inside out, I would leave home early in the morning to beat the traffic on the Hutt Road and often not get home until twelve forty-five a.m. It was not unusual for Parliament to continue sitting all day Friday and sometimes Saturday. So this apartment became my sanctuary for the small amount of time I had available. It was safe, compact and comfortable.

However, I felt a growing need to have a real garden and some cats, neither of which was possible there. Mary Sinclair and I started looking for somewhere in the country, a small cottage with land for a garden; something we could afford, where we could go on the occasional free weekend that I could manage after my electorate clinics in Wainuiomata or Lower Hutt, and also for holidays.

Because of my long-standing love affair with Nelson and its surround-ing districts, I had a very strong preference for a rural property there. Our friends Ian and Diane Grant had sold their house in Pownell Street in Greytown, and acquired a block of land at the rural end of Chamberlain Road, on the outskirts of the town. They bought a wonderful old house from Carterton and had it moved onto their new property. They then built an addition onto it without destroying its character. That was ten years ago and massive tree and shrub plantings have made it a very attractive home, garden and small holding. We four had become real friends, and Mary and I watched the developments with fascination.

While Mary's wonderful mother Mabel was still alive, we spent our

Christmases with her, in Nelson and Taupo. In Nelson we stayed at the home of my good friend Merle Hyland in Riverside Community in Lower Moutere, while she was in Switzerland. Merle's house had views to Mt Arthur and her gardening skills are legendary, so it was a very pleasant oasis after a searing year in Parliament with Roger Douglas, Richard Prebble and their cohorts in full cry.

I think that Mabel had genuine doubts when we told her we were going to stay at Riverside, and probably envisaged sleeping in a dormitory. In the event, she was delighted with the comfort and ambience of Merle's small home. Because we didn't want to overtire her, we took her exploring only every second day, and showed her the many delights of the Nelson district — potteries, craft shops, gardens, lunches at restaurants in vineyards.

By the following year, Mabel's health had deteriorated. I asked my brother to arrange an exchange, so that some Taupo person could enjoy my apartment at Eastbourne and we could give Mabel a holiday in Taupo. As it happened, the weather defeated us and rain poured down day after day. Taupo's population is expanded markedly by holidaymakers at Christmas and New Year, and for much of the time, we squelched around supermarkets and shops with other visitors.

In the year that followed, Mary moved her mother from her resthome in Pahiatua to one closer to her house in Worser Bay, and the next Christmas was spent in my apartment in Eastbourne. Ultimately, Mabel went back to her home town of Pahiatua. I was locked into the turmoil of life in Parliament as it was then, but was aware that Mabel's life was moving to its end and that Mary was having a very stressful time. When Mabel died, I wanted to attend the funeral but the National Opposition wouldn't grant me a 'pair' (grant leave), because Mabel wasn't a close relative of mine. It was the sort of pettiness that the Westminster system produced in the House in those times.

The following Christmas, Mary and I looked after the home of a Masterton woman who had gone to Australia. It was in Essex Street, which is a street full of wonderful old houses and delightful gardens with mature trees. More and more, the Wairarapa seemed to be a desirable place for a holiday home or bolthole. During the year, I had gone to Nelson to speak, and as I had a couple of hours to fill before my plane left, I went round the real estate offices. In the window of one, I saw a description of a very old rural cottage which had been refurbished, with three bedrooms, a sitting room opening out onto a wide verandah and a large kitchen with an Aga stove. From the photograph it looked charming and the half-acre cottage garden was bounded by large trees. The price appeared to be reasonable. I was very tempted, but didn't buy.

For some time, I'd been thinking that when I ultimately retired from Parliament, I wanted to get out of the city and live in a more relaxed, rural atmosphere. Because I was to be in Parliament only for six years, I wouldn't have a parliamentary pension and my finances would be limited. The cost of flying across Cook Strait would then prevent me from doing many things I wanted to do. The Wairarapa was close to Wellington and, even better, had a train service.

Whenever I could get away from Wellington, which admittedly wasn't often, we continued to look for our holiday home, from Martinborough north to rural Masterton. At those times when we were in Masterton, we stayed with the Grants and reported progress — or lack of it.

While we were staying in Essex Street over Christmas, Mary and I went to have a look at the houses which were available for relocation just over the Waingawa Bridge at the entrance to Masterton. We found a two-bedroom, rather basic cottage which we later discovered had been a family holiday home at Lake Ferry in South Wairarapa for years. It had verandahs on two sides, which appealed to us, a small sitting room, a reasonable-sized kitchen and a room which could serve as a bathroom/laundry with a separate toilet.

When we asked the depot manager why there was new weatherboarding and roofing iron down one side of the house, we discovered that they had removed a large addition to the house, measuring 4 by 6 metres, which was also available, though in a very raw state and with one side open to the elements. Mary suggested that we take that too. I was astonished and asked what use it could be. Mary said that, although she and I had our own bedrooms, we didn't have anywhere for friends to stay. I looked at this rather tatty structure and wondered what on earth we could do with it. But over the years, I had come to admire Mary's skills with houses and her ability to envisage changes for the better. The deciding factor was the depot's offer to move the extra room and put it on piles, for $1800.

Now all we needed was somewhere to put the buildings and develop a garden around them. On the last evening of our stay in Masterton, we had dinner with the Grants in a local Chinese restaurant. We described our find to them and, at their suggestion, went home for a torch and went down to the depot to view the house. The back door of the cottage had been left open, so we climbed up and walked through it, exploring its possibilities. The next morning when we met to say our farewells, Ian and Diane outlined a proposition they had discussed overnight, which was to allocate us a corner of their land (about half an acre) at the south end of their property. They couldn't sell us the land due to Town and Country Planning regulations, but they were sure some agreement could be reached.

When we looked at the land, we found that it was bounded on two sides by gums, acacias and conifers, planted by Ian and Diane as a protective boundary. Mary and I decided to accept this very generous offer, and each took on half the mortgage required to purchase and relocate the buildings. So, in March 1991, the relocation took place and work began on the development of Rangiiti, our Little Heaven.

We decided to share the responsibility of developing the property. Mary would be Officer Commanding of the house and I would plan and develop the garden. The added ingredient was that we both had strong views about our area of responsibility. In this new MMP climate, I feel that we could instruct the participants in the skills of negotiation and consensus. I knew that with my late husband Charlie's landscape gardening advice and my own experiences of gardens around the world, I had the ability to plan the half-acre garden.

I had been living in Eastbourne on the edge of the ocean and loved its myriad moods, but my early love of mountains and mountaineering urged me to be where I could see a range of mountains. The Tararuas to the west of our new abode were alternately purple and misty grey in summer and pristine and starkly beautiful in their white snow cladding. Sadly, because of the weather and illness in the winter of 1996, I seldom saw them but, when I did, they were magical. On the west boundary of our property on a neighbour's farm, there is a stand of poplars which largely hide the mountains in summer, but in the winter when their branches are bare, I can easily see the glory of the mountains. My one regret is that, with my limited lung capacity, I can't venture up those slopes or come down at the marvellous time of sunset, when shadows and the scents of the bush and the feeling of well-being make that a special experience.

Before the house was positioned, Mary made sure that it would face the sun and that the add-on room would form a courtyard also facing the sun. On the day before the move, Mary came to the Wairarapa after work, stayed with the Grants and got up in time to accompany the traffic officer heading the procession of house and truck to the site. Once both buildings were in the paddock, the piles were set in place for them. In a very short space of time, stage one of our project was completed.

The extra room sat on its piles for a couple of years, with sheets of black polythene covering the front. The winter winds and rain gradually shredded the plastic but it lasted until we were ready to renovate it. The house had been gutted, so Mary set about attending garage sales and visiting recycling yards in Wellington. Often when I got home from my electorate clinic at Wainuiomata on Saturdays, she would ring and report her latest find.

Two paddocks away to the south of our house live a remarkable family, Nancy and Charlie Baldwin and their three teenagers, Daniel, Shane and

The studio en route to Rangiiti

Anna, who became an integral part of our lives. Charlie, now a master builder, did a lot of the early renovations on the house; Daniel is now well through his carpentry apprenticeship; Shane does a wide variety of jobs in a local supermarket, and Anna is a senior student at Wairarapa College. In the early days, the boys were at college and Anna was at intermediate school. Nancy, an inspirational gardener like her mother, helped me in the garden, while first Daniel then Shane acted as chief lawnmower, helping me to develop a lawn out of the original paddock.

When I finally retired from Parliament and announced that I intended to leave Eastbourne and move permanently to the Wairarapa, friends and political colleagues were critical. To have a holiday home there was one thing, but to actually live there . . .! They told me I would be lonely and bored. I was absolutely certain that I would not — nor have I been. With exemplary and valued neighbours each a couple of paddocks away, and with new and old friends and acquaintances, the wonderful people who have helped me in so many ways, life is certainly never dull. And of course there are the people who come to visit, some of whom have been keen gardeners and have helped a great deal in the formative stages.

While I was still in Parliament, it wasn't possible to get away often, but nevertheless, the first priority was to have electrical and plumbing services installed. As we were at the rural end of our road, we weren't linked up to council water and sewage services, so for the second time in my life I was introduced to septic tank and water tank facilities, and new types of guttering.

We raided the secondhand shops for a bed each, and Ruth Dyson, then president of the Labour Party, donated a large old squashy and comfortable brown corduroy lounge suite for the sitting room. For an amazingly

With Ian and Diane Grant, Mary's mother Mabel,
and Nick Grant at Ranginui

reasonable cost, Mary found a set of kitchen cupboards and a benchtop with sink, which were installed by Charlie Baldwin. There was an ancient, rather encrusted stove which had obviously seen much service, and that was hooked up. In the early days of its existence, the house was very basic, but after Mary found a long dining table and two benches and a Kent woodstove, we were well enough equipped to be reasonably comfortable.

I was anxious that there should be a name for the place. The Grants' property was called 'Ranginui', which means 'large heaven' or 'sky'. One day I went next door from my parliamentary office to seek the advice of Koro Wetere, then MP for Western Maori. He listened to my description of our property and suggested we call it 'Rangiiti', or 'small heaven' — and so we did. We had a large rural gate made and attached a sign with the name 'Rangiiti' on it.

For some time my middle grandson Tim had been staying with me at Eastbourne. He was a qualified carpenter but had damaged his back working on huge Wellington building sites, so he had embarked on an architectural degree at Victoria University. Tim, like all my daughter Penny's boys, is very intelligent but it soon became obvious to me that he and that architectural degree were incompatible. One parliamentary recess when I was able to juggle select committee meetings and electorate responsibilities to give me some days at Rangiiti, Tim came with me.

Like all university students, Tim needed extra funds. He was not only intelligent but also very handsome, and had been doing some modelling in Wellington to raise money. I had a fax machine by my bed in Eastbourne, and his contract employers started communicating with him through that. My first intimation of this was when I arrived home after a very late parliamentary session and felt paper scrunching under my feet as I went into my bedroom. It was a fax which said, 'We need your body tomorrow at one p.m.' In my tired state, I thought this was a threat by some member of the public, but then I saw Tim's name and that of a modelling agency at the top of the fax.

When I told Tim that Mary and I wanted one end of the kitchen at Rangiiti extended and a third verandah built on the west side of the house, he said he could manage that and would welcome the money, so he moved in and began work. His ruling passion was surfing, so his building activities were dependent on the state of the surf and weather along the Wairarapa coast. In the mornings, he would ring the Meteorological Office and find out whether conditions would be right. At those times, when I rang from Wellington and got no reply, I knew that the surf was up. Sometimes, when he knew that conditions would be good in the early morning, he would pile food, his wetsuit and sleeping bag in his old car and, with his surfboard strapped on the roof, would take off for Castlepoint or Cape Palliser.

When the Waingawa freezing works closed, many Masterton men became unemployed. Some moved away to seek work elsewhere; others tried new ventures, some of which were successful. Others found life very difficult as there has been no other major industry in the town since which could employ semi- or unskilled men. Around the corner from our house is an unemployed workers' vegetable garden, which was the brainchild of Marshall Coley, a man with a highly developed social conscience. He is also an innovator. He takes young people who can't find work and teaches them horticultural skills and a work ethic. This is an organic garden and produces delicious fresh vegetables. I asked a worker who had been made redundant to do the initial digging for my cottage garden, and one of the workers from Marshall's garden came and rotary-hoed it.

We decided that it was time to have a housewarming and issued invitations to our friends. On the day, thankfully, it was fine. People parked their cars in the Grants' paddock next to the house. We had asked them to bring a cottage garden plant and a bottle and about 120 people came. It was a wonderful event. The diverse nature of the guests, their interests and political preferences, made for a very interesting mix. Comediennes Therese O'Connell and Pinky Agnew arrived in the guise of Jenny Shipley and Ruth Richardson, and their contribution was warmly received by all present, including those of a more conservative bent. Some people came on the train, and that mode of travel at weekends has become very popular with friends, many of whom hadn't been in a train for years.

We had hired a marquee for the event, and the hire people had erected

Some of the guests at the housewarming

it, but obviously expected us to dismantle it. The day after the house-warming, Mary decided to tackle this task. I, meanwhile, worked frantically with my gardener helper to plant all the gift perennials in the cottage garden before we went back to Wellington.

Among our guests had been diplomatic staff from the then Soviet Embassy and their families. They had really enjoyed their day in the country. Some days later, going up in the lift to my office, I met the Chinese

With Russian friends at the housewarming

Ambassador. She was a charming and intelligent woman whom I liked very much. On this occasion, she looked at me reproachfully and said, 'Sonja, you asked the Russians to your housewarming but not us!'

Gardening at Rangiiti was a chancy thing, because political life was not conducive to weekends away. During the Christmas that we spent in Merle's Riverside Community house with Mabel, Merle had suggested to me that while there, we should visit Pam Wratten's Lavender Patch garden at Lower Moutere. When we did, we were enchanted by the variety of lavenders and by her house and cottage garden. I had always wanted a lavender hedge and had planned one to encompass a scented garden. I ordered enough plants for this from Pam. They arrived, fortuitously, during a parliamentary recess, and I managed to squeeze enough time to get to Rangiiti and plant them according to Pam's instructions. I also planted a box hedge to border the lavender. I knew that we were facing a very busy schedule, both in Parliament and out at speaking engagements around the country. It would be at least six weeks before I could get back, so I watered the plants well and expected to find them settled in and growing next time I came. Sadly, the rabbits which populate the Grants' eastern hedgerow decided I was being very generous, and when I did come back, I found all the lavender plants pulled out of the ground with their roots eaten. It was back to the drawing board the next planting season.

Pukeko, those handsome blue-black birds, delighted me when I first saw them in the garden, stepping sprightly on their long orange legs. I soon learned that they had destructive habits, particularly with irises. I was talking on the phone one day and caught sight of two pukeko flying past the window, each with a $6 Siberian iris in its beak. Only when the cats arrived much later did they decamp.

Whenever Mary and I came to Rangiiti, we brought with us lists of things to do, she in the house and me in the garden. Our expectations of our energy plus the time needed for each task were always overinflated, and the lists kept growing longer. Mary decided we needed a garden shed, so erected one of those galvanised iron numbers that one sees in garden and hardware shops. Into this she put the old kitchen bench, paint pots, garden tools, bags of manure and the lawnmower. The next time we came up, we found the shed held down by stout ropes. Charlie had looked out of his window during one of Masterton's equinoctial gales and seen the shed rising into the air. He and Daniel had dashed up to rescue it.

I got ideas for the garden from all over the world. When I was in Kathmandu at a World Peace Council meeting, I saw in the garden of the hotel an idea I wanted to establish at Rangiiti. In the centre of the garden was a large rectangular piece of ground, surrounded by shrubs and trees.

Inside that were the tables and chairs where we drank our tea. It provided a charming oasis. I started planting shrubs and trees around the perimeter of my version. In the centre was the *Albizzia julibrizzin*, more commonly known as the silk tree or nimu. I envisaged us sitting with visitors under it, shaded from the hot sun. The nimu and the *Viburnum carlessi* were the first two trees planted at Rangiiti. The viburnum did very well but the nimu is taking its time to grow, so shaded teaparties are some way away.

I told Charlie that I wanted him to build a lychgate and a trellis at the entrance to the two Monet gardens that I was developing, to a plan devised by the artist himself. Charlie said, 'What's a lychgate?' so I showed him a picture in a gardening magazine of the one I wanted. Next time we came up, there it was, complete with wooden shingles and very handsome. Now it is smothered in spring with clematis and wisteria blooms.

In front of the house on either side of the drive, I have tried to develop a welcome to Rangiiti. To the north is a fairly narrow strip where I planted three silver birches, now quite tall and underplanted with daffodils and a soft pink prunus, a camellia and *Rhododendron fragrantissima*. When I returned from my first visit to South Africa, I found two large healthy camellias on the back verandah, waiting to be planted. They had been sent by Patrick Mahony, the Chief Family Court Judge. When we lived in Nelson, Patrick was our paper boy, and he had known Penny from the time she was a little girl going to school past his family home in Cleveland Terrace. He had learned of her death and these camellias were in her memory, his card said. The camellias are one of a number of wonderful plant gifts in the garden. I planted one on each side of the drive. I decided that the larger area on the south side was the only place I could grow rhododendrons and I've had limited success. I've become very philosophical about plants that don't survive, but failures are fewer now that I'm living here.

Water is always a problem in summer. Our 5000-gallon water tank is usually adequate, but a long hot summer makes watering the garden a problem. I use water from the water race on the south side; and washing machine and shower water is recycled for the garden.

In a gardening magazine, I saw a brick herb seat. I asked Mary if she could make one for the scented garden and said I'd plant chamomile in it and thyme round its feet. She gladly accepted the challenge. She is never happier than when she is rearranging houses, painting them, and creating new structures. In next to no time, the seat became a reality. Once it was planted with chamomile, the cats decided it was an ideal toilet facility and I had to replant and place wire netting over it. The scented garden is still developing — like the rest of the garden. Behind the chamomile seat is a

The developing garden

handsome dark green azara which in spring produces tiny yellow flowers with a vanilla fragrance. There are boronias and a white daphne, nicotiana, and a sweetly scented 'Margaret Merrill' rose. Up the centre feature of the garden, a flowering 'Mt Fuji' cherry, glorious in spring, I've trained the rose 'Alchemist', which has rich, absolutely divine creamy perfumed blooms. I have to confess that this is an idea filched from Sissinghurst, where I saw the 'Alchemist' climbing up an apple tree. The lavender hedge, now looking very healthy, borders two sides of the garden.

Mary decided that she wanted a small part of the garden as her own. She planned a feminist garden, where purple, green and white flowers would grow. She built a raised garden with a trellis behind it on the east side of the house from the lychgate. Because of its position in partial shade, she is able to grow plants there that don't do well in the sunnier parts of the garden. From time to time, as with my colour-graded cottage garden, there are glitches in the purple, green and white scheme. Birds indiscriminately drop seeds and sometimes plants aren't true to their description. Mary saw some stunning dark purple lupins in Nancy's garden and asked her for some seeds. The resulting plants were very healthy but sadly, when the buds developed, they were deep pink. I have a very handsome lupin in that colour and had given some seeds to Nancy and somehow they turned up where the purple ones should be. On the other side of the trellis, we have espaliered two 'Braeburn' apple trees and between them planted a 'Ballerina' apple, all given to us by good friends.

Furry and Feathered Friends

When we moved into Rangiiti, Mary had a small tortoiseshell cat called Pankhurst (Panky for short) who was a bundle of intelligence, mischief and daring. She had been one of two kittens which my nephew Bill was trying to foist on my brother-in-law Larry and his wife Merle when I visited them at their beach home at Waikanae. They were determined to take only one, so Bill said that as his family couldn't cope with any more cats, the other one would have to be put down.

Back in Wellington, I was regaling Mary with this story and, fanatic cat-lover that she is, she insisted she would take the kitten. So I rang Bill and arranged for him to leave it with his sister Linda at Raumati so that we could collect it from there. From the beginning, Panky was a mass of personality. As she was still very young, for the first month she accompanied Mary to work and travelled quite unfazed in the car and the fast lifts at Bowen House. She also came to Rangiiti and just loved it there. One of Mary's other cats came once. She was a city cat and was terrified of the wide spaces and the great white animals in the neighbouring paddock. She retired under Mary's bed for the weekend and never came again.

One weekend the adjoining paddock was occupied by several cattle beasts which Ian and Diane were fattening for sale. Some of them, particularly the steers, were really large and intimidating, even to me. As we walked down the paddock (later to become the garden) with friends, we saw this small tortoiseshell ball of fluff front up to a large steer through the fence. As the steer advanced towards the fence, our hearts were in our mouths. The steer started to paw the ground and its mates moved up behind it towards Panky. Panky, however, would not be intimidated. Just as I wondered if a swift rescue might be needed, the steer and its fellows, recognising a steel will, started to back off, and as soon as they decently could, turned away and started to graze as though the incident had never happened. Panky then hopped nonchalantly through the fence and started prancing around the paddock to show that she was in charge of things.

So Panky was the one feline in residence when we threw our house-warming party at Rangiiti. If she was overwhelmed by the crowd, she never let us know. The next morning, when Mary was grappling with the dismantling of the marquee, which turned out to be a very tricky business, Panky decided to assist and kept appearing from under billowing canvas.

Before I left on my South African venture, I decided it was time I acquired my own cat. I rang my friend Leone Gamet in Napier. Leone is a Siamese cat expert and I asked her to tell me where I could get a Siamese kitten of the same strain as Paeweket II, my beloved old cat who had died some time before. She told me about Norma Robinson, and I rang her and ordered a Siamese and a Burmese from the next litter, which would be ready to leave their mothers in early November. I checked with Norma when I got back and drove to Napier with Mary to collect the kittens. And there, at the cattery, I saw Paeweket II's replica. He looked just like the kitten I had placed in my husband Charlie's bush shirt pocket in 1970, and I was absolutely hooked. Sadly, the Burmese kitten had by some mischance been sold to someone else.

Back at Rangiiti, I soon became aware that Pae III was not house-trained. I had of course purchased a cat tray and kitty litter, but Pae wasn't having anything to do with that. I tried torn-up paper — not acceptable; soil — ditto. I decided to obtain some sawdust. The equinoctial gales were in full swing and I set off, taking a coal shovel and a couple of sacks with me just in case. The first two timber yards that I visited directed me else-where, but I had no luck anywhere. I looked at the huge Japanese timber-processing plant, JNL, and went through the guard at the gate to the office. In response to my query about the availability of sawdust, just a small amount, the young woman at the counter said quite firmly that JNL didn't sell sawdust. I mentioned the piles of sawdust I could see at the rear of the factory from the train, and she told me that they had their own plans for it. As I walked to my car, I met a worker whom I knew and explained my problem to him. He directed me to Whitakers Timber Company not far from Masterton's main railway station. By this time the winds were at gale force. The young woman in the office there said I was welcome to help myself and asked if I had suitable equipment. I was fool-ishly wearing navy blue trousers and sweater. For every shovelful I dug out, at least half blew onto me.

By the time I'd finished, I was completely covered in sawdust — clothes, face and hair — and rather stroppy. When I arrived home, I called Pae, who greeted me warmly from an easy chair. As I went to rearrange the cat tray, I happened to glance into Mary's room which at that time had no door. Pae had used a corner of the room for his toilet in his despera-tion the previous weekend, and Mary had pinned a sheet over the door-way in an attempt to deter him from doing it again. As I looked in this

With Paeweket the day we brought the cats home from the cattery

time, my blood ran cold, as they say. Pae had deposited a bowel motion right in the middle of the rather smart green-and white-padded quilt I had given Mary the previous Christmas. I was enraged, picked him up and rubbed his nose in it. He was appalled and told me so. I removed the evidence, scrubbed the quilt and hung it out on the line. Sadly, it was never quite the same again. I had to completely wash Pae, who complained bitterly. I dropped him into the cat tray to let him know what it was for. He was cured and used the cat tray from then on.

There was no doubt that he was the darling of my heart. Nevertheless, I still felt that he needed a chum for company, particularly when I wasn't home. I rang Val Ball, who runs the SPCA in Masterton, and told her what I wanted: a calico kitten. When I visited Monet's garden in Giverny, I was looking over into the kitchen garden and saw several calico kittens — orange, black and white, and very attractive. I'd seen them in Monet's paintings. One of the gardeners, seeing my interest, asked if I would like one to take home. For a second I was tempted, but then I envisaged Customs and quarantine and regretfully explained and refused.

Ray and Lessie came to the SPCA with me and Val showed me a seven-week-old calico kitten which was one of two that had been badly treated and dumped that morning at the SPCA. I was enchanted and said I'd have her, but Val said why didn't I take the part-Abyssinian, year-old tabby. She had been with the SPCA now for some months, had a wonderful nature and would mother Pae. She had a very aristocratic face, like one of those Egyptian cats in Nefertiti's tomb. Val said that if a home wasn't found for Abby, she would have to be put down; but I hardened my heart. Halfway down the drive, I had second thoughts and asked Ray to turn back and we'd get Abby. He said how pleased he was, because she was lovely.

And she still is. Val had told me that Abby had had one batch of kittens. She really mothered Pae and the calico kitten and they both bonded with her. She even let them go through the motions of suckling and lay passive while they did. We called the calico kitten Clawdia because of her quite vicious claws. When I took the cats to have their first inocula-

Abby preferring Monet to TV

tions, I warned the vet about Clawdia's claws. He said, 'Oh, I'll trim them for you'. It took two vets and me to hold her down. When we let her go, she swiped the vet with all her little strength. He said, 'This cat has character.'

From the beginning, Pae aimed to be top cat. If either Abby or Clawdie settled on my knee, somehow Pae sensed it even if he was outside and would rush in and climb on top of them until they gave up. He was very wilful, but also very loving.

I had said that I wanted two cats and a small dog, so when I rang Mary and told her there were three cats and the reason why, she was amazed and asked, 'What about the dog?' Brought up on a farm, she had never been enthusiastic about a non-working dog, but I had been brought up with dogs that were family pets. However, I was beginning to realise that my ability to take a dog for walks was becoming very limited.

When I was in my late twenties and finally throwing off the tyranny of tuberculosis, one of my doctors told me that, in his opinion, I wouldn't have the lung capacity to walk at all by the time I was 45. At that time, it

Feeding the ducks

seemed a long way off and I took the prophecy at face value. Now that I'm traversing my seventies, it's all coming home to roost.

When I was seventeen and climbing in the Southern Alps, I slipped on ice and fell on my back on a rock, giving my top vertebra a stiff whack. My friends insisted I saw a doctor in Christchurch who x-rayed me and said, 'When you are an old lady, you will suffer from that.' I looked at him in astonishment as, from the vantage point of seventeen, I couldn't envisage being an old lady. By the time I was 48 and living in Brooklyn, I started having alarming sharp pains all down my arms and thought I was having a heart attack. I went to the local doctor who sent me for an x-ray. After this, he told me that I had arthritis in the top vertebra; he said I should wear a collar of foam, and he gave me two bottles of Panadeine for the pain. It didn't seem like a very comfortable future, and I didn't accept that this was all that could be done. At work, I relayed the doctor's findings to Graham Kelly, who had a history of back pain as the result of an accident when he was playing cricket. His chiropractor had kept him in good shape and able to work ever since. He suggested that I go and consult Garth Cheyne, a Wellington chiropractor. The result of this consultation was that for many years, this very professional, caring man enabled me to continue to work hard. However, age, limited lung capacity, my knitted-together shoulder and my arthritis do slow me down, frustrating though that is. My Masterton chiropracter Terry Field makes it possible for me to do as much as I do. But I had to give away the idea of a dog.

When I retired, Mary's new boss, Chris Carter, who bred and sold rare breeds of chickens, gave me four Buff Orpington hens and a rooster of the same breed. Charlie and Nancy's oldest son Daniel built me a house for

A Sunday morning get-together

the chooks. The rooster was a very handsome fellow with beautiful bronze plumage. He spent his time fussing over and organising his harem and in many ways reminded me of Jonathan Hunt, so I called him Jonathan.

In spring two years ago, tiny fluffy ducklings appeared with their parents, and Mary and I had to be very firm with the cats. Until recently, there was a water race on the south side of the property and the ducks loved that and brought their babies to it. During the duckshooting season, I had around 40 mallards staying with me and demanding food whenever I fed the rooster and hens. After the duckshooting season, most of them disappeared. I soon realised that most of them gravitated to the trout hatchery in Pownall Street. One day I was coming back from the super-market when I saw a line of ducks crossing the road outside the hatchery. The man in front of me paused to let them pass and then drove on. I tried to follow him but the ducks turned back and blocked my way. I opened the car window and told them to hurry up. At the sound of my voice, a number tried to come through the window, and that night fifteen had returned to Rangiiti. So cats, ducks and chooks co-existed (for the most part peacefully) in our home environment.

In May 1996, there were major changes in the cat family. I had gone to Wellington to talk to Ken Douglas about FOL days. I had just arrived at Mary's office and was beginning to go through my notes of the meeting when the phone rang. As Mary spoke, I realised that something was wrong, and when I realised she was talking to Nancy, a cold fear gripped my heart and I knew instinctively that it was to do with Paeweket. Mary turned to me and said it was very bad news: Pae had gone out on the road and been hit by a truck and killed instantly. I had loved him so much, wicked and wilful though he was, and so had Nancy and Mary. He was top cat and was forever proving it, but despite that, he, Abby and Clawdie were best friends. I was quite devastated.

Back in the Wairarapa, Nancy met me at the station and took me to see him in her garage. There was not a mark on him. We brought him home, and Ian and Diane said they would come over in the morning and dig a grave for him. That night it rained, a fine mist, but Abby and Clawdie searched incessantly right round the garden, calling and calling Pae. I brought them inside several times, but on each occasion they searched the house and then escaped through the catdoor and continued to look for him. In the morning they were still very distressed. I decided that I should show them Pae's body. When I saw Ian and Diane and their daughter Katie coming across the paddocks, I brought Pae onto the verandah, laid him on a green silk sheet where he looked fantastic, and called the other two cats to see him. Their eyes literally widened, and it was clear that they understood. Both uttered cries of distress and decamped under the studio and peered out fearfully. I laid Pae, wrapped in the green silk, in the grave and said a last goodbye. Nancy had come to be with us, and I realised how lucky I was to have such good supportive friends. Ian and Diane brought me a Chatham Island forget-me-not, which I would have liked to plant on Pae's grave but didn't, because of our hot summers and severe winter frosts. It has survived in a cooler place.

That night I remembered what a character Pae had been. We always said he'd been here before. When I went to South Africa the second time, I borrowed a very sturdy suitcase from Ray Stewart, placed it open on Mary's bed and started to pack. I went out to answer the phone, leaving the door ajar. When I came back, Pae had taken all my clothes out of the suitcase and was sitting in it, looking defiant. He knew I was going away. On another occasion, I had taken him to the vet to have a weeping eye looked at. We came home with a small tube of ointment which I was supposed to administer morning and night. Pae hated the whole process and fought me on every occasion. I kept the ointment in one particular, I thought safe, place. Suddenly, the ointment disappeared and with it my set of keys, without which I was greatly disadvantaged. I looked every-where, even out in the garden. After a fruitless day's searching, Nancy came up and we crawled around the verandah edges to see whether I had dropped the keys there somehow. At day's end, I said that if they didn't turn up the next day, I would have to have new locks and keys. Pae had seemed most interested in all our activities, peering under the verandah with us. That night, I was deeply asleep when I became aware that something had landed on my pillow. I assumed it was Pae dropping another of his kills, as he often did. In the morning I saw my keys on their ring, and when I went out into the kitchen, I saw just inside the catdoor the packet containing the ointment, complete with toothmarks.

Another time he worked out that I needed glasses to read and write, and obviously resented the time I spent not taking notice of him. Hanging out the washing one day, I saw him streaking towards the evening primrose at the end of the garden, carrying something in his mouth. I raced out and caught him just about to hide my glasses in a place I would never have thought to look.

After his death, Clawdie,who had spent every day of her life with Pae since they were six weeks old, was still very upset and spent the first night on his grave, despite steady rain, and wouldn't be comforted or consoled.

Some weeks later, I caught glimpses of a dark shape which quickly disappeared under the house. This, it transpired, was a stray cat with a badly gashed head. I fed her under the house for a long time. Abby and Clawdie hated her on sight. I made her a warm bed in a cupboard on the verandah and, when she was in it, both cats would slink past her, growling audibly. When I look at her now, a picture of health and with plenty of confidence, I feel glad I persevered. We called her Cleo.

After some months, the same thing happened again. This time, it was a bedraggled cream and ginger cat, skinny and haunted. After I had been feeding her for some time, she developed a very fat tummy and I was convinced that she was pregnant. When I took her to the vet and asked when the kittens were likely to be born, he lifted her tail and said, 'With this equipment, this animal is certainly not going to produce kittens!' — which explained why he had shown such a keen interest in Clawdie, much to her disgust and disdain. So, he was neutered, wormed and de-fleaed and is now part of the ménage. He is called Richie after a friend of mine. He is the one who rescues Cleo when Abby tries to beat her up. Mary says she thinks there must be a sign in cat language outside our gate which says, 'A sucker lives here!'

Garden Routes

In the years since I retired from Parliament, I have gone on some memorable journeys. In mid-1994 I learned that the World Peace Council was to hold a meeting in Johannesburg in the spring. When the new government was elected in South Africa and the process of dismantling the apartheid regime began, I realised that it would now be possible to travel there. Ray Stewart, who had not long before left his position as chief executive of the WPC in Helsinki, had come to live in the Wairarapa and bought a property off Upper Plain Road and much nearer to the Tararuas than we are. We discussed the upcoming meeting and decided to go a few days before the meeting, hire a car and drive around the Garden Route. We alerted our travel agent in Auckland, and asked him to find the best and least expensive way to do this.

The night before we left, I had a long-standing engagement to open the South Wairarapa Arts Festival in the splendid old Town Hall in Greytown. My friend June Melser suggested that I should stay with her, and arranged for her son Paul, who is a great potter, and his wife Francie to collect me with my large suitcase and take us to Greytown. I woke in June's marvellous house to see the sun streaming through her beautiful mature trees, around which her architect had built the house. How I envied her those trees.

Because of the time of our flight from Wellington, Ray and I had asked Reg Boorman, Wairarapa's ex-Labour MP and now a taxi proprietor, to take us down to Wellington Airport, and they picked me up at 7.30 the next morning. At the airport, Mary dashed in to say goodbye. She and her Worser Bay friend Pauline were in the middle of running their own garage sale, which she said was turning out to be a great success. They are both indefatigable attenders of garage sales, garden fêtes and school fairs. At Auckland International Airport we had three hours to wait until our Air Singapore flight left, so I wrote cards and letters to the Grants, the Baldwins and my three grandsons. From Singapore we flew to South Africa via Mauritius. Johannesburg Airport is large and efficient, and once through Customs, we browsed through the bookshops where we found books about the struggle to defeat apartheid, and the months running up to the demise of the old system.

At Port Elizabeth, we were jetlagged beyond reason. It was 40 hours since we had started out. Nevertheless, we went for a walk along the shore and sat and ate ice-creams. After dinner, I was just sinking into a very comfortable bed when the phone rang. It was Ray suggesting I turn the TV on. I said I hadn't come all this distance to watch TV and he said, 'Well, *Bread and Roses* is showing, you'd better have a look.' So I turned it on, and there was Genevieve Picot as me having a haemorrhage from the lung. When we reached Johannesburg, I found that the delegates who had arrived early because of distance and airline schedules had seen all four episodes on four consecutive nights.

In the morning, the rental car arrived and Ray and I set out to explore Port Elizabeth before starting on the Garden Route. That city, apart from stark areas where the black African workers live, seemed to be where black and white middle-class South Africans were living in harmony. The Holiday Inn Hotel where we stayed was reminiscent of those on Australia's Gold Coast. There were huge apartment buildings, hotels and restaurants all along the beachfront.

We set out on our 850-kilometre journey to Capetown. During the day, we travelled through fascinating country with banks of mimosa, gums, weigela and a sort of huge yellow daisy lining the roads. We detoured into some of the bays, which were crammed with very expensive holiday homes, most of which seemed to have black domestic workers maintaining them. Black workers' homes as we saw them ranged from wretched hovels in built-up areas to basic and sometimes substandard accommodation in rural places. There were some which were quite good and even had electricity. We kept seeing slim upright concrete structures grouped together, and realised that they were cold showers and toilets for the workers.

We detoured again to visit Tsitukama National Park, which was on a very rugged coastline not unlike Kaikoura or South Wairarapa. It was quite spectacular. There were chalets, tramping tracks, and a shop with African goods where we bought Christmas presents for friends at home.

The first night we stopped at Wilderness; it was an idyllic, dreamlike place, although we could see already the hand of developers. During the first day we visited the historic and fascinating town of Knysa, and then on to Belvedere, a very upmarket housing estate founded in 1834 by George Henry Duthie, who established an enclave of 'gentlemen's residences' — all quite beautiful and, of course, very expensive. Each house looked out across a glassy smooth lagoon to the Outeniqua Mountains.

It was here that I first saw bushes which had purple, blue and white flowers at once. When I asked the name of this bush, I was told,

'Yesterday, Today and Tomorrow'. I asked Ray to photograph them for Mary. Back home, I consulted one of my favourite nurseries at Clareville and found that its botanic name was Brunsfelsia and asked them to order me one. Today one is planted on one side of the 'Kiftsgate' rose at the entrance to Rangiiti.

On to George, a truly beautiful town. It had a backdrop of the stark and incredibly beautiful Outeniqua Mountains. We then went over a long steep mountain road to a town called Ooutshorn, which seemed to me very redneck and conservative. That may be an injustice, but I was daunted by the rather austere Dutch Reform churches, the enormous prison (the largest I have ever seen), the huge courthouse. But there were some very handsome houses with pleasant gardens.

We were on our way to see the spectacular Kanga Caves that some people consider to be the best in the world. The caves were certainly awe-inspiring and an experience I wouldn't want to have missed. On then to Mossel Bay, or Bai as the locals call it, which has been absolutely ruined by developers. However, we had afternoon tea at a quaint little teashop which had somehow survived, and visited the Bartolomeu Dias Museum and saw the replica of the caravel used by the Portuguese navigators in 1488. On then to Smellendourn, which was a very lovely town but with no available accommodation. At Caledon we stayed at a very good country hotel. In the morning we discovered a truly wonderful wildflower botanic garden — very exciting with swathes of brilliantly coloured wildflowers. Ray is a very good photographer and all through this memorable journey had taken dozens of photos. He had what I (a rather indifferent photographer who has been known to shoot a whole reel of non-existent film) called his hotshot camera, and on this occasion used it to very good effect.

We passed through Stellenbosch, a charming university town. The university had just been told by the Government, by Nelson Mandela himself, that it was no longer appropriate for students to be taught only in Afrikaans. This seemed to be the main topic of conversation when we were there. In Capetown I saw Table Mountain and, out in the bay, the infamous Robben Island where so many political prisoners, including Nelson Mandela, had been incarcerated. We had the sense of being part of history. We walked all around the city, saw the museum, Parliament and the botanical gardens, lunched at a sensational seafood restaurant on the seafront, and drove to the southernmost tip of Africa and stood where the Indian and Atlantic Oceans meet: more photo opportunities.

We said farewell to Capetown and the rental car and flew to Johannesburg. Because we were all paying our own way, our South African colleagues had booked us into a modest but quite comfortable hotel in one of the poorer parts of the city. We were told straight away that because of violence, we were not to venture outside; that some of the African delegates (well-built, tall fellows) had disregarded this advice and gone out on foot to explore, and had been attacked, stripped of their clothes, credit cards, travellers cheques, the lot. It was rather daunting.

Albertina Sisulu had been elected president of the WPC at a meeting in Basle in 1993 which I had been unable to attend, so this was my first meeting with her. She was an MP in the new Government, the wife of Walter Sisulu, who had spent many years on Robben Island with Nelson Mandela. I found her to be a woman of great strength who had endured much as a member of the ANC, and bringing up her children alone in a harsh environment. At the same time she had a gentle and caring nature.

I was delighted that a woman was heading the organisation. I had always been concerned that so few women were involved in this move-ment. Because of their culture and chauvinism, many peace movements around the world sent only male delegates, and sometimes there were only one or two women delegates plus women secretaries and inter-preters. Because women were a vital part of peacemaking in my own country and had played a pivotal role in the anti-nuclear movement, I knew our peace movement had a more balanced view. I kept harping on at meetings about the need for more women delegates, but the result of that was pained looks from the men. Albertina and I got along very well from the beginning, and she invited me to sit with her at the top table.

For a long time, it was becoming obvious that Romesh Chandra from India, who had presided over the WPC for many years, had never really been able to accept that his role had changed. Albertina was the second person to preside over the Council since Romesh's tenure, and yet he seemed quite unable to accept that he was no longer the central charac-ter. There were uncomfortable undercurrents at the meeting, and I did not feel that Albertina was being treated with the respect that she deserved. With hindsight, probably the sight of two women at the top table freaked the men out, but it was more than that.

At the meeting, Thabo Mbeki, the Deputy Prime Minister, came and spoke to us, and also the Minister of Foreign Affairs, Alfred Nzo. Both were very impressive. As always at these meetings, representatives of local peace organisations came to meet us and we learned a great deal from them. We heard about the incredibly high unemployment rate, the monstrous homelessness of black Africans, the need for education, improved health facilities — in fact, practically everything. We realised that the Government faced massive problems with a finite budget, and were desperately seeking to prioritise and to discuss those priorities with as many people as possible. Given that scenario, it seemed hardly surpris-ing that frustration and anger had erupted into violence.

At night prostitutes came into the hotel and with them police armed with sub-machineguns to ensure that they didn't go up in the lifts. Ray and I had been having dinner with some delegates and left to go up in the lift to our respective rooms. As we got in, a police officer asked me, 'How long have you known this man?' I had an insane desire to say that I'd never seen him before in my life, but I looked at his weaponry and said where we came from and that we were friends of long standing.

Whenever I go overseas and stay in a hotel, one of the first things I do is to place my travel documents, travellers cheques and passport in the hotel safe, and this time was no exception. In the lunchbreak the next day, I went down to get some money out. Stepping into the lift later, I was joined by four men in T-shirts and jeans. It was obvious to me straight away that they were in a state of tension. They asked me which floor I was going to, and when I said the seventh, they commented that that was a pity. They got out on my floor and asked where my room was. By this time I was becoming very alarmed. They asked me to stand well away from the lift, and told me they were undercover police about to arrest a very dangerous criminal. They indicated the room that he was in, which happened to be next to mine, whipped out guns and broke into that room. I was astounded and felt that I was taking part in some TV drama. The police emerged with two handcuffed men and told me as they were getting into the lift that the men were drug runners from Mozambique. When I told Ray about this incident later, he said, 'How come this sort of thing always happens to you?' How indeed.

That morning before the meeting got underway, Albertina announced that in the late afternoon we would be taken to the World Trade Centre in another part of the city. This was where the final multi-party negotiations took place in 1994. We were told that here the Negotiating Council, consisting of 26 parties, met to hammer out an agreed constitution which would allow an election to take place. Much has been written about this process, which quite naturally was fraught with hiccups, not unexpected when one considers the shift of power that would result, and the dismantling of apartheid. In the end, after months of to-ing and fro-ing, to put it mildly, and much debate, consensus was achieved. The important thing was that these negotiations took place in public and were reported in the press and on television. There emerged not only a new constitution but also a consensus on a new flag and a new national anthem, 'Nkosi Sikelele Afrika', which would be sung along with the old one, 'Die Stem van Suid Afrika', both of which became familiar to New Zealanders when the Springboks came to our country for the first time since 1981, and again when the All Blacks toured South Africa.

We were also advised that there was to be a reception at the World

Trade Centre in the evening, where we would meet key members of the Government and of the ANC itself. At the World Trade Centre, we met the manager who, at the request of Nelson Mandela, had had to unscramble, almost overnight, a week-long church conference and find it another venue so that the Negotiating Council could move in for the duration of that dialogue. He took us into the room where the final agreement took place. Once again we had that sense of being part of history. At the reception, we met many interesting and crucial people. I had a long talk with the youthful Minister of Justice, Dullah Omar, who had a massive task ahead of him. I told him about what was being attempted in New Zealand, particularly the work of the Hamilton Abuse Intervention Programme (HAIP) which works with violent men who have been dealt with by the courts, and with their families, and has a high degree of success. Because I knew that HAIP suffered a funding crisis much of the time, I told him that, in my view, any South African replica would need adequate funding to be able to function effectively. We agreed that, around the world, violence was a major problem, and talked about the reasons for this and debated possible solutions.

I also met a wonderful black African nun who was a teacher in the crowded area of Soweto. In response to my query, she told me that she taught 96 children at a time in three separate classes each day, starting at six a.m. and finishing at ten p.m. When I asked how she managed to teach so many children at once, she said, 'By rote, of course!'

The following day, our WPC meeting discussed in what way we could further our work for peace in the light of funding restraints. I could see that, in future, the WPC's work would be largely dependent on those people who either had the personal wealth to enable them to travel, or were funded by political or peace organisations which had the financial ability to send them around the world. This trend had been developing for some time and made me feel nervous and depressed. A proposal was put forward that we should elect one or two co-presidents to share the workload with Albertina, whose parliamentary responsibilities were very heavy. She said to me that she wanted me to be one of these co-presidents, but I said that from now on I wouldn't have the money to travel and this would probably be my last appearance at WPC meetings. Despite this, she was insistent that she needed me with her, and in the end I was elected along with Jacques Denis from France and Fundoro Lopez from Cuba.

At the end of the meeting, Ray and I set off in a small plane from Johannesburg to Kruger Park, where we entered a new world. I had been on safari in 1995 in Kenya, where animals were plentiful, and looked forward to seeing what Kruger Park had to offer. Ray and I each had a very pleasant chalet complete with en suite bathroom, airconditioning and a bottle of South African wine. There was a large shop crowded with all sorts of African craft goods, which we both found very tempting. Ray bought a beautiful Masai ring for his Brazilian partner, Lessie Bacellar, and I found several gifts for friends. That night we ate dinner at the restaurant out under the stars, and had an early night as we were due to go on safari very early in the morning.

We set out as the dawn sky, streaked with pink and mauve, stretched a rich canopy above us. I soon realised that the terrain was quite different from East Africa. For one thing, the vegetation was sparser and the animals were more scattered. But we saw a wide variety of fascinating birds, various types of deer including the springbok, quite stunning herds of elephants, peaceful giraffes and zebras and lions. The two park rangers who accompanied us talked about elephant extended family patterns — how young male elephants stayed with the female herd until they became sexually active and then were sent off to be with all-male herds. They told us of elephant behaviour when one of their number died, of their palpable sorrow. We heard that there were rhinoceros in the park, but on this occasion we looked in vain. It was a rich and rewarding experience.

We had breakfast at a restaurant in the heart of the park and met people from all around the world. Back at the park headquarters, we packed and then visited the museum which told us the fascinating history of the park. Outside, we saw very colourful gheckos — one large one in particular was half turquoise and half cobalt blue. Then it was onto the small plane and back to Johannesburg Airport and the beginning of the long journey home.

Back at Rangiiti we faced a very hot dry summer, and getting up early to water the garden became the order of each day. I had developed a secret garden at the western end of the property. The main feature is a statue of a woman watercarrier, which I bought after I spoke at the graduation ceremony at St Peter's School in Palmerston North. It was such a special evening and the pupils and staff gave me real hope in a society where the main media interest is in cannabis smoking, truancy and intransigence. The watercarrier now stands under a laburnum tree, surrounded by tall salvia and with thyme at her feet, and I often think of St Peter's when I weed there. The linchpin of my gardening activities was Nancy, who has her own splendid garden. She did all those jobs that I was unable to and we developed a gardening partnership that only ended when her back seized up. But of course we still share a passion for gardens and gardening.

In 1994, Mary's fiftieth birthday was approaching, and we decided to hold a party to mark the day. About 50 people were invited, and we urged them to come on the Sunday train. I asked Mary what sort of food she would like, and she said I shouldn't go to too much trouble, just nibbles —

The first spring with the tulips

but I thought that as we would have people here for several hours, we needed something more substantial.

For some time I'd been looking for a new stove, and I saw one advertised that seemed to be what I wanted. I rang the company in Wellington and arranged for it to be delivered the week after the party. In the meantime I had to cater for the party on our old stove, so started to cook on the Friday, and had a huge pot of leek and potato soup on top of the stove and two large lasagnas in the oven when there was a knock on the back door. There was the man with the new stove. I said I wasn't expecting him until the next week, that I had food cooking for a large party; but he said that he couldn't deliver next week. He was prepared to take away the old stove, despite the fact that it was hot, and install the new one — I'd just need to get an electrician. This was late Friday afternoon.

At this point, Lauren Lysaght and Janet Frost arrived from Wellington with their pug dog, Lady Bracknell, to help with the cooking. We removed the food from the stove. When the new stove was brought in, to my horror it was slightly too big for the space available. 'You'll have to get a carpenter,' said the man, going off cheerfully. I rang the Grants and the Baldwins and asked them to finish cooking a lasagna each and the soup, and asked Nancy to get Charlie to bring his saw up. I actually managed to reach my electrician as well. Both came early on Saturday morning and completed the task. By the time people arrived on the Sunday, Lauren, Janet and I had produced a formidable amount of food, all of which was eaten.

By this time, the single room apart from the house had been re-roofed, a verandah built on the front and a toilet, handbasin and shower added, with a garden shed at the back. This gave us more space for guests and is now officially known as the studio. It doubles as a workroom.

In 1991, I discovered Claude Monet as a gardener rather than as an artist. I bought a copy of Elizabeth Murray's *Monet's Passion*, in which she presents ideas, inspiration and insights from the painter's garden. This book has beautiful pictures of Monet's garden, Giverny, and his plans for double monochromatic borders and for a *petite allée*. The borders were one of my first developments in the garden. One is blue of all shades, and the other pink. I followed the instructions faithfully and ordered blue bearded irises from Southland and some splendid pink tulips. Both of these have given lots of people pleasure in spring. Nevertheless, Mary has become used to hearing me say, 'I'm going to reorganise the Monets.'

The first couple of years were disastrous, as in both we had bad flooding throughout the garden, followed by hot summers, during which huge cracks opened up and the garden looked like the Gobi Desert. Nancy intro-

(Top) friends helping to celebrate Mary's fiftieth birthday;
(above) the house and studio completed

With Aicha Belaski (Morocco) and Marlene Haas at St George's Castle, Lisbon

duced me to mulching and in particular to pea straw — wonderful stuff.

I was determined to visit Monet's garden, and in 1993 the Labour Party sent me to Portugal to attend a meeting of Socialist International (SI) in Lisbon. I knew I could come home via France and go to Giverny. The SI meetings were quite fascinating. First we had a one-day meeting of women of the SI, where we discussed issues of great concern to women — education, health, domestic violence, incest, rape and sexual mutilation. Among others, there were women from Muslim countries and Africa, representing a wide range of views. However, there was no doubt that what we all wanted was to free women from repressive actions and policies. There was a French woman lawyer who had just successfully taken a case against an African family and a surgeon. The French-speaking family had brought their daughter to France to be circumcised under anaesthetic. Women from countries where female circumcision is practised told us about the incredible pressure put on parents and the belief that girls would be promiscuous if not circumcised. We prepared a statement and had scheduled a press conference at the end of the day, but sadly, the press were not very interested.

On the following day, I was waiting in the lobby for Marlene Haas, who was at that time the Dutch vice-president of Socialist International Women. We were going to explore Lisbon together. Suddenly, one of the lift doors opened and out stepped Nelson Mandela, the new President of South Africa. He was accompanied by media with cameras and security guards, and, as he passed, he gave me a beaming smile and said hello. Next morning as the delegates gathered in the hall, we saw on the stage not only Nelson Mandela but Shimon Peres from Israel, John Smith (then leader of the British Labour Party), a representative of Yasser Arafat, and Gro Harlem Brundtland, the Prime Minister of Norway. All these people spoke to us, and we learned a great deal about the problems and aspirations of the various countries they represented, such as peace initiatives in Israel and Palestine and the aims of the British Labour Party. Of course, the press conference held after this meeting was very well attended.

When the conference was over, I flew to Geneva and was met by Adrienne Taylor and Tord Kjelstrom. I told them about my great desire to visit Monet's garden so they gave me detailed instructions and sent me off on the huge TGV train, which seemed to me to be even faster than the Japanese bullet train. At the main railway station in Paris, I knew I had to get to St Lazare Station to catch the train to the town of Vernon. The guard told me that if I hurried I would catch an early afternoon train, so I took a cab to St Lazare. However, there was a long queue at the ticket office and I missed the connection and didn't arrive in Vernon until Monet's garden was closing for the day. I stayed at a very old hotel called La Mardiere, which had comfortable beds, low oak-beamed ceilings and hollowed-out, worn floors.

The next morning, I looked at Monet prints and other gifts in the shops and then sat on a seat on the Rue Monet waiting for his house and garden to open at ten a.m. Going back to Geneva on the TGV, I commented that it had been a very expensive visit one way and another, but I wouldn't have missed it for anything. I'd read about the history of the house, but for me, actually being there was something else. I walked round the garden in a dream. So much colour, such wonderful design. Sadly, I was too late for the wisteria, but the irises were out and hundreds of roses, and the water lilies were blissful.

As I started my tour, a New Zealand couple came up to me and said, 'You don't know us but we know you are Sonja Davies.' They told me that they had been travelling in many countries and still had some to go. He was an excellent photographer and later sent me some great photos. As I was leaving the garden, they caught up and said that meeting me had made them feel homesick and they planned to go home as soon as they could get seats on a plane. They agreed with me about the sheer beauty of Monet's garden and how well the house had been restored. Outside it was a soft pink with green shutters and I saw the famous yellow kitchen with Monet's blue and white dinner service in the dresser which was painted a deep blue. It must have been an idyllic place to live in.

As I don't speak any French, I was rather nervous about the homeward journey, but my experience has been that there will always be people, no matter how far away you are from home, to help you put your ticket the right way in the franking machine at the station, tell you the right way to get the best deal and how to get you out of the mess that you've foolishly got yourself into. And so it was on this occasion.

In 1989, the very talented and caring Diana Crossan came to see me to talk about a new charitable trust that was being established and to ask whether I would be a trustee. She explained that the purpose of the trust would be to recognise and reward the people who, for little or no financial recompense, had worked tirelessly for others over a period of time and who had improved the quality of life in this country by their work. It was to be a trust to consider the work of individuals and not organisations. Those chosen were to receive generous cheques, which they were to spend on themselves.

The instigator of this trust was a successful businessman with a strong social conscience, Tur Borren, who lived with his wife Pip next door to Diana in Orangi Kaupapa Road in Kelburn, which gave the trust its name. For a decade now, we have met twice and sometimes three times a year, mostly in Auckland where the Borrens moved to shortly after the trust was established.

It is just amazing how many people there are around the country who, without any real recognition or financial reward, are giving their time and energy for the benefit of others. The recipients never know until one or sometimes two trustees arrive to give them what the trust has decided. Vicki Carnell, whom Tur and Pip found in Auckland, does a wonderful job of finding out about the work of prospective recipients. We are sent a list before each meeting and discover as much about the people as we can before the trust meeting. So far, we've had recipients working for peace, the environment, women, Maori, the elderly, the unemployed, people with disabilities, minority groups and cultures.

There are six trustees in all, and working with them has been one of the most satisfactory and inspirational experiences I have ever had. In a society where the cult of the individual is dominant and where caring for others is not as attractive as monetary gain, it has been a privilege to be part of an organisation that recognises the work of people who strive to promote positive social changes. And taking a cheque to someone who never expected it is a real bonus. In November 1997, the trust will celebrate its tenth anniversary and will meet here in the Wairarapa at Rangiiti.

Journeying Again

When I had been retired from Parliament for a couple of years and recovered from my wonderful South African journey, Mary said she wanted to go overseas, to Europe and to visit friends and relatives and look at gardens and the Chelsea Flower Show. She wanted me to go, too, and we discussed this off and on. Warwick, my efficient travel agent in Auckland, crafted a tour itinerary to suit us both.

Mary's friend Jean in London owns a cottage on a Greek Island. She planned to spend some time there and said I'd love it. But the previous Christmas, I had talked to my friend Rae Julian who was working for Volunteer Service Abroad, based in Phnom Penh, and oversaw VSA projects in Cambodia, Vietnam and Laos. She had said that she hoped that any of her friends who were going overseas would arrange their itineraries to include a visit to her. It was a very tempting suggestion. Part of me was intrigued by the prospect of a stay on a Greek island but, in the end, I couldn't resist a visit to Rae to actually see the country about which I had heard so much. Warwick arranged for us to fly to Bangkok, where we would arrive at midnight. Mary would continue on to Greece — a long journey — and I would spend the night in the Airport Hotel in Bangkok and fly on the next day to Cambodia.

I had asked Rae about a visa and she said that she would bring one to the airport when she came to meet me. Warwick had warned me that the journey flight to Phnom Penh might be a bit strange, possibly crammed with locals with chickens and lots of hand luggage, but it was fine, and Rae was there to meet me with the visa. She took me out to her World War II American jeep which VSA had bought in Vietnam. It had an indicator which flipped out, but Rae drove it with panache!

I simply couldn't believe that I was here in this war-torn country, which was trying to haul itself back to normality by its bootstraps. Straight away, I noticed the large numbers of people of all ages who had lost limbs through landmines. Rae lived in a downstairs apartment in the city, and some Australian aid people were upstairs. The Cambodians who owned the house lived next door, a large friendly family who regarded Rae as one of theirs and were always doing little things for her.

Rae had told me she was having a dinner party the next evening for expatriate New Zealanders, and asked me which ex-Cabinet minister I would least like to be at the party. I said Roger Douglas, and she told me it was Richard Prebble, who had just come from Vietnam with his boss, Malcolm McConnell, who would be there, too. It was a very pleasant dinner. The Kiwis obviously expected fireworks when Richard and I met, but we both behaved very well, even when he told me he had been advising the Vietnamese Government on how to privatise their railway. I had to reflect on all the railways I had travelled on overseas — the frighteningly efficient Japanese bullet train, the fast French railways and the long slow journeys through the USSR — and how they juggled the priorities of profit, efficiency and people. I have fought in the past to preserve railway lines and today use the local Masterton service a lot, but since Richard privatised New Zealand rail, I cannot confidently claim that this country puts people first.

Rae told me that when VSA spoke to the Cambodian Government about sending volunteers to help with specific projects, it was advised that because of the fragile economy, it could not expect any financial help from them. New Zealand volunteers have supplemented our Government's funding by raising funds locally from expatriates and embassies.

The day after the dinner party, Rae took me to Kus commune along an incredible road — if one could call it that — full of ruts and gaps. She said that she visited regularly during the rainy season when the road was much worse. My mind boggled. The commune was situated near the Khmer Rouge territory, and they told me that they could hear gunfire as a backdrop to their activities and that local people didn't go into the forests in the nearby foothills because of the landmines. In this area there is a house filled with skulls piled one on top of the other — all local people.

We went first to a preschool seminar, organised by New Zealander Lyn Paterson. The participants came from 31 preschools in the area. It was the sort of seminar which could have been held anywhere in New Zealand, except for the absolute lack of resources, which meant that Lyn had to devise innovative ideas for the teachers to take back to their centres. She told me that these preschool teachers serve an initial three months' practical training at a variety of centres and then go to Phnom Penh for one year's intensive training. As Cambodians receive very low wages (around $US20 per month) and their transport to and from Phnom Penh and food and accommodation is only partly subsidised by the Government, the determination and dedication of the students was amazing. Lyn said that, after a year, she still found it difficult to gauge the level at which she should pitch her teaching, mainly because of the extreme courtesy of the people, who are grateful and wouldn't reveal that her teaching was possibly below their standard of competence.

Next we visited Dave Smith from Northland, who was helping local people to produce good-quality culverts to help control water during the rainy season; and latrine bases, which are badly needed, particularly in rural areas. They had also secured a contract for concrete signs to mark the work of the World Food Programme. I was pleased to hear that the Dunedin North Rotary Club had financially supported this programme.

Rae took me to visit the almost-completed health clinic, which New Zealander Jan Brown had been instrumental in establishing. A qualified nurse and midwife, she was anxious to see the clinic operational before she went home. It is a solid structure, with two examination rooms, one of which will be a birthing unit when required. There was a seminar room for health education, a secure room for drugs, a reception area and a kitchen. While it's true that buildings are not the most important thing in any endeavour, it seemed to me that for people who have had no visible health services, this clinic would reflect the virtues of asepsis when dealing with illness or for women approaching childbirth. There was one other indigenous midwife who worked with Jan. She was untrained in the clinical sense, but had a wealth of experience. Medical and nursing training was beginning again, but it would take time before trained staff were available. Jan said she had enough funding to complete the clinic, a great achievement.

Rae and I later had lunch with Jan, who told us about the health problems she faced every day, of trying to introduce safe birthing practices without offending the culture. Innoculation had been introduced. She told us about the plans for the clinic which had been drawn up in co-operation with locals. She hoped that by the time she left, locals would run the health clinic and would contribute to the well-being of everyone in the district. Volunteers are not, in my experience, well-paid, and are dedicated people. The ones that I met in Cambodia were a great example of this.

We went to look at Jeremy Ions' plant nursery. The Khmer Rouge not only destroyed buildings of all sorts in the city, they also destroyed the rural areas — trees, crops, houses, schools. So Jeremy was working with locals to re-establish forests and plantations. It is such a beautiful country, and using Kiwi ingenuity, Jeremy had created a very good nursery. It was great to see even these small beginnings of rebuilding the country.

On then to look at a new primary school. It was very basic, but the children were very proud of it. Previously, they had been taught underneath a local Buddhist temple. I met the monks who lived there; some were quite old but there were a lot of young ones. The Khmer Rouge had killed

With a local family who maintain a Hindu shrine inside Angkor Wat

the young and middle-aged monks, no doubt hoping to destroy the Buddhist religion, but today young men are joining the ranks of monks. They are very much part of the local scene. I met the senior monk who remarked, when he was told that he and I were the same age, that at least I still had my teeth. Dentures are not yet a part of Cambodian life.

On my last two days there, I flew to Seam Reap to see the famous temples Angkor Wat and Angkor Tom, a very memorable journey. I had a young tour guide who spoke very good English and was able to tell me the history of these two old stone buildings which, because of lack of funding, had been badly neglected and had huge trees growing up through the stone. Since then, I have been told that work has been done on them, so I was horrified to learn that the recent fighting in Cambodia extended to Seam Reap. I hope that those irreplaceable old buildings have not suffered.

My guide told me that he was getting married soon, and that his fiancée was still at school. I asked him if she was going on to university. He looked astonished and said no, she was going to look after him. I told him that I had heard that Cambodian men beat their wives and said I hoped he wasn't going to do that, but he said, 'What if she's bad?' I asked him if, when he was bad, his wife could beat him. 'Certainly not.'

I had seen older women with their hair shaven and was told that this signified that they were either over 60 or were widowed. I asked my guide why men were not treated the same way, and said, 'I suppose men whose wives die marry a much younger woman.' He smiled and said yes.

His story was typical of so many in this scarred country. His parents were professional medical people and his brother was in medical school. One morning when his grandmother was away with his elder brother, the Khmer Rouge arrived, pinned my guide's arms behind his back and made him watch while they killed his grandfather, his mother and father and his brother and then recruited him to work in the paddy fields. No more education for him. It says much that he ultimately rose above all this, learned English and joined the travel industry. Only tenacity could do that.

With the widows and over-60s at Seam Reap

I saw a number of weddings while I was in Phnom Penh, one under a canopy in our street. After the ceremony, the bride and groom would stand at the door of a restaurant, welcoming the guests, seeing and being seen. I watched one bride several times and saw that each time she appeared at the doorway she wore a different gown. Rae told me that brides sometimes change gowns as many as twelve times.

From Cambodia I flew to Geneva, where I met Mary. Tord took us to their home in Moens. We had a splendid weekend with these two good friends. We visited a food market which is set up each Saturday morning for four or five hours on the main street of a nearby village. The food was fantastic — all sorts of cheeses, fish, poultry, breads, salamis, even a huge pan of paella — everything one could need for weekend fare. The market was crowded with happy buyers, in strong contrast to the country I had just been to.

The next day we flew to London, Mary to her friend Jean in Queen's Park and I to Ian and Wendy in Wimbledon. Wendy's job had disappeared due to 'restructuring' and she was working from home, and Ian was at the end of his massive *History of World War II*. They were hosting a couple of overseas students. It was on this visit that they told me they were contemplating selling their house 'Hazeldene' and buying somewhere smaller. With a computer each, they could work anywhere, and talked about moving to Cambridge. With their three children living away, it seemed sensible, but I was sad because it was easier to see them on my fleeting trips through London, and it marked an end of an era.

Mary's cousin Katharine in Edinburgh had got Mary and me two tickets to Members Day at the Chelsea Flower Show, which was spectacular. We soon realised that we were underdressed. There were very stylishly dressed women there with hats and parasols, and men in formal suits.

It took us several hours to see the whole show. What I liked best were the individual gardens, some of which were quite stunning. There were dense crowds and, as I am short, I wouldn't have seen anything if Mary hadn't forged a path and got me up to the front. At one of the gardens, a man was selling garden furniture and handing out brochures. He looked at me and said, 'You're Sonja Davies.' I was stunned. How did he know that? I asked. He told me he was a New Zealander selling treated pine furniture made in New Zealand and that he'd seen me on TV. Amazing!

The next day we had lunch with another cousin of Mary's at the Parrot Club, a women's club just behind Sloane Square. Mary's cousin Rosemary lives in Oxfordshire in a manor house in a small village. After lunch, we drove out of London with her in the dense traffic and finally escaped into the open country. The manor house was very large, as was the garden, and the trees looked as though they had been there for centuries. Rosemary and her husband Robert had two children at school and several staff members came each day to work in the house and garden. It was Rosemary who took us to visit two gardens, Hidcote and Kiftsgate. Hidcote is said to be the better, and it is certainly very handsome and well-planned, but we liked Kiftsgate best, maybe because it had been designed and maintained by three generations of women. It was here that we saw the magnificent rose 'Kiftsgate', and I was immediately determined to get one.

And then we were off to Scotland to Mary's cousin Katharine and her husband Guy, who live right in Edinburgh. Katharine is an excellent gardener, the same age as me, and has created a very special garden on a steep hillside in the Leith Valley, which winds through the city, doing most of the work herself. We had a very pleasant week with them. They took us to West Scotland, where we stayed at a guesthouse looking out on a loch, and saw several outstanding gardens, one on an island. The bluebells were out, sheets of brilliant blue. I said to Katharine that I'd love to take some home and she replied, 'Why not take about 15,000, they're an awful pest here!' Edinburgh is one of my favourite cities. It has spectacular botanic gardens and is so historic that one feels it in the atmosphere.

All too soon, it was time to go home. I had been back for three days when Tony Timms rang me from Helen Clark's office and told me that there was a Socialist International meeting in Capetown and Helen wanted me to go and represent her at it. I said I was still recovering from jetlag from the last trip, but he said I wouldn't have to go until the following week! So much for retirement! When I got to Capetown, I soon saw that the level of violence had escalated since Ray Stewart and I had been there. In the taxi on the way to the hotel, the driver told me that he no longer worked at night because it was too dangerous. At the hotel, I was told not to go out alone and certainly not at night unless accompanied by a guard.

At the Socialist Women's meeting, Winnie Mandela was to be a member of a panel discussing Women and Education, but she didn't arrive. Just as we were packing up, she came into the hall with her entourage. She looked quite amazing, wearing a long green tunic in stripes of grey and black silk and a pillbox hat with black fringes which made her look like a gladiator, and a very handsome one at that. She gave her speech on Women and Education, which was very perceptive. She saw clearly what needed to be done to educate the illiterate, particularly young women.

At the main Socialist International meeting, I saw Gro Harlem Brundtland, the Prime Minister of Norway, hand Nelson Mandela (just back from Japan) a substantial cheque from her Government to help with the reconstruction and rehabilitation of his country. I presented a resolution opposing French testing at Moruroa in the Pacific. There was initial opposition from the French delegation, but we negotiated and came up with a good resolution, which was passed. We also discussed the serious problem of landmines and how we could help delegates in countries where they were a problem.

We visited black townships — something that we in New Zealand have no concept of: two families living in crowded conditions in what we would call a single room, with the kids sleeping on the floor between two single beds where the two couples slept. No electricity, just basic living. We visited District Six where the apartheid Government had destroyed all the houses of the people living there, and a women's refuge where women volunteers were facing the same problems with police about domestic violence as we faced in New Zealand in the 1970s. I told them to push for change and said that our police now recognised that domestic violence was a police issue; and I told them how our women's refuges coped.

We visited a municipality and met the mayor and saw a craft industry that was being developed. Many people were sleeping on the street and a vast number were unemployed. The Government has massive problems to grapple with, and I'm sure that, in the long run, they will manage. South Africa is such a vibrant and beautiful country and its people deserve justice and equity.

Visiting my grandson Tony while Mary and I were en route

It may seem that I was always going overseas, and indeed I have covered only some of the conferences I attended. Some, such as the 1985 Women's Conference in Nairobi, were of particular importance to me, but I said I wasn't going to write a travel book so I have excluded many of the trips I made. If there is little tangible to show for all that travelling and conferring, it is still important for New Zealand's voice to be heard internationally — we do have many valuable and unique ideas to offer and can learn a great deal from other countries. Countless reports were submitted on my returns. I established a wide network of people around the world, many of whom regularly keep in touch and we let each other know what is going on in our respective countries. My particular goal was to promote the participation of women in politics, to empower them to achieve what they believe; and I think I have contributed to this during my travels through the years. Margaret Shields is now making the relentless tours overseas in my place.

Some time after I returned from my second visit to South Africa, I was contacted and told that the Dalai Lama was to make a return visit to New Zealand, and was asked to introduce him once again to the people of Wellington. On a previous visit, I had introduced him at the Michael Fowler Centre. On that occasion, there was not a spare seat and an over-flow crowd had to listen to him over loudspeakers in the old Town Hall Concert Chamber. I had found him to be the compassionate, caring man I had read about. Despite all that has happened to him and to his people and their culture, there was not one discernible shred of bitterness or anger about him; rather he continued to seek peace and tranquillity for all. I was still in Parliament then and felt very honoured to be given this task. I had looked out over that large audience and seen how affected they were by this calm man who spoke simply of the need for us to be tolerant, to remember that we are all part of the human family; that our diversity exists, but that we should concentrate on humanity.

On this occasion, on 16 September 1996, the organisers had decided that a larger venue was needed, so they had hired the huge Events Centre on Wellington's Queen's Wharf, which holds 4000 people. When I arrived,

*A quiet moment with His Holiness the 14th Dalai Lama prior
to going on stage*

I soon saw that this too would be packed. I was taken out the back so that
I could meet and talk with the Dalai Lama before we went out into the
hall. He said straight away and accusingly that I had lost weight, which was
true, but I told him I had had a long bout of the flu and was just recovering. I was surprised and touched that he remembered me so well.

We talked about what he had been doing, and I asked him if he still felt
it was possible for Tibet to be a part of China but to retain its autonomy
and its own culture, in the same way as Hong Kong was planning to do.
He didn't actually say no, but he looked so sad that I felt he knew that it
wasn't likely. I shall never understand countries which feel that their own
way of life is so special that they can destroy a whole country and its
culture to impose their own system by violent means. Tibet did not have
powerful outside friends, as Hong Kong had. Most developed countries
were more interested in trade than in justice for the indigenous people.
We've seen it in East Timor, Tibet and Cyprus.

Once again, the Dalai was spectacular in a very understated way and
people just loved him. I had asked Don Swan, my old friend from the
Service Workers Union, to hear him. I suppose I was quite pushy. He told
me later that he wasn't terribly enthusiastic at first, but that he soon
realised what a very special man this was and that his message was so
sensible and quite clear. That day in 1996 was a highlight for me.

Epilogue

And now we are halfway through 1997. It's a glorious midwinter day, with thin lukewarm sunshine and a slight breeze from the east off the pristine splendour of the snow-clad mountains. The garden is mostly still asleep but the first harbingers of spring are beginning to appear — the crocus under the 'Mt Fuji' cherry, the mimosa bursting out on the eastern boundary, daphne and boronia just starting to open their buds.

Both Brian Edwards and Gary McCormick came at different times with their film crews to interview me in this past year, and Brian also interviewed me on his Saturday *Top o' the Morning* radio programme. Gary arrived in his huge truck, with his name clearly advertised on the side. At the supermarket, people who had seen it coming into Masterton stopped to ask me about his visit.

Now my own favourite furniture from the Eastbourne apartment is in place here in the house and in the studio. Cath Tizard was the catalyst for the shift of my goods and chattels. Shortly before she retired as Governor-General, she hosted a luncheon for Selwyn Toogood, who had fronted the long-running daytime programme *Beauty and the Beast*. This popular weekly programme had a panel of well-known women who answered questions sent in by women from around the country. All the 'Beauties' still resident in New Zealand were invited to the luncheon, including me. It was a splendid occasion — it was fun to catch up with women I had not seen for years and to see Selwyn, who had had a nasty brush with cancer. When Cath spoke, she talked about her experiences as a Beauty, about the fun we had all had; and then she said, just before she sat down, that she was retiring in three weeks' time, and on the day following her retirement she was coming to stay with me for a couple of days then would drive up to Auckland, stopping off to visit friends along the way.

I was riveted, to say the least. I had stayed with Cath at Government House, and while I knew she didn't expect that standard of accommodation at Rangiiti, I felt that the studio needed more comfort. I decided I had to move my Eastbourne furniture up here — and soon. I arranged for a furniture removal firm to come the following Friday. They said they would pack the furniture the day before, and be here by 7.30 on Friday morning. Only after I had hung up did I remember that I was due to go to Auckland on the Friday to open the newly refurbished TB ward at Green Lane Hospital. We talked to Nancy, who said she'd supervise the positioning of the furniture so long as we gave her a plan showing where things were to go. Mary devised that, and spent the rest of the weekend removing the furniture which mine would replace. I arranged for the local women's refuge to collect the unwanted furniture and other goods. As I drove to Wellington on the Friday, I saw my furniture removers passing the old Waingawa Freezing Works site, right on time. I had told them to put all the boxes of utensils, books and papers on my verandah.

At Green Lane, I was very impressed by the staff and the refurbished ward. I learned from them about new techniques; how patients usually came in only during the day, and those who stayed did so for at most two weeks. I learned also that new drug-resistant strains of TB were appearing, brought in by people from overseas, and that they were sometimes having to resort to surgery again. I talked to them about what it was like to be in hospital in various parts of New Zealand, and about the various treatments that were used 40 years ago. I am always affected when I go into a hospital, and have never lost that warm feeling towards people who work in them. Helen Clark came to listen to me between two of her meetings in Auckland. One of the things that struck me from the speeches was that because of these new untreatable strains coming in, it is essential to have an effective system of screening visitors and immigrants and of monitoring patients' movements before their disease was discovered. All of this, of course, costs money and there aren't a lot of resources put here. However, if only the powers that be could step back and see how much is saved by preventative measures — both in their precious money terms and in human terms — then they would (one would hope) be pouring money into this and other similar programmes.

When I arrived home with Mary, I found boxes piled to the roof on the verandahs, but furniture in place, looking just splendid. Needless to say, I worked frantically to clear the decks and was just congratulating myself when Cath rang. She said she was terribly sorry, she couldn't come. She hadn't realised how much there was to do before she left, and in any case, her Auckland friends wanted to give her a formal welcome home when she should have been with me. She would come at a later date.

The predictions of my political colleagues and some friends that I would be bored and lonely here in the Wairarapa have certainly not borne fruit. First of all, I have made friends here; I value my special neighbours over the paddocks on either side. And there are people I know and have

(Left) on Waiheke Island with Adrienne and Tord; (right) Paeweket and I have tea on the verandah with Katie Dewes and Pat Green

worked with, who have come to live here. My good friends from Wellington and around the country pop in to spend time with me. Once the studio was finished I could offer people their own space to stay in: Margaret Shields, who is now a Wellington Regional Councillor, usually stays overnight with me; Don Swan, my trade union colleague, has held meetings in the studio; my friend Richie Shiraishi, whom I first met in Kyoto at a peace exhibition, has come a number of times.

Richie spent 1996 in Wellington studying New Zealand history and the Maori language, and brought his wife Tei to meet me. He comes on the train, and by the time he gets to my small Solway Station, all the children in the carriage are his friends. A retired school teacher, he is also an origami specialist, and makes small creatures for the children. On one visit, he spent the day at Fernridge School with Steph Kirby, the teacher, showing the children how to make origami — his hopping frogs were a big success. I took Richie and Tei to visit Steph and John's farm at Abbotsford, and Tei was delighted to hold a lamb. She loved the Wairarapa, and in particular the animals.

Mary and Richie and me with John and Steph Kirby on their farm at Abbotsford

Many friends I have made in my various positions over the years both here and overseas have visited my 'small heaven': Rob Green from London came with Katie Dewes, and we had an enjoyable visit, as we did when Adrienne and Tord came from France. Yuri Sokolov, the last USSR

With Margaret Shields on the verandah

ambassador and now retired, came and stayed, and spoke about the Russian Federation to Rotary and to locals at a meeting at the Grants' home. Rona Ensor and Brian Small and their small daughter Hana have shared Rangiiti and given much welcome help in the garden. Their new baby son Jacob is a much-loved addition. My friend Pathma, who works for the International Confederation of Free Trade Unions and with whom I worked in Asia as well as here, came at the early stages of Rangiiti and again this year, and was amazed at the developments.

So loneliness and boredom are irrelevant.

I am now even more committed to peace. Since the demise of the Cold War, many horrible events have rent countries apart, and as a consequence, millions have been killed, maimed, starved and made homeless — particularly children, who are powerless.

But I am encouraged by the huge changes that have taken place in the last decade; the realisation by so many that violence must be dealt with at the source; that we must all respect each other's cultures, and learn to live together in peace. There will, I suspect, always be men promoting armaments, but also more and more men and women working positively for a peaceful planet.

I'm on their side.

At the end of this book, it would be tempting to write about our country as it is now: about the increasing number of dysfunctional families and the social consequences of that; about the crisis in education and health; about the continuing removal of the state from its responsibilities; about the fact that people at the top are doing very nicely in the free-market economy; that the new owners of former state-owned enterprises, while making huge profits, want more, and are putting off more and more workers; that those laid-off workers are then accused of being 'dependent' because there are no alternative jobs for them.

We know these things. What we have to do is find a way to stem the tide of privatisation, and to create a social responsibility towards people and their welfare. We are selling our children short. The interests of our sick and elderly must become of paramount importance. We need to take control of our lives so that political philosophies that pay no heed to the welfare of people cannot be allowed to prosper. Nobody wants to be dependent; nobody wants to be unemployed or on the DPB. But, thanks to right-wing economic policies, it is now likely that increasing numbers of people will be flung on the scrapheap. Families, however they be constituted, need help; parents need help, and we all have to care more about each other.

We cannot afford, because so many distrust politicians, to distance ourselves from political processes. If we don't take an active interest, we give politicians the right to do as they please. We have to insist that jobs are made available for as many workers as possible; that quality health and education services are available for those who need them; that the education of our children and the salaries of their teachers are much better funded; and that priorities are constantly reviewed, with people and their welfare always the key consideration.

Nothing is ever too difficult to achieve. Only inertia can defeat us. And when the time comes for the next election, the philosophies of constituency and list MPs will need to be closely examined and our votes much more carefully considered.

This is our country, our people.

> Ki te ui mai koe ki au
> He aha te mea nui ki tenei ao
> Maku e kii atu
> *He tangata! He tangata! He tangata!*

> If you asked me
> What indeed is the greatest treasure [in this world]
> My reply can only be
> *It is people! It is people! It is people!*